Sanity Is Where You Find It

Oklahoma Edition

Books edited by Donald Day

The Autobiography of Will Rogers

Sanity Is Where You Find It

Sanity Is Where You Find It

An affectionate history of
the United States in the 20's and 30's
by America's best-loved comedian

WILL ROGERS

Selected and edited by
Donald Day

𝕿𝖍𝖊 𝕽𝖎𝖛𝖊𝖗𝖘𝖎𝖉𝖊 𝕻𝖗𝖊𝖘𝖘 𝕮𝖺𝖒𝖇𝖗𝖎𝖉𝖌𝖊

HOUGHTON MIFFLIN COMPANY BOSTON

1 9 5 5

The Riverside Press
CAMBRIDGE · MASSACHUSETTS
PRINTED IN THE U.S.A.

WILL'S CUCKOOLAND

"CUCKOOLAND" was the affectionate term Will Rogers used for the United States. He loved every inch of it from the crook of an Oklahoma creek to "the man" in the White House, and because he loved it he joshed its foibles and follies, which he frankly admitted he shared with it.

When Will first started out with his rope he only lassoed audiences to make a living. Then after he added the more effective "rope" of words to his act he found that he could get and keep a larger audience by lassoing the "foibles and follies" of those a rung or so higher than most of his listeners. And the higher they were on the ladder of wealth, success or power the more everyone was amused.

In a democracy and in a world edging away from kingship, no matter in which direction it was moving, this was merely kidding the king.

Always basing what he said on "truth" Will salted it with a wit that kept it from spoiling before the eating.

From the few thousands which he reached in vaudeville and in The Follies Will's next step was to do the same thing, impersonally, but with equal saltiness, in his newspaper columns. Here, as he had done on the stage, he kept his remarks "strictly fresh-laid" by learning about the foibles and follies of people not from books but from daily reports of their actions in newspapers.

Not completely satisfied with what he read, his next step was, by the way of the lecture platform, to go to nearly every village and city in the United States, over and over, to see with his own eyes and hear with his own ears whether or not the newspapers were reporting the foibles and follies correctly. In this way, as America's unofficial jester, he both checked up on the people and let the people check up on him.

Feeling that he knew how they felt, and thinking that their political leaders were not doing what they wanted nor always telling them the truth about their government's relationship with foreign countries, Will made many trips all over the world to bring back to his fellow Cuckoolanders his own impressions.

Later, when the radio was perfected, his drawling, friendly voice ambled into millions of homes to report on the doings at home and abroad.

His moving pictures made his loose-jointed figure and his homely face known to millions the world over.

Probably no one, not even Franklin D. Roosevelt, "roped" so many people either by the printed or the spoken word in the United States as this drawling Oklahoma cowboy.

This book is Will's own story of Cuckooland, mostly as it appeared in his column.

Draw up a chair by the fireside and enjoy the history of the most critical period in American history as no one other than Will Rogers could have written it.

Sanity Is Where
You Find It

CHAPTER ONE

"I Am Breaking Out in a Rash Here"

December 31, 1922

Everybody is writing something nowadays. It used to be just the Literary or Newspaper men who were supposed to know what they were writing about that did all the writing. But nowadays all a man goes into office for is so he can try to find out something and then write it when he comes out.

Now being in Ziegfeld Follies for almost a Solid Year in New York has given me an inside track on some of our biggest men in the country who I meet nightly at the stage door.

So I am breaking out in a rash here.

December 31, 1922

The Ku Klux is coming into New York and kinder got it in for the Jewish People. Now they are wrong. I am against that. If the Jewish People here in New York City hadn't jumped in and made themselves good fellows and helped us celebrate Christmas, the thing would have fell flat.

They sold us every present.

The Ku Klux couldn't get much of a footing here in New York. If there was some man they wanted to take out and Tar and Feather, they wouldn't know where they live.

And even if they found out the Elevator Man in the Apartment Building wouldn't let 'em up.

January 11, 1923

They are bringing our Soldiers back from Europe. Would have

brought them sooner but we didn't have anybody in Washington knew where they were.

Had to leave them over there this long. Two of them hadn't married yet.

They went over to get in one war and come back to keep from getting in another.

Another innocent bystander shot in New York yesterday. You just stand around this town long and be innocent and somebody is going to shoot you.

One day they shot four. That's the best shooting ever done in this town. Any time you can find four innocent People in New York in one day you are going some even if you don't shoot 'em.

New York, January 13, 1923

As I go to press with this one-gland Corona of mine there is just about to be wound up in Paris what is called an economic conference which at this early day and date looks like it will be awful lucky if it don't wind up in an awful nice war.

You see, the more arguments your country is in the more publicity for the Dips.

What is it to England what France makes Germany pay, and what is it to France if England wants to tell Germany, "Kinfolks, we are even."

Germany made some sort of a proposal that there would be no more wars for a century. (I don't know whether they meant for a hundred dollars or a hundred years.) Well, anyway, it was turned down by England and France.

January 20, 1923

I launched a Ford for President movement. You see I am figuring on going in the Cabinet as he will have to be like all of them and pay off his political debts with jobs. You see all these other Cabinets are picked, not on ability, but what they have done for the Party. Well, we ain't going to have any party. It's to be called the "All over the Road Party" with Mr. Ford for Leader. Our Slogan will be "Come with Ford and you will at least get somewhere."

I will probably have to be Secretary of State although I don't think I could stand the round of Conferences. I think Vice President would be about my speed. Of course I do hate to stay hid that long because I like for people to know who I am.

I would love to see Mr. Ford in there, really. I don't know who started the idea that a President must be a Politician instead of a business man. A politician can't run any kind of business and there is no reason why he can run the U.S. That's the biggest single business in the World.

I just would love to see Mr. Ford, when Congress pulled one of those long stalls of theirs, going around and lifting up the hood and seeing what is the matter.

I see where the rest of the soldiers are coming home from Germany. I would hate to be the man to hand one of these real Soldiers his first glass of Near Beer after 4 years of German brew.

I see where they are bringing home those "unofficial representatives" we have strewn around at these various Conferences. We are the originators of the "unofficial representatives." It's like a man going to a Dinner when he was not invited. Now he may have come unofficial, but still he eats just as much as if he had been invited. Col. House was the originator of this form of entertainment.

If memory don't fail me I think we made a pilgrimage into Mexico "unofficially." All we got was Sand in our eyes. Either make it official and go in shooting, or stay out.

January 27, 1923
See where the Governor of Oklahoma fed thousands at a big three day barbecue where they killed hundreds of beef.

A lot of them ate too much and got sick. But you must remember that here was a bunch of people who had been living, or rather existing, under a Republican Administration for two years, in a Democratic State. So you can forgive any undue haste in storing away their first real meal.

The Slogan of the Feast was "Feed the children and the Democrats first." For the children of today are the voters of tomorrow.

Of course, I will admit that this generosity on the part of our Governor was not as liberal as it might look on paper. He cunningly waited until after the Republicans had been in for two years and Cattle were hardly worth killing, so the outlay for foodstuffs was practically Nil, as the Farmers couldn't sell it anyway.

Being a Dry Governor and not wanting to handle it himself, he sold the bootlegging privilege for enough to carry him through any lean years in case the Democrats should run into another layoff.

Of course, everybody brought their own as they always do in States where they vote dry. But an Oklahoman can only carry enough to last him for one day, so they had to erect emergency Stills right on the grounds to take care of extra Prohibitionists. It was the biggest success ever pulled off in any state, both Beveragelly and Gastronomically.

February 4, 1923

They are having what is called a Fillibuster in the Senate. The name is just as silly as the thing itself. It means that a man can get up and talk for 15 or 20 years at a time, then he is relieved by another, just to keep some Bill from coming to a vote, no matter about the merit of this particular Bill, whether it is good or bad.

The whole foundation of our Government is based on the majority rule, so they have done their duty when they merely vote against it or for it, whichever they like. There is no other Body of Lawmakers in the world that has a thing like that. Why, if a distinguished Foreigner was to be taken around to see our Institutions and was taken into the Senate and not told what the Institution was, and heard a man ramble on, talking that had been going on for 10 or 12 hours, he would probably say, "You have lovely quarters here for your insane, but have you no Warden to look after their health — to see that they don't talk themselves to death?"

Why, if an inmate did that in an Asylum they would put him in solitary confinement. And, mind you, if any demented person spoke that long, there would be something in his speech you would remember, for he, at least, had to be smart or he would never have gone crazy! These just mumble away on any subject.

Imagine a ball player standing at bat and not letting the other side play, to keep from having the game called against him. Why, they would murder him. Or an actor. The first one on in the show talking all night to keep the rest from going on. You know how long he would last. It's against all laws of American Sportsmanship; never mind the Parliamentary part of it.

One Senator threatened to read the Bible into the record as part of his speech. And I guess he would have done it if somebody in the Capitol had had a Bible. Now that would have been a good thing, for it would have given a lot of them a chance to hear what it says. But, of course, that was even too sensible to go through.

Instead, they just did their own act for 10 or 12 hours each, which they thought would be better than anything they could find in the Bible. To imagine how bad this thing is, did you ever attend a dinner and hear a Senator speak for 50 minutes or an hour? If you have, you remember what that did to you? Well, just imagine the same thing but only 12 times worse.

February 4, 1923

America has always wanted an adequate Coast defense, something that would really protect our shores. Well, at last we have it; twelve miles off our Eastern shore is a flotilla of ships which we never hoped three years ago to be able to produce. And, mind you, all this is done without a ship subsidy. I tell you, it is with a great feeling of security that we here in New York can go to sleep at night knowing that just a mere twelve miles away we are being guarded and protected by the entire Merchant Marine of the world.

They are so thick that an ocean liner going to Europe has to give two days notice so they can open up and make a path through to let it by.

They have the ships laid out in streets, and named according to the product sold.

Scotch Avenue is really the elite — it's the Fifth Avenue of the Atlantic. Rye Street is more solid and conservative. Gin Alley is really the Broadway of the Foam. It's the night life. To get your motor boat parked on that alley you have to reserve space days in advance.

It's worked on the same principal as the cafés on land are worked. On land you go in and drink till you get full or broke, whichever happens first; then you get out. Well, out there you tie up your launch beside one of the more popular wholesaling places, and buy till your launch is full or you are broke, same as on land.

If you are a kind of adventurous or artistic nature, they have a miniature Greenwich Village where wood alcohol is sold exclusively. It is put in copper-lined containers, where it is kept till brought ashore, and poured into the prospective corpse.

There has been some talk of hauling dirt and making an island, but they figured that there was enough stuff consumed on the premises, so that the empty bottles would eventually form their own island.

February 10, 1923

This bird, Sir Percy Baldwin, made some slighting remark about our Senate and House of Representatives. Now I resent that. President Harding and I can get vexed at Congress sometimes and say things, but we are all of the same family. We resent any foreigner coming in here and knocking our Representatives. He said if it hadn't been for Congress having something to do with the debts he could have settled it with our Reparations Committee and perhaps got the debt concelled entirely and paid something besides.

You see it's just the difference in England of a little matter of 4 or 5 billion debt. They don't like to bother Dukes and Earls with those trifles.

You see they got the King's children's wedding to go to every little while and it takes years to learn where your place is in line. So you can't expect them to be troubled with Nick Knacks.

The worst thing was, Sir Percy said our Congress were Rural and Pastoral. Now I can understand Congress not calling him

down because they were like me. They didn't know what this
pastoral gag meant. But, offhand, if I had to give a meaning
to it, I would interpret it, and would say it meant HICK.

Now, if Congress won't defend themselves, I will enter protest.
I knock 'em but I like 'em, and I understand 'em. I know they
do wrong sometimes but they mean well. They just don't know.

Sir Percy says all they know is how to raise Hogs and wheat
and sell them. He is wrong. They don't even know how to raise
hogs and wheat.

February 24, 1923

We had quite a few Notables in to our Show last Week which
I introduced to the audience. We had Stanislavsky, the head
and the principal Actor of the Russian Art Players, in to look
us over. Wanted to learn just how not to act by seeing us. I
tried to get him to speak in his native Tongue and I would interpret it for him (he speaks no English) as I do that very often
when I am introducing some Moving Picture Producer who
don't use our Mother Tongue either.

Well, these Russians are having a wonderful season here in
New York. Nobody in New York knows what they are talking
about so it has developed into a fad or game to make your
neighbors, sitting around you, think that you know.

Nothing, outside of Grand Opera in a Foreign Tongue, has
BORED the rich out of more money than these (so-called) simple
Russian Peasants.

We are a fine Nation to call some other Nation simple. The
best Acting I saw there was by the audience. When you take
three thousand people that act like they like a thing when they
don't know what it's all about, that's real acting on the Audience's part.

Keith and the Orpheum Circuit had been trying 20 years to
get Vaudeville even up to $1.50. Along Comes Morris Gest with
a Vaudeville troupe from Russia and charges $5.00 and they
have been here for two years.

You know there is a great tendency all over the Country now
to be High Brow. Everybody is four-flushing and pretending

they are not what they really are, especially here in New York.
More people should work for their Dinner instead of dressing
for it. Half the stiff bosom Shirts worn nowadays, the Laundry
is due on them yet. There are men belonging to swell Golf Clubs
today who, if their Wives ever wanted a Cook, would faint.
Their dues are paid before the grocery bill.

March 17, 1923

The Newspaper Women of all the Papers formed a Newspaper Woman's Club and they give a big Ball and I was asked
to announce the acts.

You know what an announcer at a Benefit Show is. Instead
of letting the show run along smooth and nice, one act after
the other, they have somebody come in and help drag the show
out. He is kinder like a Train Caller, only worse.

You know, Women are doing about all the writing on Newspapers and Magazines now. Of course there are lots of men
working on them too, but they mostly just put the titles under
the pictures. You know, if you are going into the Newspaper
business nowadays, don't get a Pen or a Typewriter — get a
Camera. There are thousands that buy a Paper for the Pictures that don't know the reading is in there at all.

We had there Women writers that cover everything. It would
have been the greatest place in the world for some woman to
have shot her Husband. She could have gotten a lot of Publicity out of it. There were Women Murder Writers that can
tell from the smoke the Caliber Pistol used. Then there were
the fashion Editors that could have described her Chemise Frock
while she did the shooting. Then the Sob Sister Squad who
could have almost made you feel sorry she only had one Husband
to shoot. Then, in case some man should have felt at home and
wanted to knock his wife down, why the Heart Interest Writers
would have been on the job. So you see us People in public life
want to stand in with those Girls as we never know what might
happen.

March 17, 1923

Borrowing money on what's called "easy terms" is a one way

Ticket to the Poor House. Show me ten men that mortgage their land to get money and I will have to get a search warrant to find one that gets the land back again. If you think it ain't a Sucker Game, why is your Banker the richest man in town? Why is your bank the biggest and finest building in your town? Instead of passing bills to make borrowing easy, if Congress passed a Bill that no Person could borrow a cent of Money from any other person, they would have gone down in History as committing the greatest bit of Legislation in the world.

I was raised on a Cattle Ranch and I never saw or heard of a Ranchman going broke — only the ones who had borrowed Money. You can't break a man that don't borrow. He may not have anything, but Boy! he can look the world in the face and say, "I don't owe you Birds a nickel."

You will say, what will all the Bankers do? I don't care what they do. Let 'em go to work, if there is any job any of them could earn a living at. Banking and After-Dinner Speaking are two of the most Non-essential industries we have in this Country, and I am willing to reform if they are.

Now, of course, I am not going to put these Bankers out of Business right away. It's not from a personal view that I am abolishing Banks. It's just that I don't think these Boys realize really what a menace they are. As far as being good fellows, personally, I have heard old-timers talk down home in the Indian Territory and they say the James and Dalton Boys were the most congenial men of their day, too.

New York, March 21, 1923

Manufacturers of bathroom fixtures have advanced their Art to the point where they are practically modern Michael Angelos. Where, in the old days, an Elephant Hook was almost necessary for a wife to drag her Husband toward anything that looked like Water, today those Interior Bath Decorators can almost make one of those things inviting enough to get in without flinching.

But, in doing so, they have destroyed an American Institution, and ruined the only Calendar that a Child ever had. That was the Saturday Night Bath.

Nowadays a Child just grows up in ignorance. From the Cradle to the Altar he don't know what day of the week it is.

In those good old days he knew that the next morning after that weekly Ear Washing he was going to Sunday School. Now he has not only eliminated the Bath on Saturday but has practically eliminated the Sunday School, for neither he nor his Parents know when Sunday Comes.

But, in those days, that old Kitchen Stove was kept hot after supper. And not only the Tea Kettle was filled but other Pots and Pans, and the Family Wash Tub was dragged up by the Fire, and you went out to the Well and helped your Pa draw some Water to mix with that hot. While you was doing that, your Ma, if you stayed Lucky and had a Ma up to then, was getting out all the clean Clothes and fixing the Buttons, and a laying out the schedule of who was to be first. And She was the only one could tell just how much hot Water to put in to make it right.

Now that was an event. It meant something. It brought you closer together. But now bathing is so common there's no Kick to it.

New York, April 7, 1923

Well, I haven't had much time lately to dope out many new jokes. I have been helping the Girls in the Follies make out their Income Tax.

A vital question come up, do Presents come under the heading of Salary?

You know that's a mighty big item with us. When I say Us, I don't mean Me, as no one has given me anything yet, but I stick around in case a few crumbs drop.

I have been looking for a bribe from some of our prominent men to keep their name out of my act, but the only ones who even speak to me are the ones I mention. So I guess about the only way you can get a Man sore nowadays is to ignore him.

[On April 21, 1923, Will Rogers wrote in the form of his article his famous letter to "Mr. Warren Gamaliel Harding, President of these United States and Viceroy of the District of

Columbia, Chevy Chase Golf Club, Washington, D.C.," applying for the Ambassadorship to England or "a job with the James Boys."]

I can tell by observing that it does not come under the Civil Service or competitive examination. Neither, on the other hand, is it a purely political appointment, as Mr. Harvey [who had come home to resign] adapted his Politics to fit the occasion.

Now that would not be even necessary in my case as I have no Politics. I am for the Party that is out of Power, no matter which one it is. But I will give you my word that, in case of my appointment, I will not be a Republican; I will do my best to pull with you, and not embarrass you.

Now I want to enumerate a few of my qualifications for the position of Ambassador to the Court of James (I don't know whether it is St. or Jesse). But, anyway, it's some of the James Family.

My principal qualification would be my experience in Speech-making. That, as statistics have proven, is 90 percent of the duties of a Diplomat.

Now I can't make as many speeches as my predecessor, unless, of course, I trained for it. But I would figure on making up in quality any shortcomings I might have in endurance.

Now, the way I figure it out, what one has to do is to make his speeches so that they will sound one way to the English, and the direct opposite to the Hearst readers back over here. Now Harvey was rather unfortunate in that respect; he made them so they would sound two ways, but both Nations took the Wrong Way.

Now if I wanted Mr. Balfour to take something back, I would just kid him into it; make him believe I didn't care whether he took it back or not. You know how it is, just like the Democrat Senators do with Lodge.

Another qualification that must not by any means be under-estimated is my Moving Picture experience. You see, for an official position nowadays, we must pay more attention to how our public men screen if we are to have to look at them every day in the news films. We must not only get men with screen personality, but we must get men who know Camera angles and know when they are getting the worst of it in a picture and not be caught in the background during the taking of some big event.

Europeans are far ahead of us in this line of Diplomacy, and, if you don't watch them, you are liable to be found photographed with the Mob instead of the Principals.

The thing is to do some little thing during the taking of the picture that will draw the audience's attention to you. For instance, during some Court ceremony, I could just playfully kick the King. Now you don't know how a little thing like that would get over with the public. Or, at one of the big weddings in the Abbey, I could just sorter nonchalantly step on the bride's train, as they passed by, perhaps ripping it off, or any little Diplomatic move like that. You don't realize how just little bits like that could make our Ambassador stand out over all the other Countries.

Now, another thing, I ride horseback, so the Prince of Wales and I could ride together and, on account of my experience with the rope, I could catch his horse for him.

Then I play a little Polo, just enough to get hit in the mouth, but the English would enjoy that.

Now, to offset the above mentioned qualifications, I may lack a few Social ones, but what I lacked in knowledge I could make up in tact. I would not at any dinner pick up a single weapon until I saw what the Hostess was going to operate with first. When in doubt, tell a funny story till you see what the other fellow is going to do.

Then, of course, any glaring error on my part would be laid onto the customs of my Country and not on me personally.

Now the feature that I feel rather modest about referring to, but which is really my principal asset, is my being able to wear Silk Knee Breeches — not only wear them, but what I mean, look like something in them.

It seems that the Lord instead of distributing my very few good points around as he does on most homely men, why, he just placed all of mine from the knee down.

Say, I can put on those silk Rompers and clean up. Now I

don't like to grab off a Guy's job by knocking him, but you know
we haven't had a decent looking leg over there in years. You
know you can't stay in the Follies 7 years on nothing. Well, it
wasn't my good looks. So what was it but my Shape?

That brings us down to Golf. Now I will have to admit that
my political education has been sadly neglected as I have never
walked over many green pastures. Horses are too cheap for a man
to spend half his life walking over the country looking for holes
in the ground. But as I understand this lack of Golf will not
handicap me in England as it would here, as Mr. Volstead has
not percolated into that land and the game is still fought out on
the 19th hole. And I do talk a corking Game of Golf.

Now, Mr. President, if this suggestion receives the consideration that I think it deserves, I should like to get the appointment
at once, as I want to get over there before all the king's Children
are married. If one can't attend a royal marriage, why, their
ambassadorship has been a failure as far as publicity is concerned
for that event is the World's Series in England.

Now, as to Salary, I will do just the same as the rest of the
Politicians — accept a small salary as pin Money, AND TAKE A
CHANCE ON WHAT I CAN GET.

P.S. If you don't want me, Turkey wants me to represent them
in Washington. So where would you rather have me — in
England or Washington?

[No doubt the place President Harding wanted Will in is not
ordinarily located in either England or Washington.]

May 5, 1923

The other night the Newspaper Men ond Owners from all
over the Country held their big Banquet at the Waldorf. It was
given by the advertising end of the Newspaper business. Naturally it had to be, as the advertising end is the only one which
could pay for a thing like that. If the Editorial Department ever
gave a Dinner everybody would have to bring their own Sand-
wiches.

There was 32 at the Speaker's Table. Eight must have got

caught, as I have heard Ali Baba's original cast was composed of 40.

A Bishop opened the Dinner with Prayer for the Newspaper men. I never in my life wished to know how to pray as bad as I did then, for I wanted to offer up one for you readers and Subscribers. Nobody said a word for you but me. I tell you, the more I hear these big men talk, the more I realize I am the only one that is trying to uphold the rights of the common people. Now I don't want anything from you YET, but, if things keep on, I may make a call for funds to carry on Truth.

I wish some of you Prohibition Papers could have seen your Owners and Editors during this Convention week. They got so full they couldn't hardly write an Editorial on enforcement.

According to all the Speeches it was a mighty momentous occasion, and I never felt so impressed in my life as to be able to be at a table when the affairs of the World were settled. Each said we were at a Crisis. I tried my best to get them not to settle it till they talked it over with you all, but they seemed to think if they didn't arrange it right there that they might not ever have a chance.

The reason I am telling you all this is I wasn't right sure that you know about this critical point of our Existence we were facing. I didn't, till I heard them say it. So if affairs don't go to suit you from now on you can always blame it on that dinner.

May 19, 1923

Well, there is quite a little taking place in the papers the last day or so. I bought some stock in a Chinese Bandit Corporation yesterday. I studied whether to buy that or New York Hotel Stock. Their ideas are similar; they both work on the ransom plan. We have been sending Missionaries over there for years; I knew they would get those people educated up to American ways.

As I write this, the people are still being held, and ours, and all the other governments, are threatening China with what they will do. Years ago Chinese Brigands killed two Germans, and Germany took about a fourth of China as pay for them. That was the highest price ever paid for two individuals.

Just suppose some foreign Government took part of this country every time a foreigner was killed over here. The United States would consist of Rhode Island.

These Governments ought to get together and do something about this. Those heathen Chinese should not be allowed to have bandits in their country. If you let 'em keep on, the first thing you know they will have pickpockets and taxi robbers over there. I bet you England wouldn't stand for them annoying one of their citizens. They would take their oil land away from them. And if they didn't have any, they would make 'em get some.

May 26, 1923

Church people all over the country are divided and arguing over where we come from. Never mind where we come from, Neighbor. Women living next door to you will find out where you come from, and all about you, better than all the Preachers. Just let the Preachers make it their business where you are going when you leave here.

CHAPTER TWO

"I Am at Heart an Optimist . . ."

[Will had claimed that the Democrats ran him away from
the east in 1919, to get rid of his kidding, and that now it was
the Republicans.]

Beverly Hills, June 30, 1923

I arrived at my hut in Beverly Hills just in time to keep real
estate men from plotting off and selling my front yard. They
will sell you anything or anybody's in the world as long as they
can get a first payment.

You buy lots in Los Angeles with the same frequency you
would newspapers in any other towns. After buying it, you put
it back in the hands of the Agents again, for don't think you are
going to get away with that lot. It has to be sold three or four
more times that day. Why, every lot out here has its own agent.
Agents get rich out here just off the various commissions on one
lot. If an agent handles two lots he opens up a Branch office and
has an assistant. And you call one a real estate agent and he won't
sell you anything. He is a REALATOR. It's the same as what the
old-fashioned real estate agent used to be only the commission is
different.

Your having no money don't worry the agents, if they can
just get a couple of dollars, or an old overcoat, or a shot gun
or anything to act as a first payment. Second-hand Fords is A One
collateral.

It's the greatest game I ever saw. You can't lose. Everybody
buys to sell and nobody buys to keep. What's worrying me is

who is going to be the last owner. It's just like an auction; the only one stuck is the last one.

July 21, 1923

Well, I see by this morning's papers that our old friend, Mr. Gary of the Steel Trust, after much letter writing and persuasion from President Harding, has promised the President that he would do away with the 12 hour a day work in the steel mills (just as soon as it could be arranged). He said in the letter that it would take some time to arrange it.

Now, he promised the President to do this, but you know, so many Republicans have promised him things since he has been in and then didn't make good that it is getting so that a Republican promise is not much more to be depended on than a Democratic one. And that has always been considered the lowest form of collateral in the world.

Now Mr. Gary says it will take time. You see, a man who has been working for years for 12 or 14 hours a day, and you cut him down to 8, and you have a physical wreck on your hands. You take a person who is used to the cool air of a steel furnace for half the 24 hours of each day and bring him into the stuffy atmosphere outdoors, or a home, and he can't stand it.

Now, the way the Judge is going to do is to kinder taper it down, say, the first year after the letter was written to the President, why, he will cut the men down to 11 and a ½ hours a day work. He will hold them on that for a couple of years, then, if they are still living and the shock don't kill them, he will get them down to 11 hours flat for another couple of years, and so on till about in 1940 things will be entirely on an 8 hours basis.

August 18, 1923 [*After Harding's Death*]

President Harding goes to his resting place a martyr, a martyr to the Boneheadedness of Reception Committees. You wouldn't ask your hired man to do in one week the amount of real physical work that each Committee asked him to do in a day. Imagine three long Speeches in one day in Seattle at different places, and

Parade for two hours in the hot Sun with his hat off most of the time, besides a thousand other things he was asked to do.

When the next Congress meets they should pass a law to shoot all Reception Committees, or teach them consideration for other people.

If Jack Dempsey had left Washington and undertaken this same strain, when he got back Uncle Joe Cannon could have licked him.

Any of you who have slept, or tried to, on a Train at Night and got into a Town early in the morning, you know you don't feel like speaking or Parading. You want to go to a Hotel and go to bed. Now can you imagine the President's case? Every morning at 6 A.M. to be awakened by a Band (it wouldn't be so bad if it was a good band) and you look out and there is the Town's best Citizens in Antique Hats, ready to show you the Fire House, the new Aquaduct, the High School and City Hall. The smell of the Moth Balls from the long tail coats of the Committee, morning after morning, would give a man some kind of disease.

Then, of course, he is always asked to speak out in the open. They have 60-acre Fields and put seats around them and call 'em Stadiums, and expect a man to talk in them. Anyone who has ever spoken outdoors knows what outdoor speaking does to your voice. The Town with the cheapest land and the most Concrete can have the largest Stadiums.

Now, as just an example of the trip, he loved Golf. But do you think these Committees let him do it? No, Sir, he only got out three times on the entire trip. I offered a suggestion here when they were making the arrangements, but like everything coming from a Comedian it was considered not practical. I wanted to let the Reception Committee go ahead and rent the Suits and be at the Station looking Funny just like these others he was used to day after day, but instead of dragging him off where he was going, why just say, "Mr. President, we have engaged a room at the Central Hotel. Here's a Ford Car at your disposal. Here's a Card to any Golf Course in our Town. Now we know you are tired, so you just make yourself at home these few days, do just as you please. We have no plans for you at all."

Well, my plan wasn't adopted. But if it had been even partially tried in all the Towns on this trip we would have all been happy and had him with us today. The first Town that ever does do that with their visiting Guests and treats them as if Human, they will soon be wondering where all their popularity comes from.

November 17, 1923

A race horse, *In Memorandum,* beats the great *Zev,* the International Favorite, and *My Own* thrown in for good measure. That news will perhaps interest 40 million human beings and 2000 Bookmakers, while the news of the unearthing of a Prehistoric Skull at Santa Barbara, California, linking us up with the Neanderthal Age will only be appreciated by a small minority of us thinking people.

According to Linnaeus humanity comprises four Races: the Whites, having a light colored skin, belonging to the Caucasian race; the Blacks, the completest possible negation of White; Republicans, a form of Genus Homo Ape in his earliest Prehistoric State; and, last of the four races, the Democrat.

The Democrat doubtless originated in the eastern Hemisphere. The main structural characters distinguishing him are his gait, the modification of the feet for walking instead of prehension, and the great Toe being nonapposable, and most of all, the enormous development of the brain, and smooth rounded Skull.

But what cares the man of today for the Neanderthal Age! He is of the Speculative Age. If he can get 10 dollars down on the Nose of a winner at about 15 to one, he don't care if we descend from a goat or ape.

December 1, 1923

I thought for a while, the way Lloyd George was complimenting us over here, that he might possibly be considering tossing that old Welsh Cap of his onto the White House Lawn. But I, along with various other slow-thinking citizens of our land, find that he didn't come here just to put wreaths on England's Foes of former days out of any particular love for them. He

knew that we are the champion yap Nation of the world for
swallowing Propaganda.

YOU CAN TAKE A SOB STORY AND A STICK OF CANDY AND LEAD
AMERICA RIGHT OFF INTO THE DEAD SEA.

He read the life of Lincoln coming over on the boat, and we
marvelled at his knowledge and admiration of our great Com-
moner. Perhaps he used the same Adjectives that he had many
times applied to Cromwell in England. His next jump was direct
to Mount Vernon to the Tomb of Washington.

Now you know what he thought of Washington. You know
what Firpo thinks of Dempsey.

He is a Super-A Politician. Instead of going through the
Country, doing the old Gag of kissing the Babies of the voters,
he pulled a New One. He visited all the graves of our departed
Heroes who he knew were dear to us, and he complimented
them and told what they would do for Civilization if they were
alive today. He knew they couldn't raise up and deny it.

Beverly Hills, December 29, 1923

[In an article in which he compared the soldier in the War
at $1.25 a day, which he figured boiled down to having bullets
fired at them at 5¢ apiece, and of workers on wooden ships that
received $1.00 for each nail driven, Will lashed out at those
that opposed the soldier's bonus. "You promised them everything but the Kitchen Stove if they would go to War," he reminded, "and all they got was $1.25 a day and some knitted
Sweaters and sox which after examining them they 'wore the
Sox for Sweaters and the Sweaters for Sox.' " He then suggested
that if the "wealthy men" who chiefly opposed the bonus would
submit to a tax on their "tax exempt" securities the bonus
could be paid.]

These boys helped their Country in a time of need. Tax-
Exempt Bond Buyers knowingly hindered it in a time of need
by cheating it out of Taxes.

In 1916 there was 1296 men whose income was over $300,000

and they paid a Billion in Taxes. This year there was only 246, whose income was supposed to be over 3 hundred thousand, and they only paid 153 million.

You mean to tell me that there are only 246 men in this Country who only make 300 thousand? Why, say, I have spoken at Dinners in New York where there was that many in one Dining Room, much less the United States.

That old Alibi about the Country not being able to pay is all Apple Sauce. There is no debt in the World too big for this Country to pay if they owe it. If you owed it to some foreign nation you would talk about honor and then pay it. Now what do you want to beat your own kin out of anything for? You say, "Oh, it's not enough to do him any good, anyway." If it's not enough to do him any good it's not enough to do you any harm when you pay it.

Tax-exempt Securities will drive us to the Poor House, not Soldier's Bonuses. This Country is not broke. Automobile Manufacturers are three months behind in their Orders, and Whiskey never was so High in its life.

And don't forget that there are many and many thousands of Boys who came back and are not classed as Disabled but who will carry some effect of that terrible War as long as they live. I never met 10 who were not injured in some minor way, to say nothing of the dissatisfaction. I claim we owe them everything we have got, and if they will settle for a Bonus we are lucky.

Now if a Man is against it why don't he at least come out and tell the real truth? "I don't want to spare the Money to pay you Boys." I think the best Insurance in the World against another War is to take care of the Boys who fought in the last one. You may want to use them again.

January 5, 1924

I have looked up the statistics of the Newspaper Business and I find that 92 percent perish after the first issue. The Sheriff takes the place of the Subscriber when the Bills come in after one

Edition. So we are among the 8 percent when we are able to go to Bat the Second Inning.

Now let's get down to bed rock and find out what has kept us among the elect 8 percent. Just one thing, and that is Truth. We are staking the reputation of our Periodical on the assumption that nothing in Public Life (or out of it, for that matter) is any good. Now what we have set out to do is to find the worst. It's no trouble to pick out the Bad but I tell you when you sit down to pick out the Worst, you have set Some Task for yourself.

The issue this week will be known as the Lament Number, or Hearts and Flowers Week. The week just passed has been the saddest of any known to all alleged Humorists, Paragraphers and Stage Comedians. When I picked up my morning paper one day recently and read one of the Headlines, my Wife had to pour Water on me for 30 minutes to bring me to. The Headline read, "Henry Ford not to run for President." Here I had been laying awake nights stacking up Ford Jokes and I felt better fortified for the coming Campaign than a Prize Fighter with a Rock hidden in his Glove.

I had some Gags that I had never pulled. I was just nursing them along until the heat of the Campaign come and then I was going to cut loose with them. Well, that announcement just knocked me Cuckoo. It was just like taking away a Man's bread-and-butter. You take a Ford Joke away from an Article or a Monologue and you have just about ripped the Backbone out of it.

Then also you must take into consideration that I really wanted him to be President. It was just as big a disappointment to me as it was to millions of you other folks who wanted him. Of course, outside of my personal friendship and admiration for Mr. Ford and his many great qualities, I had (I will admit) a monetary thought in mind, had he been elected. The more I see of Public affairs and Public Offices the more I realize that a Comedian has a wonderful opportunity if appointed to one of the high Presidential Appointments.

Comedians always have held those positions and there is no reason why I can't go in and do as bad as some of the rest. So you will see this Ford Boom busting a Tire has been a double disappointment to me.

Mr. Ford says, "America is on Wheels today." He means, "America is on Tick today." If an Automobile Manufacturer could make a Car so good that he could advertise it as follows, "Will last till it's paid for," he could put Ford out of business.

January 12, 1924

Now, after gathering all the returns of the New Years, I find in hundreds of Newspapers all over the United States that they devoted yards of space to what some of our Rich Men think of the business prospects of the coming year. It's the same old thing every year. It's got so a working man hates to pick up his Paper New Year's morning, for staring him in the face will be:

"Judge Gary, the head of the Steel Trust, says, 'I am at heart an Optimist, and I look to the coming year with great fortitude. I think that if everybody buckles down and gives 12 hours labor for 8 hours pay I can see nothing ahead that will affect the present prosperity of our grand nation.' "

Then Mr. Mellon is quoted and says as follows: "I am by nature an Optimist. I never want to feel Pessimistic. Because of a Presidential Election there is some uneasiness. But I look forward to one of the best years financially I have ever had."

Mr. Ford also says as follows: "There was some loose motion in the Body of our Political Life. But after I made an adjustment on the differential of the Koolidge Kampaign, and tightened up the loose parts with my declaration of where I stood, why things are oiled up, and going smoothly, unless Hiram Hearst Johnston or McAdoo carelessly thrusts a heavy Pedestrian in front of the Vehicle. But I am at heart an Optimist and I have great faith in the coming year. Speaking from a personal business angle, you just can't imagine how many people want those things, pardon me, I mean buy those things."

Then will come what Charlie Schwab has to say: "I am at heart an Optimist. I think the coming year will be the Banner year of 1924."

Then will follow a dozen other Rich Birds, depending on

where the Paper is printed and who is the richest man they have in their town.

Now these same Gags you have to read every New Years. They don't even change the wording. Every New Year holds the same thing in store for them. But they are as sure to make the front page every New Years as a Screen Star is of having her previous Husbands all enumerated every time the Papers write up her latest divorce.

Why, in the name of common sense, don't they ask somebody else what they think of the coming year? What those Guys think is pretty well established. Sure they are Optimistic of the future. If we had their Dough we would be Optimistic too. I would not only be an Optimist for that much Jack, I would even be a Vegetarian.

Why don't they ask me what the New Year has in hiding for me? Well, I want to tell you that it don't look any too rosy from where I am sitting. With every Public Man we have elected doing Comedy, I tell you I don't see much of a chance for a Comedian to make a living. I am just on the verge of going to work. They can do more funny things naturally than I can think of to do purposely.

Instead of asking Gary what he thinks, why don't they ask a Farmer? There is 10 million Farmers and only one Gary. See what the Farmer is paid every year for his Optimism. And he has to be an Optimist or he wouldn't still be a Farmer.

January 19, 1924

The Exposure is a weekly periodical devoted to Art, Commerce, Science, and anything pertaining to uplift, and for the better things in our community.

The past week 9 Women in various parts of the U.S. shot and killed their Husbands. In no line of our modern Scientific advancement has progress been more marked than in the Marksmanship of our Weaker Sex. Husbands are being hit in these days and times who in years past were just merely shot at.

It is true that Woman is the weaker sex physically. But the Automatic (with its sprinkling of Bullets) has proven to be the great stabilizer between the two Sexes. Remington, and Smith and Wesson, have done more to advance the cause of Woman's Sufferage than all the arguments of its millions of believers. Man used to be bigger than Woman but now Woman carries the difference in her Vanity Case, neatly oiled and loaded.

If you will notice in any of your Towns you will find located as near as possible to the Marriage Bureau a Firearms store. In some cases the Gun is bought with the License, but in most cases the Pistol is procured the day following the betrothal.

If you see a Woman or a young Girl at a shooting gallery at any of our Resorts or Amusement places, you will know at once that she is Engaged, and is practicing for the inevitable. So The Exposure, after carefully examining the steps made in all Scientific lines, awards the Palm to the Woman's Marksmanship.

Now we must go from the scientific standpoint to the practical side. What has been accomplished by this continuous parade to the Cemetery? Has it improved the Character of our Husbandry? No, it has not. The Exposure believes that the Type and Stability of Husbands were never lower than at this particular Era. This rattle of Musketry in the Homes has made more Dead Husbands, but has not made any better ones.

Beverly Hills, January 19, 1924

So far, the The Exposure is the only Paper of any magnitude that has not made Editorial comment on this small-time War being argued out in the Episcopal Church. It's bad enough to have to expose the Political affairs without having to give our version of the Bible.

How the Lord got here on earth, whether by Virgin Birth, or Via the familiar Stork, has nothing to do with it. He must have been a pretty good man after he did get here.

If some of those Birds would spend their time following His example instead of trying to figure out His mode of arrival and departure, they would come nearer getting confidence in their Church. Their is no argument in the World carries the hatred that a Religious belief one does. It seems the more learned a man is the less consideration he has for another man's belief.

Speaking of not believing, I don't believe that Noah took a pair of every kind of Animals into the Ark, for I have seen Men, since Prohibition changed their drink, claim that they saw Animals that Noah never even heard of. But just because I don't believe Noah's African Adventures maby others do, and besides with my small experience with Animals I don't believe Noah could round up all the Animals in one Herd without the Skunk causing a Stampede.

That is no reason why I should go around shouting about it, and be arrested for Heresay. I can enjoy a good Zoo as well as any one. Whether the Animals come here by Ark or by Subway makes no difference to me. If they are going to argue religion in the Church instead of teaching it no wonder you can see more People at a Circus than at a Church.

January 26, 1924

I see by the Papers that they say "Germany is going insane." I wish you would name me a Nation that is competent of judging insanity.

Russia wants us to recognize them. Our government say they won't recognize them. We will sell them something but we won't let on that we know them. Russia wants us to recognize them so they can send over an Embassy. Then they can get in on this Bootlegging.

Russia should take a tip from Mexico. Mexico got along fine that last few years till we started to recognize them, and immediately they broke out into another Revolution.

January 26, 1924

They are having an argument over Mr. Mellon's Tax Bill. Mellon wants to cut the Surtax on the Rich, and leave it as it is on the poor, as there is more poor than rich.

Beverly Hills, February 9, 1924

[When the Teapot Dome oil scandal boiled over and got into a Senatorial Investigation Will remarked that "statistics have proven that the surest way to get anything out of the Public mind and never to hear of it again is to have a Senate Committee appointed to look into it."

Will himself suggested that a "wet nurse" like that looking after the morals of Hollywood be appointed for the oil industry. His opinion was that "scandal for scandal" the oil people were worse than the Movie people. In addition he had an interesting suggestion]:

Now, what I propose is for the Women's Clubs to take action the minute a thing like this happens and have that particular Brand of Oil banished. Let each State act separately and if a man is suspected (make it like the Movies, he don't have to be convicted), why get busy at once and don't allow any of his Oil to be publicly sold.

For there is one thing that we want to inculcate into the minds of the Youths of this Country: that honesty and fair dealing with our own Government is the foundation of this nation.

Our history honors no man who betrayed, or attempted to betray, a government trust.

I don't want the patriotism of my children endangered by driving around in a car that is propelled by Gasoline manufactured from profits derived from tampering with the integrity of those Noble Officials whom we Trust with not only our lives but our oil.

Now, mind you, I am not against the good work that Club Women are doing for the Public good. I am in favor of them carrying it further and embracing some industry where it will do even more good.

The Public is always after the Stage and Screen for some unfortunate happening. But can you imagine for a minute Sir Harry Lauder sending a Hundred Thousand Dollars to a Man, by way of a Suit Case, and not having a Note or Mortgage to show for it as security? We of the screen are supposed to be very careless of our English, but never have I heard one of us mistake $68,000 for 6 or 8 cows.

The very day that all this testimony came out in the Papers there was in the same Paper a picture showing a Negro with one of those Truth Machines fastened on his wrist. They are supposed to make you tell the Truth, or rather to tell when you are lying. They had brought this Negro out of Jail where he had been sentenced for 99 years. Now if he admitted that he killed the Party he would get Life. It meant either life or 99 years to him, and they waste all of this time on him.

That very day in Washington here were Guys testifying with nothing on their wrists but Silk Shirts. God bless America for a Sense of Humor.

If they had ever taken one of those Truth Machines to that investigation there would have been more Americans sailing for Europe than went during the War. What's become of the old-fashioned Felon that used to be arrested for Perjury?

Now I am in favor of appointing a keeper for the oil business like the Movies have. I would off hand suggest William J. Bryan. What they most need is someone whose Reputation is above reproach, and someone who will add a certain Dignity to the Oil Business which is sadly lacking now.

Now I think Bryan would be the best as it would get his mind off this business of descending from a Monkey. Then he could not only add a certain prestige to what has degraded into a Greasy industry, but he could also advise them when and with whom to place their Bribes where they would not be apt to creep out.

April 5, 1924

I have a Scheme that I think would be very beneficial and add to the efficiency of this investigation. That is, have certain days for certain things. Now, say for instance, Mondays, that is for Confessions. Everybody that wants to confess come over and confess on Monday. Tuesday, is for Accusations. If you want to accuse anybody come Tuesday, and accuse from 9 A.M. to 6 P.M.

Then that leaves Wednesday, Thursdays, Fridays, and Saturdays for Denials. You see it takes longer to Deny than anything else. That would make it a lot easier on the Spectators. They would know then just what days to go.

They could sell the House out Tuesdays. Everybody wants to

hear Accusations, and nobody wants to hear Denials. So you are just taking up spectators' time by having them there on days when all they hear is, "It's absolutely false. I didn't receive the money, and if those 18 witnesses have testified that I did they must have been mistaken." Or here is another favorite line: "I don't remember."

I tell you, Folks, if American Men are as Dumb as some of them have Appeared on the witness stand this year, Civilization is Tottering.

If I am called I will remember and will tell 'em more things than Vanderlip told the Rotary Club in Sing Sing. I won't hide behind my Vast Wealth and refuse to answer. I will tell 'em some things about Hollywood that will rock the very foundation of Censorship.

Beverly Hills, April 27, 1924

Just last week out here in Los Angeles they dug up a lot of old Human Bones that are supposed to be hundreds of years Older than old King Tut and the fancy Undertakers who flourished about his time. Now there were three of these old Fossils dug up out here and among them was a Rock Gavel. So the supposition is that they were holding a Committe meeting investigating somebody, and one of them as the Chairman had a gavel.

It only shows you how Bad things are getting out here in the Bored Spaces when they have to dig down 200 feet to find a Sucker.

Generally we await them at the Depot or at the Community Camping Ground.

CHAPTER THREE

Political "Follies" of 1924

[Will attended both the Republican Nominating Convention at Cleveland, a Convention held "for no reason at all" since Coolidge could have been nominated "by postcards," and the Democratic Nominating Convention held in Madison Square Garden in New York.

The latter Convention, hopelessly split by the Drys under William G. McAdoo and the Wets under Al Smith, was the longest in history. He wrote that "they nominated everybody but the four horsemen" and described in his Follies Routines and in his articles the delegates getting old and reminded them that here in the Garden they were depriving New York of its annual bath. In final desperation he sent out in his newspaper reports "a speech" that he was going to make, so he said, but warned the public not to wait for it. In a masterpiece of political oratory (written) he put into nomination the name of the only man they could win with]:

OH, MY FRIENDS, I am too good a Democrat not to be appreciative of what the party has done for me, not to try and warn you while there is yet time.

We are not gathered here just to name a nominee of the next election, but we are here to name the next President of the grand and glorious United States, of which this party today is the sole refuge for the true patriot.

In naming a man for this high and lofty office there are certain traditions and specifications which we must hold in mind, if we want to reach a successful victory in November.

The man we name must be a man who is not now connected with those intersectional fights and feuds here on the floor. The man I am about to name is absolutely aloof from them.

The man we name to carry us to victory must be geographically strong enough to carry a majority of New England. The man I am about to name knows these mysterious canny people.

The man we name must be able to go into the far Westland and reap a majority. The man I am about to name possesses the attributes to do that very deed.

The man we name must be able to remove any doubtful States into the realm of certainty. The man I am about to name can give you a majority that will look like a census report.

The man we name here must be a man who never earned outside of public life a fee of over $10. The man I am about to name has that honorable reputation.

The man we name here must have no taint of Morgan or Wall Street. The man I am about to name never saw Wall Street.

The man we name here must have absolutely no affiliation with the Klan. The man I am about to name is not a member of the Klan.

The man we name must be of no minority religious creed. The man I am about to name belongs to the creed whose voters are in the majority.

On account of the present length of the convention, the man we name must not be of too many score years of age. The man I am about to name has many useful and unworried years of public service ahead of him.

The man we name must have had no connection with oil. The man I am about to name never used oil, except at Government or State expense.

Oh, gentlemen of the grand and glorious Democratic Party, let us not make a mistake. We have our greatest chance this year to bring home victory. That great scandal in our opponents' party and their close affiliation with predatory wealth has given us an unbounded opportunity.

over

Don't let us disrupt the party when we can win. We will go to a sure Democratic defeat if we name the wrong man. Oh, my friends, let us be connected with a victory in this glorious year of 1924. Why court defeat?

The man I am about to name is the only man in these grand and glorious United States who, if we nominate, we can go home and have no worry as to the outcome. Don't, oh, my Democratic Colleagues, listen to my friend Bryan. He named ten candidates; ten men can't win! Only one man can win. Oh, my newly made friends, have confidence in me. Trust me just this once and I will lead you out of this darkened wilderness into the gates of the White House. Oh, my tired and worn friends, there is only one man. That man I am about to name to you is Calvin Coolidge. *Is a Republican*

July 4, 1924

Met at One O'clock and My Friend, Mr. Augustus Thomas, the Orator and Playwrite, read what was called the Declaration of Independence. Nobody knows how they ever found a Copy of it. The J. P. Morgan Private Library has most all those old things, so guess he loaned it to them.

The Delegates seemed mildly amused as he read this strange old Legend. On its completion a Delegate at Large from Georgia offered an amendment to the Declaration of Independence. Ohio called for a Poll of their Delegation in case the Declaration came to a vote.

Mr. Thomas explained before starting to read it that it was written by Thomas Jefferson, a Democrat.

Had its Author happened to have been a Republican it would have been denounced as a Senatorial Oligarchy and a Tool of the Interests written for the sole protection of predatory Wealth.

August 23, 1924

There are two things that I don't care how smart you are, you will never understand. One is an Alienist's testimony, and the other is a Railroad timetable.

New York, September, 1924 Follies Routine

I see today where the Pope appealed to the men to see if they couldn't use their influence to get the women to wear more clothes.

I don't know just how whole-heartedly that request will be entered into by the men.

If men do start interfering with women's clothes the Vatican will have some more marriages to declare illegal.

They say that women's clothes are a disgrace. One minister said he never saw such indecency in his life. I never saw such legs.

If some of them will look backwards over their shoulder in a mirror it will do more good than all the persuasion.

Then the goloshes, they wear 'em loose and they sound like a mule with buggy harness on running away.

I am going to get 'em some of these wrapped puttees to go from the bottom of the skirt to the top of the goloshes.

October 4, 1924

Last week the Holy Name Society, that as you know is a Society formed to prevent the taking of the Lord's Name in vain — well, last week 100 thousand of them went from New York down to Washington to see President Coolidge to get him to use his influence with Dawes to keep him from cussing.

Well, President Coolidge broached the subject to Dawes and all he got for an answer was, "Hell-and-Maria, you can't learn an old dog new tricks. If I have to give up cussing to be Vice President, I would rather not be one. The job itself is enough to make a man cuss."

November 2, 1924

The Income Tax has made more Liars out of the American people than Golf has. You should get out a new kind of Tax every year or two, so they don't know how to beat it. When this one first come out, the first year, every man's name on it was down for two or three times the amount that he pays today.

We had no tax experts, no Lawyers that made a specialty of

showing you what you could take off. You simply had a Wife
and so Many Children and that was about as far as you knew
what to charge off.

Why don't we have a sales tax. That is the only fair and
just tax. Have no tax on necessary foods, and moderate priced
necessary clothes, but put a Tax on every other thing you buy
or use. Then the rich fellow who buys more and uses more certainly has no way of getting out of paying his share. Collect
it at the source, that is, at the manufacturer's. Don't depend on
the retailer. That way it would not cost much to collect. Canada
has tried it and it has proven absolutely satisfactory. Do it that
way and every time you see a big 10 or 12 thousand dollar
Limousine going down the street you would know that the
fellow in there has already paid the government a big percentage
of tax on it to help run the country. You would know the Government has theirs. Put big taxes on everything of a luxury
nature. You do that, and let the working man know the rich
have paid before they got it and you will do more than any one
thing to settle some of the unrest and dissatisfaction that you
hear every day — not by the Reds or Bolsheviki, or even Pinks,
but by real citizens and every day people of this country. They
know there is something wrong with taxation, and I have yet to
meet one person, since those lists were published, that didn't
think so. No slick Lawyer or income tax expert can get you
out of a sales tax.

It is so much a dollar on every luxury you buy. Then if you
like to live in wealth and luxury, the poor fellow knows you are
paying for it and he will not feel envious of you. He will even
Encourage you to buy more so it will help out the Government.

The beauty of the plan is if you don't want to pay any tax
just don't buy anything outside of bare necessities and you pay
no tax. But the minute you want a pair of those Knee Golf
Breeches, why let the Government pop it to you for about 50
cents on each dollar. That would cure you of looking funny.

Children's plaything, no tax! but Golf and Polo, hang it on
them with plenty tax. If a man really feels like he wants to
swing something Sunday morning, give him an axe and head

him towards a woodpile. Let his wife give him a broom and
see how many strokes he can go round the room in.

You do this and you wouldn't have to wait until just before
election to know what your local rich man paid in the way of
tax. If you saw him with high priced things during the year
you would know he had paid every cent of his share. Now that
is what I call a real Issue. Taxation is about all there is to
Government. People don't want their taxes lower near as much
as the Politician tries to make you believe. People want JUST
taxes, more than they want lower taxes. They want to know
that every man is paying his proportionate share according to
his wealth.

November 15, 1924

Well, the election is finally over. The result was just as big
a surprise as the announcement that Christmas was coming in
December. The Republicans mopped up, the Democrats
gummed up.

November 29, 1924

Heard a lot about Ireland and am all excited about going
there. That is where some of my folks come from. There is a
fine breed for you, Irish-Indian. Ziegfeld says I have a touch of
Hebraic in me too. Which would make me Irish, Jewish, Indian.

My family crest would in that case be a Shillalah with a
Tomahawk on one end, and a percent sign (%) on the other.

December 15, 1924

In parts of India they have a Law that if a Man is married
and is unfaithful to his wife, her family can take him out and
publicly shoot him. There is no trial or anything. It is just
their religious and State custom (and we call them uncivilized).
Well, anyway, if that was the custom over here, I would take
every cent I make and put it into an Ammunition Factory.

January 18, 1925

If somebody wants to do something for the Automobile Public, let him invent a car that will sell second handed, one week after you bought it, for at least one fourth of what you gave for it.

I see where the fleet got back with a girl aboard. If a girl with Dresses could sneak on Board and no one see her all this time, what could the enemy do if they happened to dress like sailors?

February 1, 1925

New Yorkers know nothing about the Sun. The moon and sun mean nothing to a New Yorker. You can't see the sun out of the Subway and you can't see the Moon through the top of a Taxicab. So when the two passed in this eclipse it meant nothing in their lives.

New Yorkers were so used to Traffic Stops that they could not realize how any two objects could pass peacefully by each other without hitting. It was also the only thing ever took place back here that went off on schedule time. I wish those Scientists run the Railroads. It's funny those Guys can tell you just to the minute when something is going to happen 10 million miles away and none of them has ever been smart enough to tell you what day to put on your heavy underwear.

New York, February 22, 1925

We are today celebrating the birth of George Washington. George was not only Father of our Country, but was the most celebrated Woodsman that ever lived. He gained more fame with a hatchet than Lincoln did with an Axe.

America celebrating for Washington — a man who was so truthful — seems kinder sacreligious. A lot of Lying Americans get together and celebrate!

Americans celebrating a truthful man's Birthday always reminds me of a Snake Charmer celebrating St. Patrick's Day.

Holidays in America are celebrated just to give Theatres a chance to raise their prices.

If Coolidge ever chopped down a Cherry Tree it wouldn't be just to try out a hatchet.

March 21, 1925

[In his weekly article Will discussed the bill which raised the

Senators' and Congressmen's salaries from $7,500 to $10,000, from both the standpoint of the men getting the raise and the fact that President Coolidge signed it. "Personally," Will commented, "I think he signed it to try and encourage them in HONESTY. You know, it's not what you pay a man but what he costs you that counts."]

Then another thing, I see where Congress was just asked for $50 thousand to put a new roof on and redecorate the White House. So you see it was kind of a trade. He was tired moving his bed every time it rained and he figured, if I do right by these boys, they will do right by me. Then again there is liable to be a Presidential raise come up again at any time and those are the boys who have to o.k. it. Now, as to whether they should have it or not, that is kinder hard to say. I believe they should, and the Illiterate Digest in saying that is kinder going out of its policy. Because we generally can't see any good in the whole shebang. But I figure if we pay 'em good it might encourage them to do better. They do like flattery, and if we raise their pay and sorter kid 'em along they may amount to something yet.

Another queer thing about this extra gyp, the President has always wanted to know when he signed a bill for an appropriation, just where the extra money was to come from to pay it. He wouldn't pass the Postal raise until they showed him where the money for the raise was to come from. But he didn't ask where this was to come from. I propose that to raise this, they put a light tax on all liquor sold on the Capitol grounds to Senators and Congressmen. In that way the tax would fall on the bootleggers who are getting rich out of these same men. There is no reason why they shouldn't bear the brunt of the tax. Increased salary means increased sales for them. I am sorry the President didn't demand something of this kind.

The bad part about the whole structure of our paying public officials is that we name a sum and give them all the same, regardless of ability. No other business in the world has a fixed sum to pay all their employees the same salary. Take, for instance, Borah! If our Government was run as a business and not as a charity organization, how much would you have to pay him? How many Congressmen and Senators is he worth to us? Yet he has no chance to get any more money than some bird who, when sent there, it takes him two years to find the Capitol with a Guide Book. Even his kin folks back home have to think twice before they can remember where he is. If some efficiency expert would work out a scheme where each one would be paid according to his ability, I think we would save a lot of money. I don't know why Mr. Coolidge, as one of his economy measures, has not thought of that. But I guess a fellow in a high position like that can't think of everything.

But take it all in all, I believe they ought to have their raise. We are a rich nation (ON PAPER) and our officials should be the best paid in the world. The principal bad feature is that it will make more men want to hold office, and once a man wants to hold a public office he is absolutely no good for honest work.

There should be a tax on every man that wanted to get a government appointment or be elected to office. In two years that tax alone would pay our National debt. Half the people in the United States would rather collect one dollar from the government than get $10 from an individual.

[Will then commented caustically in his Follies Act on what most of the Congressmen did in regard to the bill]:

Most of the Congressmen run away and wouldn't vote on their salary raise. They run on a "fearless ticket," not afraid to come out into the open on anything, and then they run away from this.

I am going to hold a meeting and vote myself a higher salary. Can you imagine me voting myself more Money and Ziegfeld not knowing it?

Looks like with Congress charging more, the PEOPLE are getting harder to displease than they used to be.

March, 1925

Our Vice President is for abolishing the Senate. Now that is no doubt a splendid idea, but I think that I can improve on it fifty percent. Abolish Congress too, and I really think there is one reason why we don't do it. We have got the building there and we haven't got anything else to put in those rooms. If somebody would just think of some use we could put their rooms to, I doubt if we would ever send any more of our worst characters back there.

Statistics have proved that only one half of one percent of the speeches made in Congress are listened to. A great many Congressmen speak IN but not TO Congress. But every speech is published in the record. They send the records back home to show "What they told 'em up there in Washington." Now the people back home think Congress heard their "Lem tell them this."

Now here is a scheme to stop speech making. A bill reading as follows: "Congressional Record must not only contain speech but numbers of members and names who listened to speech and why." For instance, "Congressman Post Hole arose to a point of information and spoke at length on 'Is Locarno a town or is it a Treaty?' Length of speech without waiting for applause, four hours, thirty six minutes; attendance, Gout, Rep. N.Y. Unable to get out; Sixtyforty of N.J., case of reciprocity, he listened to mine; Lowbrow, Dem. Mass. I was asleep, even the good speakers haven't woke me up." Now I claim that will stop some speech making. The minute it gets back home that "Lemmie" is talking to himself up there, "Lemmie" will stop talking.

There is two or three things you can't get anywhere on kidding a man, one is his station in life at Birth, another is his lack of Educational advantages, and the other is his careful handling of his money. People will laugh at it but it is a kinder dry laugh where they stop, and study a minute, and then admire instead of ridiculing him.

April 11, 1925

Everything nowadays is a saying, or slogan. You can't go to bed, you can't get up, you can't brush your teeth without doing it to some advertising slogan. We are even born nowadays by a slogan: "Better Parents have Better Babies." Our children are raised by a slogan: "Feed your baby Cowlicks malted milk and

he will be another Dempsey." Everything is a slogan and of all
the bunk things in America the slogan is the champ. There never
was one that lived up to its name. They can't manufacture a new
article until they have a slogan to go with it. You can't form a
new club unless it has a catchy slogan. The merits of the thing
has nothing to do with it. It is, just how good is the slogan?

Even the Government is in on it. The Navy has a slogan:
"Join the Navy and see the world." You join, and all you see for
the first 4 years is a bucket of soap suds and a mop, and some
brass polish. You spend the first 5 years in Newport News. On
the sixth year you are allowed to go on a cruise to Old Point
Comfort. So there is a slogan gone wrong.

Congress even has slogans: "Why sleep at home when you can
sleep in Congress?" "Be a politician — no training necessary."
"It is easier to fool 'em in Washington than it is at home, so why
not be a Senator?" "Come to Washington and vote to raise your
own pay." "Get in the Cabinet; you won't have to stay long."
"Work for Uncle Sam, it's just like a pension." "Be a Republican
and sooner or later you will be a Postmaster." "Join the Senate
and investigate something." "If you are a lawyer and have never
worked for a trust we can get you into the Cabinet."

All such slogans are held up to the youth of this country. You
can't sit down in a street car after a hard day's work without
having a slogan staring you in the face; "Let the Bohunk Twins
do your work." "Chew Wiggley's Gum; the flavor lasts." Now
they know that it don't last when they tell you that. In two
minutes after you start anybody's gum you might just as well
have an old rubber boot to chew on as far as any flavor is concerned. I know because that's all I have done for 20 years is to
throw old gum where someone will step on it. I have to talk a
great deal to the public, and I use gum just to keep my jaws in
good shape. If it wasn't for gum my jaws couldn't go through a
rigorous season of truth telling. So gum has its place but the
slogans are all wet.

Even if you want to get married a sign will stare you in the
face: "You get the girl, we will furnish the ring." That has led
more saps astray than any misinformation ever published, outside

of the prize one of all, which is: "Two can live as cheap as one."
That, next to law enforcement, is the biggest bunk slogan ever
invented. Yes, two can live as cheap as one if one don't want to
eat or wear anything during its lifetime. Two can't even live as
cheap as two, much less one.

Then the preachers say: "Let no man put asunder." And two
thirds of the married world is asunder in less than three months.
Then comes the furniture slogan: "A dollar down and a dollar a
week." It's few wives that last with the same husband until the
cook stove is paid for.

"It's cheaper to buy than pay rent." That's the next bunk
slogan that attracts the love-sick boobs. Half the people in the
United States are living on interest paid by people who will never
get the last mortgage paid out.

Even political campaigns are run and won on slogans. Years
ago some fellow run on "the Full Dinner Pail" and after he was
elected and they opened it there was nothing in it. Another
slogan went wrong. Then William J. Bryan run on a slogan:
"16 to 1." He was defeated, of course, because he didn't explain
what the 16 meant. It meant 16 defeats to one victory.

We even got into the war on a slogan that was supposed to
keep us out. After we got in we were going to "Make the world
safe for Democracy." And maybe we did — you can't tell, because
there is no nation ever tried Democracy since. Our boys went
over singing "Over There" and come back singing "I am always
chasing Rainbows."

The next president was elected on the slogan "Back to Normalcy." Back to Normalcy consisted of the most Cuckoo years of
spending and carousing and graft we ever had. Another slogan
knocked crosswise. Last election, out come the slogan makers
again. Some fool that didn't know American politics had J. W.
Davis run on "Honesty." Well, that had no more place in politics
than I have in the Harvard Faculty. It was one of the poorest
selections of a slogan that was ever invented, and I bet you as long
as there are political parties in this country you will never see
another one ever make the mistake of picking such an absurd one.

Coolidge ran on "Economy" which is always good for the boobs.

It's like getting up at a dinner and saying, "I am proud to be here." It's an old gag but it always goes. Economy beat honesty by 8 million, and as soon as he got in he raised Congress' and the Senate's salary and redecorated the White House. So away goes another slogan!

P. T. Barnum come nearer having a true slogan than anybody: "There is a sucker born every minute." And Henry Ford is right there to take care of him the minute he becomes of age. General Pershing said, "Lafayette, we are here!" and France sent him a bill for the use of the grounds.

Kaiser Wilhelm's slogan was "Germany Uber Alles." I don't know what that Uber means, but whatever it means he was wrong, and it's too late to look it up now.

You see a fool slogan can get you into anything. But you never heard of a slogan getting you out of anything. It takes either bullets, hard work or money to get you out of anything. Nobody has ever invented a slogan to use instead of paying your taxes.

But they *will* fall for 'em. You shake a slogan at an American and it's just like showing a hungry dog a bone. We even die by slogans. I saw an undertakers' sign the other day which read, "There is a satisfaction in dying if you know the Woodlawn Brothers are to bury you."

May 2, 1925

You almost have to be a Lawyer in Washington to hold your own. It's kinder like Bootlegging in Washington. You have to be one down there to keep someone else from selling it to you and also in that way you get wholesale prices from another in the same profession.

New York, May 2, 1925

[In April Will went to Washington and both attended and spoke at his first Gridiron Dinner. "It's the one day in the year," he wrote, "when Newspaper men tell the truth about the men they know. That's considered a great novelty for them. But for me it is no Novelty. I tell the truth about them 364 days, and to be original, instead of telling the truth I will switch my yearly routine and I will Lie about our prominent guests tonight. I am going to compliment them."

Will tried to but long before he got through his speech he reverted to form. He later told about meeting President Coolidge before the dinner]:

I had heard so much of Calvin's not saying anything, that I already had my mind made up on some of the jokes I was going to tell after meeting him, about what a clam he was, and of how I had to button up my coat to keep from catching cold while in his presence. I really wanted this to happen as it would make good joke material for me, and perhaps pay for my trip.

Now you can't tell me that Calvin hasn't got a kinder quiet sense of humor that he can use when it will do him the most good. I will always believe that he had figured out just about what I wanted him to do, and he was smart enough to doublecross me and do the opposite. When Nick and I come in he got up (I won't say he "jumped" but he "got" up) and come over and shook hands with us, and offered us chairs, and said to me that he was very glad to meet me (He didn't say this to Nick. I guess he had met him before.) And he shook my hand — instead of just taking it and letting it drop as I had heard he had done with other people's hands. Some have told me he dropped their hands so quick they fell on the floor before they had time to recover them.

He said he wanted to hear me speak that night, and of course I had to return the compliment and tell him I would stay and listen to him also. I said I was looking forward to this dinner as I had heard of them for years and I thought that they were the most celebrated dinners in the world. He said, yes it was but it was kinder "hard on the President." I thought of course he meant the jokes and sketches they put on about him, but he said no, it is the time it "keeps me there till after 12."

Now there was a joke right there. You see the subtle thing about a joke is to make it look like it was not a joke. I told him I was very anxious to see one of these dinners as I had heard they put on great stuff. He said, "Yes the singing is good." Now there is another kind of a subtle one.

Vice Pres. Dawes had been called away suddenly that day and wouldn't be able to be there, so we spoke of that. I told him that would be a big disappointment as Dawes was to the Gridiron Club what Ford cars were to comedians. Well, he got a laugh out of that, really a better laugh than it deserved, because it was not especially funny.

He was as agreeable as an Insurance Agent.

Now what am I to do? I can't go out and knock a man and say he won't talk when he was as pleasant as he was. So that is why I just figured he crossed me. He outsmarted me. He says to himself, "Here is a smart aleck guy coming in here to get a lot of jokes on me and speechlessness, so I will just fool him. I will talk for 15 minutes, IF IT KILLS ME." Nick said going out to me that he had never heard him so gabby in his life.

Well, at the dinner that night he laughed at all my stuff on him. So I will always believe he purposely doublecrossed me.

The D.A.R. reunion was there that week and there was hundreds waiting to form in line to go by and shake hands with the President. Nick Longworth's female secretary said the D.A.R. stood for "Darned Annual Rumpus." Spanish American War is as far as we can trace back and I can't find any of us in it. But it gives these women something to do to get away from husbands perhaps who are terrible to live with.

I got lots more to tell you about Washington but the children's and my horses have just arrived from California. So me and the kids got to do some riding and roping.

June, 1925 [Follies Routine]

Fellow sent me some elk meat the other day. I have seen a lot of these Elk Conventions but I never knew the meat of one was worth eating before. So that is just about liable to solve this food problem — eat up these elks for I have seen some of 'em as fat as hogs.

Well we are having a terrible time with Prohibition.

The Papers are running a Straw Vote on Wets or Drys.

A Straw Vote is like betting on a race in your mind. When it's all over you are in the same shape you were at first.

The Drys claim them and the Bootleggers are not voting.

I don't see how the wets can win. I don't see how it's possible to get it any wetter than it is.

You will never get people back on light wines and Beers.

June 27, 1925

[In a column entitled "Meddling in Mexico, a Summer Sport," Will illustrated how diplomacy was carried on. Kellogg had just been appointed Secretary of State and Will reported his calling in an Under Secretary and asking if any Notes had been sent lately.]

"Most of the Secretaries of State gained fame by sending Notes to some other Nation. Whom can we send one to?"

The Under Secretary suggested that a Note might be sent to France or Italy. Kellogg replied, "No, we can't do that. That would interfere with Diplomatic relations. We have to be very careful with them as each of them has a Navy and Army, and their feelings are very sensitive. By the way, what about Mexico? I have heard that when the U.S. couldn't find anybody else to pick on that they picked on Mexico."

"I know, Mr. Secretary, but Mexico has not done anything. In fact they have been behaving themselves almost beyond recognition. They are so peaceful you would hardly think they were a Republic."

It was found out that Mexico did not owe the country anything as a country but did owe damages to individuals.

"Well, you send them the following: 'America is getting very tired of your Nation down there not paying us what you owe us for land we claim was taken by the Revolutionists from some of our respected Citizens. It's funny to me you can't control those Revolutions. Now, we want Americans protected. Remember, MEXICO IS ON TRIAL BEFORE THE EYES OF THE WORLD. Remember this is a friendly Note.'

"Put a Special Delivery stamp on that, boy, and send it down at once. Where is my Golf Clubs?"

"I know, but Mr. Secretary Kellogg, why don't you send a note demanding the protection of our American Tourists in France? They have been skinned alive there for years."

"Yes, I know they have but France has an Air Force and a Navy. You have to be Diplomatic in these things. That's why I am able to be Secretary of State. Don't ask me any more questions, please."

Now all the above is just what took place, and we were very much excited when Mexico replied and told us that as they were paying the Taxes in Mexico naturally they felt they should have some saying as to how their Country should be run, and that as for the EYES OF THE WORLD being on them, the World was Cockeyed nowadays anyway.

Now what Ye Old Reliable Illiterate Digest wants to know is what the Devil business is it of ours how some other Country runs their business? How does Kellogg and Coolidge know what the EYES OF THE WORLD ARE ON?

As a matter of fact, the Eyes of the World are on a $1 bill and especially if somebody else has it. Outside of the Oil Interests and Americans who want to make money out of Mexico, the rest of the World's Eyes don't even know Mexico exists (and incidentally Mexico is not worrying about them).

There is only one way in the World to prevent war, and that is, FOR EVERY NATION TO TEND TO ITS OWN BUSINESS.

Trace any war that ever was and you will find some Nation was trying to tell some other Nation how to run their Business.

There is a war in China now. They don't want the Foreigners in there. There is a war in Morocco. They don't want the French and Spanish in there. All these Nations are interfering with some other Nation's personal affairs, BUT with an eye to business. Why the mischief don't we let the rest of the World act like it wants to?

Look at Switzerland! There is an example of a Country minding its own business. No Wars, No Notes. Just tending to its own business.

July 4, 1925

Well, it's been quite a week for wars. China seems to be putting on about the best one. An Irish history in some roundabout way must have fallen into the hands of the Chinese, and as they read it they started loading their guns; and as they finished it, they started shooting. You might ask, Who did they shoot? Well, if you get your schooling from an Irish history, you shoot anybody. The theory is (and they are just about right) that everybody that ain't shot, should be shot. The motto is, "When in doubt, shoot!"

Every nation in the world has always felt privileged to dictate some particular policy to China. They would hold a conference and decide that China should have an "open door," while they went back home and even plugged up their own key holes.

They all grabbed off territory in China for what they termed as a Coaling Station, or Eastern Naval Base, always claiming that it was necessary for their protection. They gobbled up Hong Kong entirely. A Chinaman himself can't get into Hong Kong without a passport. But, oh boy! What a wail would go up if China decided she needed a Coaling Station or Naval Base to protect her interests at Liverpool!

Now the Chinese have given all this and didn't say anything about it, but they did think that they still owned Canton, which was supposed to be their own. So they went up there and started what they thought was a private war among themselves. But No, all these other nations must go up and get in it. I even read where a Portuguese Gun Boat fired on a Chinese mob. That was done for an advertisement to let the world know that Portugal had a gun boat.

Now what we want to know is, what was half of Portugal's Navy doing away out in Canton, China? Of course the British were there protecting their interests with a fleet, as is usual in any private argument held anywhere in the world. They even had two Dreadnaughts covering the Dempsey-Carpentier fight to protect their interests, and are now trying to get a gun boat to Dayton, Tennessee to see that British Ancestral Tails are not trampled on. If it wasn't for these big nations having to cover private disturbances in somebody else's country, they wouldn't need any fleet at all.

Even America is stealing their stuff. You can't pick up a paper without seeing where the Marines were landed to keep some Nation from shooting each other, and if necessary we shoot them to keep them from shooting each other.

No wonder the Chinese all come to 'Frisco and New York to carry out their Tong Wars. It's the only place where they can shoot each other in a friendly way without having some nation join in to protect their interests.

The world is coming to a fine point when lesser nations have to emigrate to another country before shooting each other without interference. Instead of Article 10, which seemed to be the chief drawback in the League of Nations Covenant, let us substitute in its place the following:

"Any nation can have as many private wars as they choose without outside interference, so long as all shooting is confined to the home grounds."

July 18, 1925 [The Scopes Evolution Trial]

Andrew Jackson brought undying fame to the glorious state of Tennessee. He did it by personal bravery and unmatched native intelligence. He reached the White House, the highest prize in the gift of the American people, but it remained for a product of the corn tassels of Nebraska and the under-water Realtor from Florida to bring a dignified commonwealth onto the comic pages of every periodical in the world.

"Hickory" Jackson's work of a life-time has all been undone by the self-advertisement of William Jennings Bryan. It is generally conceded that it was done to advertise Dayton, but why make a monkey out of Tennessee? Tennessee claims they didn't descend from a monkey, but their actions in this case prove otherwise. If a man is a gentleman he don't have to announce it; all he has to do is to act like one and let the world decide. No man should have to prove in court what he is, or what he come from. As far as Scopes teaching children evolution, nobody is going to change the belief of Tennessee children as to their ancestry. It is from the action of their parents that they will form their opinions.

Bryan says he is appearing there for no pay, but you just let

every newspaper in the United States decide not to say a word
about this trial and Bryan will be back in Florida so quick you
will think he has been nominated for something.

Bryan *should* appear for nothing. He ought to pay Scopes' fine.
It has been almost like a Democratic Convention year for Bryan.
It's the most publicity any politician ever got on an off year.
Why, it's just like Peggy Joyce finding a new millionaire husband.

If Darwin hadn't died before Bryan was old enough to maneu-
ver, I would have bet that Bryan framed up the theory with
Darwin, but as he didn't he should at least thank him and give
him the credit, and when he dies leave all his money to some
animal institute.

Bryan says if he fails in this case that Christianity is through
why, even when our Savior came down to earth he didn't make
it that assertive. There is nowhere in the Bible any prediction of
what would have happened if he had failed.

You can't stop a man thinking; neither do I think Bryan could
start a serious man thinking. These fellows who honestly believe
that their great, great grandfathers were as proficient with their
toes as with their fingers, they have that right just as much as
Bryan has the right to seriously believe he is a second Messiah
and that Nebraska was the modern Manger.

Now, all joking aside, can you seriously imagine the future of
Christianity (which means the whole world) depending upon
what Bryan proves at this trial? Darwin started this thing years
ago, and Christianity hadn't done much tottering up to the time
Bryan began to have fears for it.

There is a terrible lot of us who don't think that we come from
a monkey, but if there are some people who think they do, why,
it's not our business to rob them of what little pleasure they may
get out of imagining it. Most people are proud of their ancestry
and it is a touchy thing for even a Bryan to cast reflections on
any man's forefathers, even if he did arrive here on all fours.
What good will it do at this late date to argue over how or who
we come from?

Why don't Bryan and a lot of other people let the world
alone? What has been the matter with it up to now? I can show

you millions of people that think it is great, and are not worrying even if we arrived here from a tadpole. If the Lord had wanted us to know exactly how, and where, and when we come he would have let us know in the first place. He didn't leave any room for doubt when he told you how you should act when you got here. His example, and the Commandments are plain enough, so just start from there, never mind going back any farther. If he had wanted Bryan to have all the details he would have told him.

The Lord put all these millions of people over the earth. They don't all agree on how they got here, and ninety percent don't care. But he was pretty wise when he did see to it that they all do agree on one thing (whether Christian, heathen or Mohammedan) and that is the better lives you live the better you will finish.

No great religious revival will ever be started from an argument over where we come from. The religious revival of the future, when it is started, will be people's fear over where we are going.

Bryan is not going to be able to scare the world into believing that the Lord is going to send anybody to Hell just because they don't know how, or from whom, they arrived here. I don't know how I got here, but I will just stay ignorant and take my chances at the end, rather than Bryan's chances if he willfully stirs up religious hatred among his fellowmen.

July 25, 1925

Coolidge is a better example of evolution than either Bryan or Darrow, for he knows when not to talk, which is the biggest asset the monkey possesses over the human.

July 25, 1925

Ye Olde Reliable Illiterate Digest thought we had disposed of Dayton, Tennessee, in our last issue, but Bryan and Darrow bobbed up in another tree, so now we will have to go over there and shake 'em out of it.

If I was in either one of those men's places I wouldn't spend the best years of my Chautauqua life trying to prove or disprove my ancestry. With the condition the Democratic Party is in at present, instead of trying to prove he didn't come from a monkey, Bryan had better be spending his time trying to prove he didn't descend from a Democrat.

Monkeys are better off than Democrats this season, for they are feeding monkeys gratis. Republicans appropriate money in every big city that has a zoo just for their upkeep, but I never heard of them appropriating anything for the upkeep of "ex-Democratic office holders." If I had the two things hanging over me — Simian or political ancestry — I would certainly try and disprove the latter.

What Darrow should be doing and trying to disprove is that he didn't come from Chicago.

You hang an ape and a Chicago ancestry over me and you will see me taking it into the Supreme Court to prove that the ape part is O.K. but that the Chicago end of it is base libel.

An ape can go through life and never be murdered or robbed by its own kind, but in Chicago no man has ever been able to live there long enough to die of old age. Pork used to be Chicago's chief commodity; now automatic pistols and floral offerings are its leading industries.

I started to the trial but I couldn't find a pair of suspenders, and I knew a man with a belt would be burned at the stake for being a Modernist.

In many ways it was the most unique trial ever held. When they started the case every man in Tennessee would have disclosed the whereabouts of his Still to get on the jury. When the twelve were selected they were more envied than Ziegfeld's front-row girls. Then fate arose and slapped a wet dishrag right in their faces, because the minute they were selected they were sent out of court and weren't allowed back again until they brought in their verdict (which they had made up before they were sworn in).

Everybody in the world was invited to sit in the courtroom but the jury. Every time a counsel, either for ape or for rib, would arise, the judge would remark:

"Gentlemen of the Jury, you will please retire, as you wouldn't know what the learned counsel was saying."

August 15, 1925

Been reading a lot in the papers about our fleet that visited Australia and the wonderful reception given our boys. Since we passed that Japanese Exclusion Act there is a bond of sympathy between America and Australia. They both figure it's a good time to stand in with each other. You can talk all you want about a bond of feeling, and "blood thicker than water" and all that, but the thing that really makes any two nations a little more "sympathetic" toward each other is the fact that they may be able to use each other. Japan turning out airships over there every minute like Fords don't set so nice around the adjoining Pacific.

This trip was planned with our Pacific fleet to impress Japan with the size of it. That was not necessary. Japan knows more about our war strength now than either of our Secretaries of War or Navy.

October 17, 1925

I appeared one night in Canton, Ohio, and we had several preachers in and one of them has the biggest Sunday School in the United States. So the Minister asked me to come up the next morning and see this wonderful Sunday School and to say a few words at his church service. Well, I did, and it seemed to be going pretty good, nobody was converted, but everybody seemed to be laughing. When I would stop, he would tell me to go on, and I kept on — me hesitating and him encouraging — until when I finished he didn't get up and preach at all. I had preached and didn't know it.

That preacher just used me to conserve a sermon of his that morning, or else he didn't have one. But I enjoyed it, and the church audience applauded, and I think it made me better, for on my way back to the Hotel I passed a Beggar selling lead pencils, and I know I passed him with more feeling and just kinder wished I didn't write with a fountain pen so I could have helped him.

You see I hold the distinction of being the only one that ever preached a sermon in a regular church and didn't know it. And I don't even know what denomination the church was.

But I am having a wonderful trip, meeting and looking out into the the faces of Taxpayers, instead of Bootleggers.

Lexington, Kentucky, November 1, 1925

It sure was a pleasure to hit the first old southern town where you could see two men talking and neither one trying to sell the other something.

People go to Europe and prowl around over there trying to find something pretty to come home and tell about to impress their neighbors, when there are those Stock farms around Lexington, Kentucky, with those thoroughbred mares and colts grazing on that old blue grass and all those white Board paddocks. Say, Europe looks like a railroad freight yards compared to that.

Visited Man o' War. Say, there is more people visits his stable than there is visits the White House in Washington. He is a bright golden Chestnut sorrel. He is the most beautiful living thing I ever saw in my life (and I come out of the Follies where we have some thoroughbreds).

If Flo could land some Girl with his speed and looks he could put out a No. 2 Follies.

They got an old Negro fellow lives with him and takes care of him all the time. That old boy can tell you what the horse is thinking about.

When I saw all those wonderful horses, I wished there had never been an automobile invented.

I have never yet seen a man in such a big hurry that a horse or train wouldn't have got him there in plenty of time. In fact nine tenths of the people would be better off if they stayed where they are, instead of going where they are going. No man in America if he didn't get where he is going would be missed.

People take themselves too serious. They think if they don't break their neck from one place of business to another then the World will stop. Say, all they have to do is just watch some man die that is more prominent than they are, and in less than 24 hours the world has forgot he ever lived, so they ought to have imagination enough to know how long they will stop things if they left this old earth. People nowadays are traveling faster, but they are not getting any further (in fact not as far) as our old dads did.

January 10, 1926

Now, I would advise you not to read this Article. You are just wasting your time, and again it will just make you about half sore. I doubt if there is five people in the United States that will agree with me on what I am going to tell you in here.

I know you will say, "What's the idea of writing a crazy thing like that then?" Well, I will tell you why. All you hear in Washington and all you can read in the papers is "Cutting down the taxes." Everybody is howling, "Cut the taxes."

Every Industry and business in the world have rushed battalions of Experts and Lobbyists to Washington the last few months just to show the government that theirs was the very Industry that was "just RUINED by the taxes, and wouldn't they please take them off theirs and put them on something else."

Will you tell me any good reason (OUTSIDE OF POLITICS) why Taxes should be lowered this year? I know it's good politics to lower taxes. In fact, did you ever figure it out — TAXES IS ALL THERE IS TO POLITICS? I bet you tomorrow if you started a Political Party and had this as its platform, "No taxes are to be paid at all. We will borrow money on our National resources for all current expenses. Remember the Slogan, 'No Taxes as long as we can borrow,'" well, I will bet you you would have the biggest Political party in America.

Now, on the other hand, start a Society on the following Platform: "Everybody try to borrow all you can personally, and save up nothing. Leave your children plenty of debts." Say, you wouldn't get 10 to join that. You would be arrested for being crazy. But you will let the coming Generation pay 70 percent (of each dollar they pay in) just for what you borrowed during your Generation. Our children shouldn't pay for the wooden ships we tried to build during the war, and the millions of dollars we spent on aviation that didn't aviate, and the Hog Islands that REALLY HOGGED us. That was not the coming generation's fault. They will have their own wars to look after, without paying for ours.

January 17, 1926

Never look at a town with one of its prominent citizens and think you have seen the place. You have just seen what he wants you to see. I always get me a Taxi and go "prowling."

February 27, 1926

The Countess of Cathcart, and the Earl of Cravem grabbed the Immigration Department by its ears and shook it out publicly before the Scandal-Hungry Mob.

Somebody found a clause called Moral Turpitude, or something that sounded like that.

It means you told the truth when you ought not to.

It seems she had been in Africa with this Lord Cravem. Now you can go to Atlantic City and Palm Beach accompanied by a misplaced Husband, but they don't like to have you take one as far away as Africa. That's what constitutes Turpitude. If it's a week-end trip it's only indiscretion.

Well, they held her up, and she told them, "Well, why didn't you hold up the Lord?" (Or Earl or some minor League title like that.) "Well, we would have held him up but we didn't know what Moral Turpitude was then. We just got a Dictionary. Besides we don't know for sure he was down in Africa with you."

"Yes, but you are keeping me out for being down there with him."

"No, we are keeping you out for *saying* you were down there with him."

"But suppose I say I wasn't down there?"

"Why, that will be all right. You can come in then. The idea is, Lady, we just don't like to have people do anything and then *admit it.* You can go to Siberia with Mussolini and spend the winter and come back by here and get in, if you tell us you haven't been there."

March 13, 1926

Well, they are having a big stir out there, and in fact all over the United States, about Tia Juana and Mexicali, Mex. They want President Coolidge to clean these places up, or make Mexico do it, and if they won't why go to war with them and make 'em clean 'em up. It seems they sell drinks down there right over the bar. You don't have to have a fellow leave it at your place or anything. You just pay for it by the drink, and not by the bottle, and they Gamble right there before your own eyes, and they claim it is ruining the Youth and Manhood of this Country. That it is a disgrace to have these things done right there in Mexico, where the Americans can go right over and see all this.

Americans don't want to drink and gamble. They just go over there to see the mountains, and these scheming Mexicans grab 'em and make 'em drink, and make 'em make bets, and make 'em watch the race Horses run for money. It seems that Americans don't know these places are over there at all, and when they get there these Mexicans spring on 'em and they have to drink or the Mexicans will kill 'em.

All in the world we have to do to keep our Citizens pure and good like they have been all this time is to not allow them over the line. If we have to admit to the world that we are raising people that don't know enough to take proper care of themselves, we will have to do it by another Amendment, as follows: "Americans are not allowed anywhere where they will be subject to evil influences."

You put a Church in every building where there is a Gambling house and Saloon now, in Tia Juana, Mex., and I lay you a bet there wouldn't be five people cross the line a year.

Well, I talked to newspaper men who covered that whole Tia Juana case. One of the head Mexican Police officials of Tia Juana pulled the best bit of philosophy in regard to America and all her protecting influences, I ever heard. "You never make a Dog good, by keeping him tied up."

April 17, 1926

Here is some South American Editors up here in our midst. Mr. Kellogg (our clean shaven Hughes) got the first crack at them the other day. It wasn't a hands across the sea speech. It was an elbow crooked around down through the Canal to try to reach them. He said he hoped to see the time that all National Problems were settled by arbitration. That is the champion Apple Sauce speech of the world. Nations should get together and discard that from the Diplomatic Vocabulary.

If I was a Diplomat and asked to speak at an International Dinner and that was all I could think of, I believe I would plead Bad Cold. Sounds like a Sunday School teacher saying just out of force of habit, "Go home now children, and be good little Boys and Girls and don't do anything naughty, and don't fuss, and mind your parents. Do that now." He told Peru and Chili that they should settle their dispute over that disputed territory and set an example in liberal statesmanship. And here we are on the verge of war with Mexico because Mexico wants to make her own laws! Those Editors would rather he would have explained that to them. Anybody knows all their sympathies are more with Mexico than with us. They hadn't quit smiling up their sleeves when the President took another Apple Sauce jolt at them the next day, with the Power of the Press and how much they could do to bring on international friendly relations.

Why do people want to continually hand out a lot of Bunk that they don't believe themselves and they know the other side don't? These Editors are a bunch of keen business men. They come here to see how we got so many Ads in our Papers. They come to learn something about their own business. They want the Pictures of our leading Murderers and Divorce Principles. They are here to find what it will cost to transfer Mutt and Jeff into Spanish, and can Jiggs eat Chili the same as Corn Beef. They are not here cementing any good feeling. To tell you the truth, they are just here slumming.

CHAPTER FOUR

An Un-Innocent Abroad

[From the opening of his first lecture tour at Elmira, New York, October 1, 1925, until its triumphal close on April 24, 1926, at Carnegie Hall, New York, Will had had the time of his life. He had met and talked with the "real bird," the men and women of the little towns and cities which make up the backbone of the United States. Heretofore these people had only seen him in moving pictures where he was playing a part. They, too, had seen "the real bird" and from now on he was their man.

Now, with hardly a pause to catch his breath Will was to broaden both his experience and his audience to across the seas. And, as he did everything, he did it with an audaciousness that was breath taking.

In his own article, and in carefully planned publicity, it was announced that Will had seen George Horace Lorimer, editor of the *Saturday Evening Post,* and that he was going to Europe for that magazine.

In his Letters of a *Self-Made Diplomat to His President,* a report of this trip, Will says in an "Author's Note"]:

THIS IS UNIQUE in Memoirs or Autobiographies. I am publishing what was done and said while all the Parties concerned in these narratives are alive. I could have waited a few years till some of the actors who stalked across the stage in this great drama of human events were dead. But I said No. These are facts, and if there is a man connected in anyway with them who dares to dispute them, let him rare up on his hind legs and proclaim himself. I have always felt that a man can defend himself better than his remaining relatives. Then besides there was always the possibility of me passing out first.

[Will also warned that what he wrote about was only that which came under his own observation. "The President and the Cabinet have dealt with many little minor affairs that is not dealt with in these narratives at all, because I couldn't see personally after everything. So naturally I just took up the more important."

He set up the basis of his relation to the President]:

Now comes the most remarkable thing about our relation, and that is we have no personal contact or agreement about taking up this work for him. In other words, our understanding has been so perfect between each other that we haven't even had to talk it over. There is a kind of mental telepathy between us.

I just felt that he needed a foreign Diplomat that could really go in and dip, and he didn't even have to ask me to do it; that same intimate understanding that had told me he needed someone, had told him that I was the one that he needed. And that's all there has ever been between us. We just feel that our ideas are so mutual that whatever one does the other agrees with.

Of course we have foreign Ambassadors over there, but they are more of a Social than a Diplomatic aid to us.

[So Will went to Europe, in May, 1926, and remained until the end of September. His "reports" on Europe came in the form of either "letters" or "wires" supposedly to the President. He even satirized this]:

We only had one understanding before I left and that was that everything between us must be carried on in an absolutely confidential manner, and not get out to the General Public.

So it was decided to carry it on by postcard. Just another example of typical American Diplomacy.

Aboard the Leviathan, *April 30, 1926*

My Dear President:

Everybody received Flowers and Fruit and Candy. If you sent anything it hasn't been sent to my stateroom yet. But there is a lot of Bundles and baskets up there yet that haven't been delivered, and I will give you the benefit of the doubt till I find out otherwise.

Yours devotedly,

Col. William Rogers

P.S. Have you done anything for the Farmers yet? Certain news is so urgent that it is necessary for me to cable you, so from time to time you may get something "Collect." I hope there is an appropriation to cover this, look under the heading "Ways and Means."

Willrog [diplomatic code name]

Radiogram: Somewhere in the Middle of England's Ocean. Date — What's time to a guy in the middle of an ocean.

My Dear President:

Will you kindly find out for me through our intelligence Department who is the fellow that said a big Boat didn't rock. Hold him till I return.

Yours, feeble but still devotedly,

Willrog

Aboard the Leviathan, *May 3, 1926*

You ought to come over some time. It used to be quite a fad for the President to run over for the week-end. If you decide to come, let me know and I will give you a letter to Billy the Head Steward. If you come on some of those French or other lines, you wouldn't know what you were eating. Pancakes got some crazy name.

Marcus Loew and Lee Shubert, the two biggest theater Owners in America, were on the boat. They both said they wished you would go to the Theatres more; that they thought it would have a good effect on the rest of the country. I told them a pass including Self and Party might have some effect on you.

So if you get anything in the way of an Annie Oakley in the next few weeks you will know that I am working in your interest every minute.

Hope they haven't forced you too strong on that Farmer relief thing. That seems to be about the only thing they have been able to corner you in. Watch it both ways, because both sides vote.

We are just off France. I hear a noise. I think it's the Franc dropping.

Your devoted accomplice,

Col. William Rogers

[Will landed in England after the General Strike of 1926 had gotten under way. He described what he saw on the way from Southampton, where he disembarked, to London]:

It's about 80 miles through the most beautiful Country you ever saw up to London; every field planted and plowed and raising something. And by the way there is no Farm relief problem over here. These fellows looked like they had solved their Farm problems by working them.

You see, they have figured out the Jimson weeds and Cockleburs and Sunflowers and all kinds of weeds take up as much room and as much nourishment out of the ground as wheat or oats do, so they just don't raise them. They don't drive to town till they drive in to sell something. Gloria Swanson proving that virtue will triumph in the end is taken as a matter of fact. They don't have to go every night to see it proved. Leaving the field and going to a Lion's Luncheon is another thing they have never figured as an actual farmers' accomplishment toward less weeds and more Porridge.

Just imagine! I was in a Farmer's house here and he and his family had a Book instead of a Radio.

[Will wanted to go to the House of Commons. But even the head of the Associated Press could not manage it for him. He went to see an official and was not making any progress until he showed him his Press Credentials where he was writing for the *Claremore Progress,* of Claremore, Oklahoma. "The minute they saw that they not only gave me the pass but asked all about Claremore; said they had always been interested in the marvelous development of the town, and that it had often been suggested that they send men from London to study our method of running the town."

Will was surprised at the number of policemen at the Parliament building. He compared this to Washington where they only had "one on duty in that whole end of Washington" no doubt, as he said, because "if you are going to have a lot of Policemen around, how are the Bootleggers going to get in — without splitting?" He made some pithy remarks on the Chaplain that opened the meeting]:

Well, they met, and a man who was just engaged for that business prayed. He incidentally mentioned the King more than he did the subjects. That struck me as kinder odd, because from what I had seen of the King and the house he was living in, and what I had seen of the subjects, I thought the King was doing pretty well, and didn't particularly need any help. At least, to be fair, I thought the Subjects should have an even break.

But I am not one to go around criticizing anything connected with religion. If you knew enough to keep out of the Klan fight, I certainly ought to know enough to not mix up in any of England's religious prayers. I am not the fellow to go to a Country and then start criticizing it from our angle at home.

[With the General Strike in full swing Will had ample opportunity to look things over.]

Well, this Commons didn't lose any time about getting down to the strike. If it had been over home and a strike had been on all over the Country, they would have met and argued Prohibition. Finally Lloyd George got up. He belongs to what is called the Liberal Party, whose standing is now about what the Populist Party is in America. I sho was glad to be there and hear him.

Well, the Union Party on the other side — they are what the

Republicans are, if they all stuck together over home — they got to hooting and riding Lloyd George. Well, that didn't seem hardly right to me. Here was a man that had brought them through the most critical times in their History as Prime Minister, and now they rode him just because he happened to degenerate into a common Member of Parliament — M.P. — that's about like you, Mr. Coolidge, being in Congress after you had been all these years in the White House.

If you help the Farmer, remember what I tell you. Be careful at who's expense you help him.

London, May 13, 1926
MY DEAR PRESIDENT:

Say, I told them about you over here. During all this calm and no excitement [over the General Strike], everbody asked me, "How would you Americans take this if it were happening over there?"

So I just told them, "We would have all been cuckoo and crazy and shooting and rioting, and everybody up in the air — all but one man. He would have been just like your House of Lords. He might every few days ask, 'Is the strike over yet?' But he would have been the sole individual that would have not turned a hair."

Then they all would ask, "Who is this remarkable man that you speak of?"

I remarked, "Calvin Coolidge."

I wish you had been here. It was just your kind of stuff.

I will go and see if London Bridge is falling down. I have heard somewhere it was.

Watch the farmers. They are tricky.

London, May 16, 1926
MY DEAR PRESIDENT:

The strike was carried on something like this: Some government man would approach a man and ask, "Could I get you to drive a Tram for us? We are really in great distress at not being able to perambulate."

"No, sir, I can't drive it for you; I am on strike. I am a Tram driver by profession. However, I should be very glad to assist you if it's not presuming too much on your short acquaintance. I will see who I can find that is not on strike and send them around to you."

"Well, that's very nice of you, old chap. It's deucedly awkward to have to approach a strange man and ask him to assist you without at least a previous introduction. But on learning that you were a striker I knew that you would be in sympathy with my position and do all you can to assist me in this awfully embarrassing position of having to ask a perfect stranger for aid. Here is my Card. I don't like to hasten you, but I should be very much obliged if you would get me the man as quickly as he is procurable. Beastly old Tram and everything; looks awfully unsightly just standing there not doing anything."

The whole thing from both sides was handled like a well-organized Funeral, by an old well-established Undertaker.

And by the way, Mr. President, who owns Coal mines anyway? There is always trouble in the coal mines, both over home and here, and nobody knows who the Coal Mine Owners are. The Miners can't be wrong all the time. In fact their wages don't prove that they are a lot of plutocrats. So let's find the mine owners in both countries and see just what type of man he is, and who he is.

Nobody should be allowed to employ labor that can't deal with them Personally. So kindly take this up at the next Cabinet meeting and see what we can do about it.

Calcool, Washhousewhite: Special Cable
London, May 17, 1926

Don't put too much faith in rumor that peasants of Middle West will defeat you.

They change with the wheat crops, and you have two to go.

Calcool, Whitehousewash: Special Cable
London, May 18, 1926

You can pick an American bootlegger out of a crowd of Americans every time. He will be the one that is sober.

London, May 18, 1926 [At a Dinner Given by Lady Astor]

There was another outsider at the Dinner besides me that Mrs. Astor told me she wanted especially for me to meet, and she sit him right by me, and what a wonderful little man he is, and meeting him will always remain one of the high spots in my memory. It was Sir James Barrie. I think he is a Syndicate writer, or Strip Cartoonist, or Paragrapher, or something like that. I think he has a Cartoon running called Peter Pan, and a little Comedy Character called the Little Minister. They were afterwards made into Books.

Well, we had a great time. He said, "Are you a writer?"

Well, that did bring the big Guffaw. I had to bust right out at that. He was such a nice and pleasant little man that I wanted to be honest with him and tell him no. Then I happened to think of the three typewriters I had worn out, so I said, "Yes, Sir, are You?"

He said, "No."

I said, "Well, I am, if you ain't, because we are certainly opposite."

He said, "What did you write?"

I said, "Tobacco ads."

Then I asked him what he wrote and he said, "Peter Pan." And then he said, "I should like to read your ad book."

Well, come to find out, Mrs. Astor had of course tipped him off about me, and the Rascal was kidding me all the time. But, anyway, we broke even, for neither one of us had read anything the other had written.

[After the dinner was over Will went with Sir James Barrie to his apartment where they had a gay evening. Sir James told him all about his discovery of Maude Adams, and about other things connected with his interesting life.]

London, May 19, 1926

My Dear Mr. President:

England has the best Statesmen and the Rottenest coffee of any Country in the World. I just hate to see morning come because

I have to get up and drink this coffee. Is there nothing can be done about this?

Personally, I will be perfectly willing to sign over my share in the debt settlement for just one good cup of Coffee. Dam it, we give 'em good tea, and all we demand is reciprocity.

Look into this, will you?

Next to Farmers' relief, it's one of the big problems that is confronting us today. For every Fool American is coming over this summer, and it's the fool vote that we have got to watch for.

I would even drink New Orleans Coffee if I had it now.

London, May 19, 1926

MY DEAR MR. PRESIDENT:

The American Club in London, on Piccadilly, wanted to give me a Dinner, and you know what I think of these Dinners. You remember the one you and I attended at the Gridiron Club in Washington. I remember we were both equally bored. It took us till almost one o'clock to eat what little they had, and the speeches outside of yours and mine was terrible; if I remember right, even yours wasn't so good. Well, I went here.

[By the time that Will left London he was able to report that he had had a great time, "met everybody. The old Prince phoned me and had an hour over at his Boarding House." "It looked about like an Oil Millionaire's home in Oklahoma, only more simple and in better taste. And Long Island Homes? His whole place would have got lost in their what they humorously call their Main Saloon."

The Prince shook hands with him "like a Rotary Club President that has been coached in the best ways to make friends." After a long talk with the Prince, about many things which he reported, Will ended with, "But just between you and I, Calvin, he don't care any more about being King than you would going back to Vice-President again."

Will flew from London to Paris, on June 5, 1926, and got thoroughly airsick on the way. "We hit France finally, and somebody hadn't paid their poll tax, and we hit more Air pockets, or Chug holes. It reminded me of motoring in Virginia."]

By continuous gulping and main force it looked like I would make it with my original cargo, when all at once I looked and there was an airplane field below us, and he didn't coast down to it. He just dropped right down into it. Well, he broke my clear record with the last 500 feet that he dropped. Well, airships are great, but take it from me, it's the last 500 feet that's the hardest.

[Will had the same trouble with taxicabs in Paris that most tourists have. They had the lowest start in the way of money of any in the world and one of the most expensive finishes. Also, just coming from an "unloading" airplane trip, the way they missed objects was hair-raising. "All at once here comes a truck loaded with French wine, labeled 1888. You say we can't meet in this narrow place, and you can't, but you do." In the cafés he also found that they all spoke English (as they did in the stores) when they sold you something but when you complained about getting gypped they suddenly forgot how to speak it.

From Paris Will went to Italy.]

Rome, June 1, 1926
[Will was sitting around a hotel lobby after night trying to figure out what to do when "why in blows the Barnum and Bailey's Circus of American Tourists. It's the Hotel Men's Association"]:

They have been over here for over two months, three hundred of them. They have been the Guests of the Hotel men over here. Everything paid, even to their Railroad fares. Well, maby you think I wasn't glad to see them. Here was a bunch of Highbinders that I had paid toll to all over the United States for years, and just when I wanted to see somebody else getting back at them and making them pay the freight, why they were the Guests of somebody. But I was glad to see the Rascals, for after all they are a fine bunch and we can't live without them, and for a bunch of all around good fellows I guess we haven't got a race over there that beat them unless it is the Bootleggers, and that profession embraced most of these.

They played a town every day, and a Banquet that night. How the Ladies stood it is more than I will ever know. But they seemed to look great and all in fine shape. They got up at eight o'clock to go to the Palace and see the King. Now that is pretty early just to see a King. But he spoke good English to them, in fact too good for some of them.

Rome, June 1, 1926

MY DEAR MR. PRESIDENT:

Well, I come clear to Italy, as you know, Boss, just to see Mussolini, and see for you if his style of Government was as bad as the Republicans over home. He is the busiest man in the world today and I didn't know if I would be able to see him personally.

[Will *did not* have a letter from Coolidge to Mussolini but letters which Nick and Alice Longworth had given him took care of the situation nicely. In fact Will hinted that they worked better than if Coolidge had written a letter.

He summed up his visit]:

I had felt as much at home with him as I would with Dinty Moore on 46th St. I was as much surprised, Mr. President, as I was the first time I ever run onto you, when Nick took me in there and you laughed, and pulled a few yourself, and we had a good visit, and I come out thinking you wasn't as sober as you make yourself look. It's a wonderful thing to meet people and see about how they all are about the same when you can get their minds off their Life's work.

Well, you got to be in Italy to really understand the fellow. The trouble with America is we can't ever seem to see somebody else only through our eyes; we don't take into consideration their angle or viewpoint.

Now you, Mr. President, with your one last year's suit, your speech on Economy while stepping off the Mayflower, your little quiet yet just as effective way of getting what you want done;

well that and you would be just as funny to Italy as he is to us.

He gets up in Public and tells Austria and Germany what to do. You have Kellogg send Mexico a note telling them what time to quit work that day. He comes into the House of Deputies over there and tells them the measures that shall be put through. You have five or six Senators for breakfast and the same thing happens.

You see, everyone of us in the world have our audience to play to; we study them and we try and do it so it will appeal to what we think is the great majority. We all have our particular little line of Apple Sauce for each occasion. So let's be honest with ourselves, and not take ourselves too serious, and never condemn the other fellow for doing what we are doing every day, only in a different way.

Venice, June 3, 1926

If the tide is high they can row you right up to the desk in the lobby.

There is no such thing as any cats squalling in the alleys of Venice. If there is a Cat there he is a catfish.

There is one square in Venice which is apparently land, but the Pigeons apparently have that.

A street cleaner is my idea of an easy job in Venice.

Venice used to be a nation, now it's only a Life Buoy.

Rome, June 5, 1926

My Dear Mr. President:

Calvin, I wish you could see Rome. It's the oldest uncivilized town in the world. New York is just as uncivilized, but it's not as old as Rome. Rome has been held by every Nation in the World at one time or another for no reason at all. Between you and I, I think some of them give it up without much of a struggle.

Rome has more Churches and less preaching in them than any City in the World. Everybody wants to see where Saint Peter was buried, but nobody wants to try to live like him.

Rome was built on seven hills. Every prominent Roman had a little hill all his own. History records, and local gossip has added to history, that coming home after a hard and exciting night at the baths, there has been Romans that didn't find the right hill. There is only six of these hills left today. Some Roman went out of the back window so fast one night that he took the hill with him. That's the inside story. History says that the Barbarians took not only all the assembled Romans but the hill as well with them.

I tried to find out who the Barbarians were. From the best that I could learn, Barbarians were a race of people that stole from you. If you stole from the barbarians, you were indexed in your History as Christian.

Rome wasn't built in a day. It's not like Miami Beach by any means. All Tourist agencies advise you to spend at least 10 days seeing it. The Hotels advise you to take four months.

I am, I bet you, the only one that ever visited the city that didn't run myself ragged dragging from one old Church to another, and from one old Oil Painting to the next. In the first place, I don't care anything about Oil Paintings. Ever since I struck a dry hole near the old home ranch in Rogers County, Oklahoma, I have hated oil in the raw. I don't want to see a lot of Old Pictures. If I did I would get D. W. Griffith to revive the Birth of a Nation. Charles Dana Gibson can assemble 'em good enough for me.

Now we call Rome the seat of Culture, but somebody stole the chair. Today it has no more culture than Minneapolis or Long Beach, California. They live there in Rome amongst what used to be called Culture, but that don't mean a thing. Men in Washington you know yourself, Calvin, live where Washington and Jefferson and Hamilton lived, but as far as the good it does them, they just as well have the Capitol down at Claremore, Oklahoma.

Then another thing you got to take into consideration. If a town has any culture and Tourists commenced hitting it, your culture is gone. Tourists will rub it out of any town.

Then another thing, I didn't know before I got there, and they told me all this, that Rome had Senators. Now I know why it declined.

Rome has what they call a river. It's the Tiber, and of all the overrated things! You would think a River that is good enough to get into History for all these years would have something to back it up, wouldn't you. History don't say a word about the Verdigris River, and here this Tiber couldn't be a tributary to it. The Tiber don't flow; it just oozes along.

Nice, France, June 8, 1926
My Dear Mr. President:
It's pronounced neece, not nice; they have no word for nice in French.

Cablegram: RUSH: President
Monte Carlo, Monaco, June 22, 1926
Please send money. Unexpected Diplomatic relations have suddenly arisen here which no one could foresee. Please rush, as French Taxi Driver is waiting. They are unusually impatient when you owe them. Willrog

Geneva, Switzerland, June 23, 1926
Mr. President:
Have found Pullman car window that will open without crew of Porters. Biggest discovery made in Europe so far on entire trip.

Paris, France, June 24, 1926
Dear President:
I arrived in Paris late at night. The next day we had Briand Premier for breakfast; Herriot Premier for Lunch; Poincaré for Dinner; and woke up the next morning and Briand is back in again.

This is not a Government; it's an old-fashioned Movie, where they flash on the screen, "Two minutes, please, while we change Premiers."

I have had a date to interview every one of them, but they were thrown out before the Interview time come due.

[The last of June Will made a trip through Spain on which he interviewed both Primo de Rivera and the King. He said of de Rivera, "He is not the live go-get-'em-knock-'em-down-kid like Mussolini, but he gets some of the same things done in a quieter way." He also watched the King play polo and also a stable full of handsome mules. "Well, they looked so natural I wanted to go in and kiss one. Here was St. Joe, Missouri, Boonville and Sedalia right under my nose."]

Calcool, Whitewashhouse: Special Cable
London, August 2, 1926

A bunch of American Tourists were hissed and stoned yesterday in France, but not until they had finished buying.

Calcool, Whitehousewash: Special Cable
London, August 3, 1926

When Borah asked England and France what had become of that 400,000,000 acres of land they divided up after the war, that stopped all debt arguments over here. He is always thinking up some question nobody can answer. He even sticks you. Regards to "Cuckooland." WILLROG

[Will made a Moving Picture, *Tip-Toes,* in London in which he appeared with Dorothy Gish and Nelson Keith. He also appeared in the *Cochran Revue,* a musical show. At the time Americans were very unpopular in Europe and there was doubt as to how Will's banter — à la the Follies — would be taken. He did his usual stunt and spoke freely about how he felt. *Everybody's Weekly* suggested bluntly that he go home. But in spite of that the first night was a sellout and after that the show was a sensation, particularly after it was learned that Will had gone on the show to help pull out a flop for his old friend C. B. Cochran. Here is a sample of what Will said]:

English Friends, and you, too, Shylocks.
All Americans that come to Europe have to sooner or later work their way back. Now I was working in Moving Pictures here all day, but I had nothing to do with my nights, so I says

to myself, who can I annoy in the evenings. So I happened to think of all the English Lecturers that have been over home — that was before we put the Emigration Law in to stop English authors from Lecturing or reading us their books. Every man that ever wrote his name on a Hotel Registry slip come to America as an Author. So I says to myself, I am going to get even with those Birds by going and talking to England.

Now I don't know what I will talk about. I will talk about anything that you pick out. I have no set subject. If I don't know it won't make any difference to me.

Dublin, Ireland, August 25, 1926

[Will, upon hearing about a fire in a moving picture theatre in Drumbolloger, Ireland, went to Dublin to play a benefit for the victims and their families.]

Well, they only had two days to do it, but they did it, and they took over a big fine Theatre (the man donated it) and we had our show. They put on their wonderful Military Band and a Lady Singer, and I want to tell you I have been mixed up in all kinds of shows but this one last night was the greatest one I ever was in. You talk about an audience! They were packed in! And you talk about "Getting" your stuff! Say, you leave it to these Irish. They get you and they get you good. If there is a speck of humor or fun in anything you say or do they will dig it out, and they won't be all day digging. They were without a doubt the most appreciative audience I ever saw in my life, and at moderate prices we got their fund about four thousand dollars.

Had President Cosgrove in the Box and introduced him. He is doing a lot for Ireland. You take the time he has had and the funds he has had to work with and he has accomplished more than any other Nation I have been in in the same length of time.

A lot of people who are always prowling around looking for some place every year and wind up in France, where they are not wanted, ought to come here. Ireland welcomes you, even if you don't buy something every minute.

CHAPTER FIVE

"Trying to Tell What Russia Is . . ."

[In August, 1926, Will spent a couple of weeks in Russia. "Now there has been more said and written about Russia than there has been about Honesty in Politics," he wrote, "and there has been just as little done about it. I am the only person that ever wrote on Russia that admits he don't know a thing about it. And, on the other hand, I know just as much about Russia as anybody that ever wrote about it. Nobody knows anything about Russia. It's too big; nobody could tell about it. Trying to tell what Russia is is like trying to tell the difference between a Conservative Republican and a Progressive Democrat. If you are a visiting Communist, or have Communistic leanings, why, naturally you will write of it from their accomplishment point of view, and are liable to — accidentally — leave out any little defects you might have seen. Then, on the other hand, if you are not the least bit in sympathy with any part of their program, why, you naturally are not liable to let yourself see anything that has any merit in it. So if you are looking for me to solve the Russian Problem, you are not going to get it done." Will did say what he was going to do]:

I AM GOING TO be like a prisoner at the bar when some wise, old good-natured Judge who wants to get the facts asks, "Will you please tell the Court in your own way and your own language just what happened on the entire night of June the twelfth?" Now that's what I am going to do. I am just going to tell you everything I saw and what happened in Russia in the last few weeks.

[Will flew from Berlin to Moscow in a Russian plane with a Russian pilot.]

I constituted Russia's sole aerial immigration that day. Well, in one way, I am generous. If I am going to drop, I don't want to have the pleasure all to myself; I want to share it with somebody.

As I got in I commenced to think of all the jokes I had told about Russia. And then I remembered that people had remarked to me they didn't know why I had been given a passport into Russia when it was so hard to get one. Then I thought, maby they know about some of the jokes and this Aerial Cossack is about heading right off to Siberia with me.

We was flying nice and low and you could see all the people out in the fields working — well, not exactly all the people, but the ones that were women. Then every time we would pass over a little town or village you would see a kind of market place, and all the men would be gathered, or you would see them driving in or out of town in little wagons with one horse.

I think the men are pretty good that way in Russia. They make mighty good husbands. If the wives raise anything, why the Husbands are perfectly willing to take it to town and sell it.

Now everybody had said to me in going in, "Don't take anything in with you; they examine everything."

Well, I stripped myself down till I didn't have a single piece of paper about me but my passport. I tore up two handfuls of cards people had given me of people in Russia to look up for them. I took in only one suit and four extra shirts, as I was told if I took in too much I would be suspected of capitalistic tendencies. I even didn't get a shave for a few days, figuring I might pass as a native.

Now, as a consequence, I didn't have a soul in the world to go to, or a single address.

We went into Moscow right on the dot — not a minute late.

That field was full of Airplanes; there must have been eight or ten single-seaters up doing their stuff.

Well, due to the expert advice of those who told me what not to take into Russia no one ever knocked on the portals of Sing Sing any lighter equipped than I entered the city of Moscow. I didn't even have my Shriner pin or my Elk Tooth Fob. I tell you I was practically Neglige.

I went into a little customs office. They took my passport, give it a peek and shoved it back to me. I opened my grip. He got one peek — didn't even feel in there. And as for looking to see what you had in your pocket or had on your person, why, I could have had a bass drum in each hip pocket, a Saxophone down each leg and two years' collection of the Congressional Records in my coat pockets.

People had warned me not to say much or laugh at them. Funny? Say, I was just about the saddest looking thing you ever saw. Claremore, Oklahoma's favorite light Comedian was in no jovial mood to derive merriment from a Bolsheviki regime that far away from home. So if I thought of an alleged Wise Crack, it was immediately stifled before reaching the thorax. The whole system of Communism might have openly appeared to me Cock-eyed and disastrous, but if I thought so, I would have said it to myself.

No, come to think about it, I wouldn't even have said it to myself. I would have been afraid some thought reader would pick it up.

I looked, I absorbed, but I didn't utter.

[Will had also been told that he would be escorted around Russia and watched every moment. "I don't think," he admitted, "there was a soul in Russia that knew I was in there. In fact it kinder hurt my pride when I found nobody was watching me or paying me any attention. I felt kinder like every new Congressman when he first comes to Washington and looks for Mr. and Mrs. Coolidge and the Cabinet and Alice Longworth and Walter Johnson all to meet him at the train. Then he comes and prowls around for a week before anybody but his Landlord knows he is there."]

Well, I went all over the country; drove out to villages, went to other towns, got on the train and made a night's journey from Moscow to St. Peterburg — or Leningrad was the name of it that week — and wasn't stopped or asked a question.

I talked to various Government officials connected with their Foreign Department, and everywhere had the greatest courtesy and consideration. They explained anything that I would ask them about the government or the country.

I wanted to go in the Kremlin, the old-time Czars' Castle and Fort and I went. They give you a Guide who speaks English. But that was the only place where they furnished me one.

You know how it is yourself, Calvin. I bet you have had Political enemies and you would think from your impression of them that they ought to be quartered in the zoo in the reptile house. Yet when you met them you could see their side and find they wasn't so bad, and that you were both trying to get about the same thing in the long run.

But I found out the real reason I didn't get to see Trotzky. Trotzky is not in so good with the Present Government. It may seem rather funny to some to hear he is too conservative for them.

A Conservative among Communists is a man with a Bomb in only one hand; a Radical is what you call a Two-Bomb Man. They have one in each hand, and will spit a third one at you if possible.

Before coming in here I read everything. I read so many of that fellow Marx's books that I don't want even to see the Marx Brothers. I have come to the conclusion that the reason there is so many books on Socialism is because it's the only thing in the world that you can't explain easy. If the Socialists worked as much as they talked, they would be the most prosperous style of Government in the World.

Liberty don't work as good in practice as it does in speech.

You got to figure that bunch of fellows are playing with the biggest Toy in the world, and they are naturally going to have a lot of short circuits and burned fingers before they get the thing going.

Course it won't be such a terrible disgrace — on them — if

they don't make it, for there is Nations with men trained from childhood in government that look like they were getting practiced on. It's just tough on the people, that's all. It's no disgrace not to be able to run a country nowadays, but it is a disgrace to keep on trying when you know you can't.

You see, the Communism that they started out with, the idea that everybody would get the same and have the same — Lord, that didn't work at all. That has all been changed — the idea that the fellow that was managing the bank was to get no more than the fellow that swept it out. That talked well to a crowd, but they got no more of that now than we have.

I don't suppose there is two men in Russia getting exactly the same salary. They get what they can get, and where they can get it.

When the government runs anything, as they do practically everything over there, there is always about twice or three times as many working in the place as would be found in private enterprise.

During these hard times they have had so much dishonesty among the people working where they could get their hands on any money that it takes about two to watch one, and then four others to watch those two.

The Russians can vote but they can't get them counted.

It seems the whole idea of Communism, or whatever they want to call it, is based on propaganda and blood. Their whole life and thought is to convince somebody else. It looks to me like if a thing is so good and is working so fine for you, you would kind of want to keep it yourself. I would be afraid to let anybody in on it, and that generally seems to be about the usual brand of human nature everywhere.

But the Communist has so many good things he just wants you to join in and help him use some of them.

They are trying to foster art and culture, but all of it is of the Revolutionary type. If it is a painting, the main character has one foot on a capitalist's neck and is punching another capitalist in the jaw. But the main thing that dominates the thing is to spread propaganda.

Talk about some of our states guarding what their schoolbooks contain — these children never get a chance to read anything only about how terrible everything is but Communism.

And you'd better do something about aviation in the United States. They're doing it there. The next war you don't want to Look Out: you want to Look Up! When you look up and see a cloud during the next war to end wars, don't you be starting to admire its silvery lining till you find out how many planes are hiding behind it. I just want you to know what even Russia is doing.

Now the main question that I know strikes you is, Has Russia changed much and is it better off? Say, that is the one answer you can go and bet on. Russia hasn't changed one bit, and a Communist's whole life work is based on complaint of how everything is being done. Well, when they are running everything themselves, why, that takes away their chief industry. They have nobody to blame it on. Even if he is satisfied with it, why, he is miserable because he has nothing to complain about. Same way with Strikes and Revolutions. They would rather stir up a strike somewhere than eat. So, naturally, in Russia, with themselves, they feel rather restrained, for they are totally unable to indulge in their old favorite sport of going on strike and jumping up on a box and inviting all the boys out with them.

You know, that is their whole life, and that is why I don't believe they will ever be satisfied to run their own country, especially if everything runs smooth.

You make one satisfied and he is no longer a Communist. So if they ever get their country running good they will defeat their own cause.

Now, mind you, I may be wrong about these people, for you can never tell about a Russian. They all may be just having the best time in the World over there and enjoying it fine. You know, that is one thing about the Russian — he thrives on adversity. He is never happy in his life as when he is miserable. So he may be just setting pretty, for he is certainly miserable.

CHAPTER SIX

*"Pretty Near Good Enough to
Live In"*

[Will was not happy over what he had learned in Europe. He wrote]:

WE KNOW that Europe don't like us, we know that Europeans make fun of us. An American is a joke to every European. They may cater to an American for his money, but socially or any other way they either ignore us or just tolerate us. They went so far as to throw rocks at them last summer, and the more they hit them the more the Americans come. Just let it be known that some country has acquired a dislike for us and Americans will mortgage their home and let the car go back for unexpired payments, call up the furniture man and let him come get his bedstead for they are going to hike to Europe to see this new form of enemy.

If they meet you on arrival at their border and strew your path with poison ivy, why, the more interesting it will be and the more gifts you will buy to bring to your friends. Laughs at you in Europe is a compliment. The more we are ridiculed, the more we like it.

[Out on his lecture tour, as befitted a person who had mingled with the Old World, he announced, "This is going to be a dignified Lecture. It is not going to be one of those Jazz and Apple Sauce Affairs that I had last year. Jazz has died out and this one is to appeal to the intelligence of the few. Chances are it won't be enjoyed by but only a few." He then gave "the ignorant ones" a chance to leave the Hall and go to their caliber of entertainment, "the Movies or Church or a Political meeting" and those that wanted to could "ask for their money back." He immediately added, "I say you can ask for it back, but TRY and get it. That's where you showed your ignorance was by coming in here in the first place."

Then, after looking over the crowd, and noting that nobody had left, Will went right on and gave them one of his greatest talks. Come midnight, if they still wanted to go on, he would be sitting on the edge of the stage still talking, kidding them about their "follies" and getting started again when someone asked a question.

"Everyone has said to me, 'Will, what does Coolidge think about your letters? Reckon he ever read 'em? Have you seen him?' Now how was I going to tell 'em what Mr. Coolidge thought of them or of anything? I had no reason to believe that he would declare himself on my correspondence any more than he would on prohibition, World Court or Farmer's relief. Did you ever know the smaller a man is the more definite he is?"

Will's competitor on the lecture platform was Queen Marie, "the roving Rumanian," who, as Will said, sort of intended to spear a few loose dollars while here. Will challenged her to join his campaign for "Farmer's relief" and he would show her "more of America than Rand McNally." Above all he was grateful to her for "running Peaches Browning and Aimee McPherson back among the want ads."]

Montgomery, Alabama, October 31, 1926

It took two weeks to coach New York politicians how to dress and act to meet the Queen so they all looked like twins and spoke the same little piece.

Americans are getting like a Ford car — they all have the same parts, the same upholstering and make exactly the same noises.

November 3, 1926

England is holding their fleet maneuvers in Italy's front yard. That's what you call courtesy among nations.

If individuals did that kind of thing to show-off how strong they were in front of someone they didn't like somebody would shoot 'em and everybody else would cheer.

Suppose Tunney exercised in front of your window every morning for no reason at all.

November 13, 1926

President Coolidge brought out Mr. Harding's idea about the conscription of all wealth in case of war. That sounds fine after the war is over. Funny nobody thought of it before the last war started, and I doubt if you hear anything of it just before the start of the next one. If they did do it it would be a great enlistment boost for war, as we all know thousands that would go themselves just to see some of the money taken away from the ones that copped it during the last war. It would be an interesting experiment and would add novelty to the next war, as we have lots more fellows ready and willing to give their lives than we have ones that would be willing to give their fortunes. You would have more suicides and heart failures on your hands than you would have shot by bullets.

It was a great idea when Mr. Harding recommended it, but it's like a campaign promise, it's too good to ever come true. It would be worth a war just to try it out.

Why not postpone having the next war till the cause of it is so popular that you won't have to conscript either of them? If you will wait till we are invaded and everybody knows what they are fighting for, you won't need conscription.

Say, they had a big meeting in Washington last week. The Preservation of Wild Game, and I was a Delegate from Hollywood.

The President said that all "Wild Life" is of public concern, and any time you could preserve one it was a public service.

Preserve 'em! We pickle 'em out in Hollywood.

Atlantic City, January 28, 1927

Missionaries went over to announce to China that there was a heaven, and now the Chinamen want to kill them to give them a chance to prove it.

But some of the missionaries are showing a little doubt themselves.

Roanoke, Virginia, February 1, 1927

I am down in Old Virginia, the mother of Presidents when we thought Presidents had to be aristocrats. Since we got wise to the limitations of aristocrats, Virginia has featured their ham over their Presidential timber.

February 5, 1927

China! those poor people! I never felt as sorry for anyone in my life as I do for them. Here they are, they have never bothered anyone in their whole lives. They have lived within their own boundaries, never invaded anyone else's domains, worked hard, got little pay for it, and no pleasures in life, learned us about two thirds of the useful things we do, and now they want to have a Civil War.

Now we had one and nobody butted in and told us we couldn't have it. China didn't send Gunboats up our Mississippi River to protect their laundries at Memphis or St. Louis or New Orleans. They let us go ahead and fight. If a package of dirty shirts got pierced by a bullet, and it made button holes in the wrong place, the poor Chinaman had to make it good himself. His Country didn't send warships to protect the washboard. If they rendered up his flat irons into canon balls and heave 'em at each other, China didn't demand restitution.

No, sir, China told them if you can't watch your own ironing board and wash tub, you better stay home. They told them, "You are going there, why? Because you can make money. Well, take the extra money you make and pay for your own protection."

Now the Chinese, I bet you, have had about more people of their race killed innocently, and have stood for more insults and property damage in all foreign countries than any other race. But they have never let a squeal out of them about it. Yet every other Nation in the world has always took upon themselves some particular claim to help run China. Every Nation in the World have their own land, and every other Nation recognizes it. But China, everybody looks on theirs as public domain.

England holds one of their towns. Now what right has England to hold one of their Towns any more than China has to make a Laundry out of Buckingham Palace?

Japan used to have these other Nations tell them what to do too. Then they went out and got them a Navy, and now England and France and America take off their coats and spread 'em down for Japan to walk on. Japan is CIVILIZED NOW. THEY HAVE A NAVY. We don't send any more Missionaries there now. Any Nation is a heathern that ain't strong enough to punch you in the Jaw.

Why, the Chinese as a race have forgot more honesty and gentlemanness than we will ever know if we live another Century. If a bank fails in China, they behead the men at the head of it that was responsible. If one fails over here, we write the men up in the Magazines, as how they started poor, worked hard, took advantage of their opportunities (and depositors) and today they are rated as "up in the millions."

If we beheaded all of ours that were responsible for failures, we wouldn't have enough people left to bury the heads. Us and England, even collect their customs for them. We can't trust them with their own money.

Can you imagine having charge of another Countries customs? We said China must maintain the "Open Door" policy. What they meant by the open door is everybody could come in and do what they wanted but China. Suppose China wanted to have a "Moral Turpitude" Clause in their immigration laws. Why, I doubt if even our Ambassadors could get in!

It's a cinch a Marine couldn't get by that test, and if he could he wouldn't be much of a Marine. You just as well not land him.

So poor old China wants to have their Civil War. But no, they can't do it. It would interfere with British and our trade. We can't allow them to do anything that would interfere in any way with our commerce.

England had a strike that stopped every wheel of Industry and Commerce for weeks. Did China tell them they couldn't do it? Maby China had boats at Liverpool's docks waiting to unload. But do you suppose they could even suggest anything about their business being hurt?

The prize two old "Busybodys" of the world is England and America. If Dempsey and Tunney exercised their physical superiority as much as England and America do their Naval superiority, why they would be walking along punching guys in the nose every five minutes, or at least telling them what to do.

Even Brazil, I see, has a Gunboat over there "protecting their interest." Now what could their interest be? China don't eat Nuts and don't drink Coffee. Portugal has a Gunboat there. They are doing it for the ad, just to let people know that they have a Gunboat. Can you imagine Portugal trying to stabilize the Government of China? When I was in Madrid, Spain, last summer, Portugal had three Revolutions and three different Presidents, all in 24 hours. They only worked eight hour shifts.

We have Marines in China and none in Herrin, Illinois.

We haven't even got a Missionary in Herrin.

Between our Missionaries and our Oil men we are just in wrong all over the world. Mr. Coolidge says if China ever gets a stable Government that we will give them some new Treaties, admitting right then that we must have been wrong with the old ones.

How is any Nation capable of judging when another Nation has a stable Government? Boy, they are all Cuckoo!

Poor old China, they just ain't going to allow them to have a nice little private war of their own. No, we must get in it.

[Will got more disturbed about our interference in the affairs of other nations. "China owes us four million and we take over their custom revenue," he said. "France owes us four billion and we are afraid to send them a bill for it. What a great difference in diplomatic relations an army and navy makes!"

"Going to break off diplomatic relations with Mexico and lift the arms embargo and allow arms to be shipped in to any Revolutionist!" "Here we are the Nation that is always hollering for disarmament and peace, and just because we are not smart enough to settle our differences by diplomacy (because we have none) why we are going to make it possible for somebody else to exterminate the faction that we don't like."]

Portland, Oregon, April 4, 1927

Headline says "British Kill Fourteen Chinamen in Shanghai." If our missionaries had already saved these fourteen, why that ought to make it all right, but it certainly will be terrible if they died heathens.

Hurrah for self-determination of nations!

Butte, Montana, April 5, 1927

A nation is just like an individual. If a man's neighbors all hate him and he is continually in trouble, and all his fights and troubles are always over in the other fellow's yard, he must be wrong.

If he won't stay at home what he needs is a good licking or a muzzle.

Hastings, Nebraska, April 6, 1927

Everybody is excited over who will win the election in Chicago. The side with the most machine guns will win it.

We send Marines to Nicaragua to tell them how to run an election and send missionaries to China. No wonder we are funny to the rest of the world.

Yours for law and order — in China!

Milwaukee, April 8, 1927

See by the papers today that the Phillippines wanted just to vote to see if they wanted independence. But we told 'em, "No, you can't even vote to see if you want it or not, and furthermore we urgently request that you don't even be seen thinking about it."

What was that slogan the whole country was shouting just

exactly ten years ago today? Does this sound like it, "Self-determination of small nations."

Yours for memory.

Chicago, April 11, 1927

Buried a bandit here yesterday. Had thirty-five thousand dollars' worth of flowers.

It's the florist that's backing this crime wave. Undertakers advertise their high-priced coffins, "Fit for a bandit." Glorified crime.

Vincennes, Indiana, April 13, 1927

It's all the rage now to hold a debate on prohibition, if you can find a crowd drunk enough to pay to hear it.

I hereby challenge Billy Sunday on the subject: "Resolved: That the talk and arguments used for and against prohibition are worse on the public's morals than the drinking."

Billy can take either side, affirmative, negative, progressive or farmer's relief.

At the finish we will split 50–50. He can take the decision and I will take the gate receipts.

P.S. Let me hear from this, Billy, over in Aurora, right away. If you don't take me, why Aimee will.

Providence, Rhode Island, May 16, 1927

When American diplomacy gets through messing us around over in China, I can tell them what has caused this hate of us over there.

It's our missionaries who have been trying to introduce "chop suey" into China.

China didn't mind them eating it there, but when they tried to call it a Chinese dish that's what made them start shooting at us.

Yours for corn bread, chitlins and turnip greens.

Oneonta, New York, May 17, 1927

When I am playing in a town and it looks like there is not

going to be much of a house, I announce through the papers that
that night I will read passages from "Elmer Gantry," that Baptist
sheik, and the house will be packed with Methodist and Presby-
terian women. Old Elmer sure had it.

Beverly Hills, June 10, 1927

There are two types of men in the world that I feel sincerely
sorry for. One is the fellow that thinks he "knows women," and
the other is the one that is always saying, "I know the Mississippi
River."

The Bolsheviks used to sponsor bomb throwing. That's when
they were doing the throwing. Now that they are on the receiving
end, it's inhuman.

[On June 16 Will reported that "a stomach ache which the
Mayor inherited from the last Administration was erroneously
reported in the press today as nervous indigestion." He stated "it
has been found to be nothing but the effects of home cooking"
and that he had started "eating in a different restaurant every
meal now, and my stomach thinks I am in a different town every
day, so I am back to normal again." He was a little worried since
one doctor had thought he had had a prosperous enough season
"to call a bellyache appendicitis."

The upshot of it all was a diagnosis of gall bladder trouble
and Will was sent to the hospital for the removal of his "surplus
gall."

"I am thrilled to death," he said. "Never had an operation, so
let the stones fall where they may."

Will's condition was critical for a few days but he managed to
survive and to write a book about his experiences, *Ether and Me*,
which got him back the money that he spent on doctors and hospital expenses.

While sick, Will received thousands of wires and letters including one from President Coolidge. "People couldn't have been
nicer to me if I had died," he said.]

Beverly Hills, July 14, 1927

Today I got my official document from the Red Cross headquarters of being made a life member. Well, sir, I am just crazy about it for two reasons.

One, of course, is that it is the greatest organization in the United States (including the world). I think it's greater than the Republican Party (including government salaries). But the other reason is it looks like a diploma.

You know I never had any kind of diploma. I never finished from anything. I always did want something that looked important. I never even had an oil share.

I waited all these years to get something to frame. And if Congress don't help the Mississippi Valley this next term I will devote my few remaining years to telling the truth about them. P.S. the pay season on Oklahoma Fords entering Beverly Hills is closed, sine die, positively.

Beverly Hills, July 15, 1927

This morning lots of people will feel discouraged over the disastrous ending of this disarmament conference without doing anything. But I don't.

I think it was the most successful conference we ever attended. It's the only one where we lost nothing, promised to give up nothing. It's the first one in our history where we come out as strong as we went in. If we would just do nothing at all of them, I wouldn't mind us attending them.

Fight, if necessary, but don't confer.

Beverly Hills, July 28, 1927

Lots of people don't know the difference between the two songs of America and England — "Columbia, Gem of the Ocean" and "Britannia Rules the Waves."

Here is the difference: "Britannia Rules the Waves" is a fact; "Columbia, Gem of the Ocean" is just a song.

[When Will returned from Europe in the fall of 1926 he was made "honorary" Mayor of Beverly Hills. Then, as he said, "the State Legislature of California passed a law saying that no one not a politician could hold office." This deprived him of his mayorality. "I hereby notify the world," he wrote, "that Beverly

Hills has left my bed and board and I will not be responsible for any debts contracted by said municipality." Will signed his notice with, "just a good man looking for something better."

On his way East to accept an appointment from the National Press Club as Congressman-at-Large he stopped in Kansas City and addressed the Ex-Mayors' Association which had made him its President. This group he described as "an earnest body of men trying to come back, all placed where they are by the honesty of the ballot. What this country needs is more ex-Mayors."

In his talk, in the Union Station, Will began by saying, "My Lord, look what the towns have escaped from." He then went on to say that "sometimes we lose confidence in the American form of government, and think that our system of voting is wrong. But I want to tell you that after looking at you and the position you occupy today, there is 'justice in the ballot.' The American voters are like the Canadian Northwest Mounted Police, they gradually get their man, and I see you have all been got."

In Washington Will told the National Press Club, when he was presented with a scroll designating him as Congressman-at-Large]:

More Congressmen have talked themselves out of a job than ever talked themselves into one. I certainly regret the disgrace that's been thrust on me here tonight.

When a Boss wishes to fire a man or lower his position he calls him in privately and does it. When a man is to be hung it is done practically without a flurry. They don't hire a hall to publicly acclaim his downfall. So I am sorry you have made this a public festivity.

I certainly have lived, or tried to live my life so that I would never become a Congressman, and I am just as ashamed of the fact that I have failed as you are.

And to have it Presented by a Senator is adding insult to injury. It is like a Second Lieutenant reprimanding a General. Why in private life a man from the great State of Oklahoma wouldn't associate on the same stage with a man from Arizona, much less a Senator. Why we got a thousand bushels of Wheat to every cactus in your State, a million barrels of oil to every rattlesnake you got. Why, he was elected because the Gila monsters voted Democratic.

When I used to read about Walter Johnson I thought, if this ever happened to me, I would get a bag of money, like he did. And here it is a sheepskin. There is millions of men in America that have a sheepskin that haven't even got a sheep, and in ten years working for the skin it hasn't told them how to get the sheep.

This thing is presented by the Press Club while all the best men are in the Black Hills watching to see if Coolidge catches a perch. We have nothing left here but the riffraff. The best ones are out there trying to get a scoop — a scoop is a reporter that can tell the sex of a fish.

Coolidge got to be President by knowing enough to keep his mouth shut, so I DON'T CHOOSE TO SAY much.

A bandit at large is one they haven't caught, a Congressman-at-Large, or for that matter any Congressman, is one they haven't got wise to.

Hollywood, October 23, 1927

Dwight Morrow is on his way to Mexico to become a diplomat. His diplomacy started early; in fact, at the border, when he got into an armored train. We needn't worry about him. Those Morgan boys can generally take care of themselves. If the train is held up by bandits, I bet you the outlaws come out second best in any financial transaction. If the worst comes to the worst he will float a loan and take their guns and horses as collateral.

If Dwight gets away with Mexico in good shape, I hereby propose him as first ambassador to Russia.

Beverly Hills, October 25, 1927

The American Bankers' Association are holding their annual benefit at Houston. It's their biggest benefit year. The Government has contributed permission for them to consolidate to freeze out the little fellow. The public will contribute something else, so really the only problem before the convention is "How much bonuses on loans will we make 'em pay above the legal rate of interest?"

Branch banks are all the go now. They realize they have got to bring the bank nearer the robber. He won't be annoyed by driving through traffic just to rob one bank. The branch bank is the robbers' only salvation.

P.S. Every banker that could afford a failure during the past year is there.

Beverly Hills, November 24, 1927

If you think we are not prosperous and cuckoo both, read these: "Three hundred thousand dollars for seat on Stock Exchange." You pay that for a seat where nobody sits down. They stand and yell and sell something they haven't got, and buy something they will never get. You can get on the Curb for forty thousand. All you have to do is make signs to a guy in a window, and try to keep from being run over by a truck.

In the next column we read "Kentucky prohibits betting on races." You can gamble on how high people pay for their bread but you can't bet on how fast a horse will run. We must appear odd to the foreigners.

Beverly Hills, November 25, 1927

All the day's news comes from Europe.

Rumania's dictator died. So that helps Prince Carol's case. He is only two wives removed from the throne now.

Another headline says, "One Hundred Million More Men Under Arms in Europe than 1914." "England sends word to Italy to lay off Jugoslavia."

It's taken a long time for Europe to get back to normal, but it's slowly doing it.

CHAPTER SEVEN

"The Country is Prosperous As A Hole ..."

[In January, 1928, Will appeared with Paul Whiteman, Al Jolson and Fred Stone in the first national hookup on radio. Will was at his home in Beverly Hills, Paul Whiteman was in New York, Al Jolson was in New Orleans and Fred Stone was in Chicago, which was the center of the hookup. All of their voices went to Chicago and were then broadcast from there. Will's family, in the next room, heard his voice, which had gone to Chicago and come back, within a fraction of a second. Each of the participators had on head phones so he could hear the others.

In Will's own personal broadcast he did the famous imitation of President Coolidge which created a national sensation. Here is what he said]:

LADIES AND GENTLEMEN: It's the duty of the President to deliver a message to the people on the condition of the country. I am proud to report that the condition of the country as a whole is prosperous. I don't mean by that the whole country is prosperous. But as a Hole it's prosperous. That is it is prosperous for a Hole. There is not a "hole" lot of doubt about that. Everybody that I come in contact with is doing well — Hoover, Dawes, Lowden, Curtis, and Al Smith are all doing well. But not as well as they would like to be doing this time next year. Mellon has saved some money, for the country, and done very well for himself. He is the only Treasury that has saved faster than Congress could divide it up. Congress is here now though to grab what he has got. It would have been cheaper to have sent each Congressman and Senator his pro rata share and saved the expense of holding this Congress.

Just a few words on the public issues of the day. They won't seat two Republican Senators. The Democrats didn't mind them buying their seats but it was the price they paid. It would establish a price that would have made it prohibitive for a Democrat to even get standing room much less a seat in the Senate.

I sent Dwight Morrow to Mexico. Smart Boy Dwight, one of the two smartest boys in our class at Amherst where we were preparing for College. Lindbergh is busy in Central America. We seem to get in wrong faster than he can get us out. I wish he was twins.

I made a statement last summer in which I said I didn't choose to run. It seems to have been misunderstood. So months ago I clarified it by saying, "I still don't choose to run." If they misunderstood "Choose" in the first place I don't very well see how they could do it again.

On farm relief, I give 'em rain and a good crop. That beats all the McHaughen bills for relief. Fill a Farmer up, that will stop him from hollering quicker'n anything.

On our Foreign Debts, I am sorry to state that they are just as Foreign as ever, if not more so.

Cuba and South America, I am going there at once to try and show them that we are not as bad as we've been.

Nicaragua, we are still having a little trouble down there, but I think we will gradually get it all Buried.

Prohibition, prohibition is GOING DOWN about as well as usual.

Radio audience, I thank you.

Beverly Hills, January 3, 1928

See where they got a bill in Congress to make a road from Brownsville, Texas, up along the Rio Grande to El Paso, then on out to San Diego along the Mexican boundary.

It's a good idea and should be built, but it's called in the bill a "military highway." Now, if we was building a road along the Canadian border we wouldn't insult our neighbors by calling it a military road. Can't you get Government aid without calling it military?

No wonder it takes all Lindbergh's time to try and make friends, as fast as our State's lack of courtesy loses them for us.

This case is like calling a hospital "the home for incurables." There is a tactful title for you.

Garrett, Indiana, January 9, 1928

You can kid about Chicago and its crooks, but they have the smartest way of handling their crooks of any city. They get the rival gangs to kill off each other and all the police have to do is just referee and count up the bodies. They won't have a crook in Chicago unless he will agree to shoot at another crook. So viva Chicago!

Washington, D.C., January 13, 1928

I found on my arrival in Washington that some people had censored me severely for leaving the impression the other night that Mr. Coolidge was on the radio. Well, the idea that any one could imagine it was him uttering the nonsense that I was uttering! It struck me that it would be an insult to any one's sense of humor to announce that it was not him.

So I wrote Mr. Coolidge a note explaining, and received a two-page letter within thirty minutes from him, written all in his own longhand, saying that he had been told of it, but knew that anything that I did was done in good-natured amusement, and to not give it a moment's worry. He also thanked me for my kind reference to him on various occasions which he had not heard.

I knew my man before I joked about him. It's as I have often said: You can always joke good naturedly a big man, but be sure he is a big man before you joke about him. What I did over the radio on Mr. Coolidge I did on my tour of every State last season, and I knew it didn't offend good taste.

I want to here publicly thank Mr. Coolidge for that lovely letter, for I am personally very fond of him. With an election coming on, I know of no man connected with either party who I have ever had the pleasure of meeting for whom I have a greater regard.

When there is no malice in your heart, there can be none shown in your humor. But between you and I there is a lot of people in this country who should never be so absentminded as to refer to their sense of humor.

Atlanta, Georgia, March 22, 1928

Why try to be funny when an association does it for you? This week's prize for humor goes to the Maryland Racing Association for barring Harry Sinclair's horses from races. Be a good joke if the Senate investigated them.

I suppose all the touts at Maryland tracks will have to live at the Y.M.C.A. and the bookmakers will have to show their church cards. They will have Governor Ritchie making prohibition speeches.

It's a great country when you are down and out. Well, Harry, I hope Oklahoma don't get so pure that they refuse your taxes. If they do we will all the rest of us go to work.

March 24, 1928

We have courses in Business administration, Salesmanship, Public speaking, Etiquette, Banking, Dairying, Fertilizing, Everything that a person can think of we have a course in it that you can take at some College. Now what I want to propose is a course in "Public Testifying."

Most of our public men spend over half their time testifying on the stand, especially the Republicans. Now what has brought forth this idea of mine is the testimony that has been delivered on the stand. Did you ever in your life see men get as flustrated and tangled up as these fellows do on the stand? It looks like the smarter the man the bigger Sucker he is when he is being questioned. You know the greatest testimony in any case and about the only convincing testimony we have, is some Child's testimony, or some old ignorant Farmer or Laborer. They are the ones that always make the hit on the stand. They can answer every question without flinching, and in a simple direct way. But the minute a witness has had any education, or thinks he knows something, why the less convincing he is on the stand.

I think of all the bunch on the witness stand that Lawyers are the worst. You never read a Lawyer's testimony on the stand in any case in your life and could tell heads or tails of it. They think they are so smart that they have to hide something, and they are generally more scared than any other class of witness there is. The reason the child, or old Lady, or ignorant workman make such good witnesses is they only have one story, and the prosecuting Lawyer knows they only have one, so there is no chance of tying them up in cross examinations. But the smart fellow has so many different angles that he is trying to use a little of all of them, and winds up by making everybody believe that he didn't tell half he knew, and didn't know half he told.

So I am going to start a school of "Public Testimony." Instead of being layed out like a School it will be layed out like a Court. Instead of teachers we will have 'em made up as Sheriffs, and Bailiffs and Jurymen, and Judges. The minute a man is elected to office like Senator or Congressman, why we will have him come and spend a few weeks in the school and then when he goes on to his public office he will be all set for the first investigation. We will teach 'em not to be nervous, not to let the other fellow get 'em rattled, and have 'em all trained to tell where they got every dollar they used in their campaign and how much they paid for each vote.

June 3, 1928

Just when Secretary Kellogg had his "no-more-war plan" all going good and about ready to sign up, why England, Japan and France came through with the old usual diplomatic clause which says:

"We agree in principle, but . . ."

Well, there was the but. "We are heartily against all wars, unless, of course, we should see fit to do a little fighting ourselves. Then, of course, this agreement would be null and void. But we certainly join you in preventing others from having the pleasure of fighting."

If Kellogg can get all us four big nations to agree that Monday follows Sunday without them having "I agree in principle, but . . ." in it, he will be the world's greatest diplomat.

[The Republicans in Convention at Kansas city nominated Herbert Hoover and the Democrats in convention at Houston nominated Al Smith as their respective Presidential candidates. After attending both conventions Will suggested censors to operate as a control on both political conventions to make them painless by providing, first, that if a speaker has an idea let him give it to the convention provided it hasn't been given by other speakers all week; second, to take out all histories of the parties and reference to the names of their founders ("In fact I think a lot of our past great men would be a lot bigger in public estimation if it was made prohibitory for them to be referred to by some of our Politicians"); and to eliminate or put under strict censorship all references to "past records" ("All Legislation is put through by the aid of swaps and trades. They are just a lot of horse traders. So make 'em leave out all the so-called Party accomplishments from the speeches.")]

Beverly Hills, July 11, 1928

Mayor Jimmy Walker gave a lot of the film people an awful roasting out here for being Republicans, and I am like Jimmy.

I think any of us that are in the amusement line should naturally be Democrats.

August 18, 1928

[In his weekly article Will gave his own story of the organization and history of the famous Bohemian Club and the Bohemian Grove of San Francisco.]

This Bohemian Club, or Gang rather, is just about the most unique organization that was ever held up for the arrival of a corkscrew. It started exactly fifty years ago. It started over an actor. About the only things that actors can start is a fad or a divorce. But this Actor had lost his job in Frisco and had to go to New York to work where all the other actors laying off could see and criticise him. Frisco gave him a dinner, and they give it in a grove out in the Country, and they had such a good dinner nobody woke up all night and when daylight come they found

they had communed with nature, and it being the first time they
had ever slept under anything but shingles and mortgages, that
they said, "Let's come every year and get so we can't get back
home that night."

And that was the start of Actors and Artists sitting down and
eating with white folks. And the thing has grown till now they
own and preserve three thousand acres of Red Woods, and over
250 Bank Presidents, and no telling how many ferns and Vice
Presidents there is. It's the biggest thing of its kind in the World
today where all classes speak to each other FOR THREE WEEKS.
They have a great time. Hoover belongs when he is not a Candidate. The play on the last night is the most wonderful thing ever
staged. I want to thank them for having me there as a Guest.
It's awful hard to get into. It was a question whether I or Coolidge would get in, and I want to thank them.

[In August, 1928, Fred Stone, who was going to open a show in
New York with his daughter Dorothy, had a plane wreck which
put him into the hospital for an indefinite time.

Will canceled what amounted to $500,000 in lecture and other
commitments to go on in Fred's place and pinch-hit for him so
that the show would not be a flop. His telegram to Fred read]:

If you don't want Dorothy to wait until you are entirely recovered I will go into the show with her, just to sort of plug along
till you are able to rejoin, and I will do the best I can with your
part. Dorothy can keep telling me how you would have played
it.

Dorothy, of course, would be the star, and I don't want any
billing. Anything you, Dorothy and Dillingham says goes with
me.

[Will, of course, in the show did pretty much as he had done
in the old Follies. Here are some of the things he said]:

There is no Country in the history of the World that ever lived
in the high class manner we do — Radio, Bath Tubs, almost an-

tique furniture, Pianos, Rugs — Course other Countries could have had all the things but they can't buy 'em on credit.

This Country is not prosperous. It's just got good credit. We live better and owe more than anybody in the World. All you got to do in America to enjoy life is to "Don't let your next payment worry you."

You can get all the Luxuries of life in this country, no matter how poor you are, if you just don't mind buying on credit.

If you can just get a dollar a Luxury to pay down.

August 29, 1928

I have a scheme for stopping war. It's this — no nation is allowed to enter a war till they have paid for the last one.

September 4, 1928

I have been libeled by my friend Brisbane. He says that at one time I was a Sunday School teacher. Now, he is wrong. I went, but didn't teach. I didn't even take up the collection.

Some banker always did that.

New York, September 17, 1928

Just had dinner tonight with Thomas Edison, Henry Ford and Harvey Firestone and their wives. Say, there is the ones you want to meet. These three famous men, we know all about them, but you ought to meet these wives that made them famous. No frills, no put on, just three lovely wholesome family folks. Talked children and grandchildren all evening.

And say, Thomas A. pulled a good one. As you all know he is very deaf; well, he walked over to the window overlooking Broadway, and says to us, "Broadway seems so quiet." I think he was looking at it to see if his lights was working O.K.

[As the 1928 Presidential campaign got under way Will became more and more disturbed as the religious question surged to the front. Much was made of the fact that Al Smith was a Catholic. Will particularly did not like what the preachers were doing. "On Sundays the preachers all start out by saying, 'The Church

should not enter into politics, BUT . . .' Then they try to show
that in their case it is different, that they are not entering politics,
they are just advising, that people are so flighty nowadays that if
they are not advised properly why they are so apt to be led astray
by the opposition."

This is what Will feared. When Al Smith nailed Hoover by
showing that "the Republican Farm relief plank was exactly the
same in the 1924 platform and in the 1928 one," he applauded
that. But he said that the Republicans would squirm out of it
and anyhow "the farmer up North" would go on voting Republican and the farmer down South would go on voting Democratic
when in reality they ought to line up against the city. The reason
for this, of course, was an alignment made during the Civil War
which had no sense nor even nonsense at the present time.]

October 13, 1928
We never have a man so crooked that he would like to ruin the
country, we may run onto one or two every once in awhile that
want to grab off part of our possessions. But they feel there is
plenty left where they got that. So the old country just rambles
along, not because of the politician but in spite of him. Anyway
politics is a business where most of the men in it are looking for
glory and personal gratification more than they are money. It's
one of the easiest ways of horning into something publicly.

Why these old birds that are on all these national committees,
and are always delegates to conventions why you could no more
pry one of those jobs loose from them even if they had to pay
their way and the convention was held in Moscow, Russia. They
like to say, "Well, we are going to put Seth Bohunk over. I been
talking to all the boys in my state." Now here is forty-eight
states and he thinks poor soul that the whole thing is all on his
shoulders from this one state, then the credit they do take afterwards, now mind you two thirds of the people who voted don't
belong to any of these things, they just pick 'em out a man and
go vote for him, nothing in the world any of these regular politicians could say would influence them any more than a goat.

But we got it and we will always have it, there is nothing else

that they could get that much publicity out of, and they think
they are running the country and are directly responsible for
what little we may have to eat, so we won't put 'em out of business, they are a harmless sort, and really at heart mean well, and
I think at heart most of 'em are really wise to themselves, but it's
gone so far they can't admit it.

New York, November 1, 1928

We sent our marines not so much to supervise Nicaragua's
election Sunday as we did to keep them from being at our election Tuesday and getting into real serious trouble. We won't
vote on Sunday, as we are holding our last political sermons
then.

Those Nicaraguans are just about ignorant enough to have
nothing in their election about bigotry, religion, prohibition,
pro-British, brown hats, bad English, 100 percent, or any of those
great issues that we know mean the life and death of our country.

Nicaragua is perhaps so backward and primitive that they don't
know enough to believe in campaign promises.

November 13, 1928

[Will predicted rightly before the election that it was "going
to be the greatest lesson in geography that New York City ever
had. They never knew how many people live west of the Hud-
son." He was correct. New York's candidate, Al Smith, was
snowed under. Will also gloomily stated that it would take "two
generations to sweep up the dirt." He went on to say, "You will
please pardon a Comedian for lapsing into seriousness, but there
was no reason for all this religious gab, and all the threats of
what would happen if certain things were brought about."]

Been reading editorials on President Coolidge's debt and arma-
ment speech. Several papers have asked, "What would Europe do
if we were in difficulties and needed help?"

So this is in reply to those inquiries: Europe would hold a celebration.

December, 1928 [*Routine on Fred Stone Show*]

I have given this corruption and crime situation a good deal of study. You know not only here but all over the Country there is an attempt being made by the "so-called Better Citizens" to stamp out corruption.

I am not an authority, and am a member of no Commission, but the only way I know of for the good citizen to stamp out corruption is for the good citizen to quit drinking.

Without somebody to sell it to there can't be any corruption. This goes for the "better element" also.

A seat on the stock exchange is worth half a million dollars. That's not a seat, that's a license to hold a Sucker up when he buys and blackjack him as he sells, to commit petty larceny when he buys, and grand larceny when he sells.

December 31, 1928 [*Routine on the Fred Stone Show*]

The old year will go out tonight through the necks of millions. It's a good thing the drys won. New Yorkers couldn't have carried any more. There's not an idle flask in the city tonight. The show is getting eleven dollars. One fellow got a ticket at the Box Office and dropped dead with amazement. It would take Coolidge, Smith and Hoover playing the Three Musketeers in Yiddish to be worth eleven bucks.

If it keeps on getting more expensive to celebrate every year, it will take what you make to see the old year out.

If the New Year stays as wet as it starts, the Nation will die of delirium tremors by July.

New York, January 3, 1929

Everybody is picking on that poor boy out there in California that run the wrong way with that football. If I was an editorial writer I would ask how many out of the hundred and ten million of the rest of us are headed the wrong way? How many out of us have even had the presence of mind enough to pick up a fumble? How many grabbed out of the scramble what they think is success and don't know till they reach the goal line whether it's the right one or not?

New York, January 4, 1929

Mr. Hoover lands at Old Point Comfort tomorrow. That's about the last comfort he will get for the next four years.

January 5, 1929

Education never helped morals. The most savage people we have are the most moral. The smarter the Guy the bigger the rascal. And the minute a thing is high priced, you immediately create a desire for it. You give liquor away tomorrow like water and the novelty of being drunk would be over in a week, and nobody would touch the stuff. It's like Golf, you let the poor all get to playing it and you watch the rich give it up. So make the Government make it, and give it away, and we will all be disgusted with it. Americans don't like common things.

February 9, 1929

They will tell you how Washington's farsightedness is exemplified in the broad street of Pennsylvania Avenue, that he knew that some day the merry Ford and the frolicsome Chevrolet would be flitting hither and thither.

They credit all these to the foresight of Washington when, as a matter of fact, the width of the Avenue was determined to give a Senator or Congressman room to stagger to his lodgings without bumping into a building.

He made the Street wide for another reason. He could look from the White House up the Avenue and see when some Congressman was coming to call on him, and would know when to hide.

New York, February 15, 1929

Somebody just left Yale eight million as an endowment to study humans, including senior classmen. They want to figure out what kind of a heart beats under a raccoon coat.

Yale wants to know why Notre Dame can throw a forward pass further than they can a green apple.

It's to study "group conduct" and human behavior. Chicago is the place for that.

All this stuff would have been a kick to Abe Lincoln, wouldn't it?

A college President's work nowadays consists of thinking up new things for the students to play with that looks like studying. A kindergarten teacher ain't in it with schemes in trying to amuse.

New York, February 18, 1929

Truth comes out mighty slow. Florida wants the Federal Government to pay all the expenses of putting a windbreak around Lake Okeechobee so the water won't all blow out.

Religion didn't drive that State Republican!

New York, February 24, 1929

All we seem to celebrate Washington's Birthday for is so we can revive the argument as to what he had to say about "entanglements" in Europe. Every speaker makes him say just what that speaker wants him to say.

Coolidge says it was Jefferson that made the "wisecrack" about not messing with outsiders.

So it looks like added to all his other accomplishments Washington was a diplomat.

A diplomat is one that says something that is equally misunderstood by both sides, and never clear to either.

New York, February 18, 1929

The war didn't scare the Senate as bad as Jim Reed's joke that he was going to tell who voted dry and drank not only wet, but anything (whether it was wet or not). Some haven't slept since he threatened to do it. No man that has left that Senate in many a day will be missed like Jim.

Ain't it funny how many hundreds of thousands of soldiers we can recruit with nerve. But we just can't find one politician in a million with backbone.

New York, March 26, 1929

Hoover gets rid of something useless every day. Wait till he sees the Senate and Congress.

He sunk the Mayflower without warning; took the White
House stables and made a garage for fishing poles out of it; sent
six horses to the museum that had never been able to be ridden
since Taft got through with them; traded the mechanical horse
for a medicine ball, and makes everybody catch it before they
can get any breakfast. That's to discourage Senators eating there.

New York, March 27, 1929

I told you Mr. Hoover did one good deed every day. I see
today where he is going to clean up the Republican organizations
in the South. That's going to take a little over a day. Maybe a
day and a half.

He will find it's easier to change the color on some of them
than it is the morals on others. If he holds a clinic over 'em he
will find the blackest ones are the whitest ones after all.

The only way that situation can be remedied that I can see is
to ship in some better Republicans from the North, and there
just ain't any to spare.

March 29, 1929

You know Women are getting into more things that are embarrassing to the men. You see the first idea of giving them the
vote was just to use the vote. But the Women, contrary like they
are, they wasn't satisfied with that. They started to take this
equality thing serious. They begin to think they really was
somebody. The women figured that "While we may not be as
good as a Man, we are at least as good a Politician." So the
Scamps commenced to want to get in on the loot.

As soon as they found out a Political Job took no experience
to hold, that it only took experience to get, why they commenced
to making themselves rather embarrassing around the Political
employment Bureau.

It was all right with the men when the women took the little
Committee assignments where there was NO salary connected, but
when they started to want to put their powdered nose into the
feed trough, why that brought on complications. Now they are
wondering, "Was the Women's vote worth what they are asking
for it?"

Women that used to wouldn't think of gossiping anywhere but over a back fence, now won't say a word about you till the meeting has been duly called to order. It's scattered Scandal around more. It's brought it more into the open. It's changed lots of things around. Families that used to didn't know there was a Restaurant in town are looking over the Menu cards on days when the Ladies Auxiliary of the "Pork Barrel Political Society" is in session.

April 6, 1929

A bunch of Congressmen landed in New York from Panama Canal where they had been at Government expense to see if it really did connect the two Oceans, or was it just propaganda.

Well, they got back here to New York and they only searched one of their baggage and found four Quarts. He had forgot to claim Government privilege (that's a gag where if you leave the Country, you can come back with anything you want and they can't search your baggage). The other 14 had claimed it and they got home with theirs. All but Congressman La Guardia, an Italian American (and a good one). He admitted that he had started from down there with a few steins of Grog, but had drank it up before arrival at Quarantine, purposely. Now he will be ostracised in Congress for honesty.

New York, April 14, 1929

Tomorrow is a historic day. Mr. Hoover, all during his career, has had men almost lay down their lives to aid him in carrying out some good work. That all ends tomorrow, Congress meets, and his faith in human nature will start waning before sundown. We will find no tinge of Red Cross spirit on that hill. Six hundred gathered there from all over the country, just waiting for somebody to suggest something worthwhile, and then show him what happens to it. I can hear Mr. Coolidge laughing to himself away over in Northhampton and saying, "Well, I'm glad I didn't try to relieve 'em."

Boston, April 15, 1929

Just read the farm relief bill. It's just a political version of Einstein's last theory.

If a farmer could understand it, he certainly would know more than to farm. He would be a professor out here in Harvard. The farmers will die in the poorhouse before the guy that wrote it can even get the Senate to understand it.

In my dumb way it read like it was all based on doing away with the middleman. That's a great idea and has been tried ever since the snake came between Adam and Eve. He is unnecessary, but he is here yet.

Then if this did work next year we would have to give relief to the middleman. But it will give 'em something to argue over.

New York, April 16, 1929

England is taking the tax off tea. It's been on 300 years.

Now, why don't they take the quinine or assafitity (or whatever it is) out of their coffee? It tastes like something that has been in there 300 years, too. Poor coffee and no bathtubs have drove more Americans out of England than unfamiliarity with their language has.

Winston Churchill's party is running on "no tea tax and no betting tax." Lloyd George's gang is running on "more employment." Churchill will win. If an Englishman has got tea and can bet on a horse, what does he want with employment?

Boston, April 23, 1929

Say, that speech of Mr. Hoover's yesterday was just about one of the strongest things a President ever said when he said life and property is less safe here than any other civilized country in the world.

The only difference of opinion we can have about that is, do we come under the heading of "civilized"? I doubt that more than I do the statement.

One thing, he hadn't spoken two minutes till you could tell the same man hadn't written that speech that had been in there. It was about the condition of the country, but not the same condition that Calvin used to enumerate to us.

Boston, April 25, 1929

See where some society visiting President Hoover said for

human reasons they didn't have him shake hands with them.

Well, that's fine. Now, why didn't they go further with their good idea and not visit him and take up his time? Then they would have been 100 percent correct.

Boston, April 30, 1929

Did you see the figures issued by the Department of Commerce about the amount man spent on cosmetics to beautify themselves? Didn't I tell you they are getting vainer over their looks than women?

They spent over $1,000,000,000 and there is more bald-headed ones and more ugly ones and more funny-looking ones that we ever had before. They will try anything in the world a woman does. They will have dresses on in less than ten years.

Beauty parlors are thicker than filling stations, but more power to the people that run 'em, for they earn it having to listen to people with nothing on their mind but wanting to look better.

Boston, May 2, 1929

Say, what's this May Day thing? We used to look on it as a beautiful Spring day when we had a picnic and fastened ribbons to the top of a pole and danced around and sang and played. We had no mass production (only in children). We had no Federal Reserve or Farm Relief. Everybody was just poor and ignorant enough to be happy.

But now May Day, with all our modern accomplishments, is for the dissatisfied. He puts in his only hard earned day of the year. He arises early so he can denounce longer, prints an obituary notice on a banner of everybody that has tried to make him earn his living during the year, and he just has one of the best times of his life. Hurrah for progress!

Philadelphia, May 11, 1929

Just flew down to Pimlico, Maryland, to see the great "Preakness" race. Bucked a head wind but not as strong a one as the horses I bet on bucked. Forty thousand people there, counting Senators and Congressmen.

Farmers got no relief today but the mutuel betting machine

cleaned up. Handled over a million and a half on one race.

Lucky for me I ran into "Doc" Admiral Grayson. Through his medical influence he got me in the inclosure where the Republicans were, otherwise I would have had to stay in the center field with the Democrats.

It was the one place where the Democrats couldn't join with the loose-moraled Republicans and put over anything.

Philadelphia, May 12, 1929

As I paid for this joke, I want to see it in the papers. At Baltimore Friday in the big race I bet on four horses, all to win, place and show. Blue Coat was tipped me by Governor Ritchie, who I think was working on commission. One was called the "Nut."

Well, birds of a feather must back each other. I bet on Earl Sande's Hermitage because Sande is a friend of mine. There was a horse called Soul of Honor from Oklahoma; there's real humor for you.

I had all these tickets in my outside coat pocket and some Republican Senator or Congressman pinched 'em. I discovered it just as they got to the post, so my only hope was to pray for 'em all to lose, and they did. They all four run last, so imagine that Republican scoundrel's embarrassment. The Lord is with us Democrats.

Philadelphia, May 15, 1929

The old farmer is getting his relief. I see today where they put high tariff on "shingles and flaxseed." Heretofore every time a farmer raised a good crop of "shingles," why, he had to compete with the Argentine-grown "shingles," but with two new tariffs, why, the old agrarian is sitting pretty. They have taken the "shingles" off his roof so he can see the Republican viewpoint. He puts a flaxseed poultice on his head and prays that he will never be so unfortunate as to be relieved again.

Philadelphia, May 16, 1929

Postscript — Farmers get more relief today. Tariff was raised on window panes. Cheap glass from Glasgow has always hurt our agrarian glass growers.

Philadelphia, May 17, 1929

This Al Capone that is supposed to be Field Marshal on Chicago's western front blew into our little City of Brotherly Love here yesterday and before his valet could unpack his machine gun why he had been sentenced to a year in jail for wearing his pistols instead of a vest. That's one of the worst blows against our new aristocracy we have had.

Detroit, May 21, 1929

Everybody that I know kicking about the Federal Reserve is someone trying to make money by speculation. So I about come to the conclusion that the Federal Reserve might accidentally be working in the interests of the hundred million who don't know a stock from a stockyard.

If 1 percent raise in rate can upset the whole of Wall Street, then they are working on a mighty slim margin.

Detroit, May 24, 1929

Did you know that the only bill that has really passed the House and Senate and been signed by the President is the bill appropriating the salary of the members of this extra session?

The farmers can grow whiskers, the orphans can grow up, the tariff can tear out the vitals of the consumers' purse, but the boys there want theirs in advance whether they deliver any relief to anybody else or not.

Pittsburgh, May 31, 1929

A sure certainty about our Memorial days is as fast as the ranks from one war thin out, the ranks from another take their place. Prominent men run out of Decoration Day speeches, but the world never runs out of wars. People talk peace, but men give their life's work to war. It won't stop till there is as much brains and scientific study put to aid peace as there is to promote wars.

[The Fred Stone Show, after a most successful run, was closed in Pittsburgh on June 1, 1929. Will headed immediately by plane for Beverly Hills, and home.

"If you have missed anybody around their old haunts in the

East," he announced on his arrival on June 3, "and have no idea where they are, they are right here in Beverly Hills trying to get in the talkies, and the ones that are in 'em are trying to learn to talk. I haven't had a chance to say a word since I got home for people just practicing on me to show me they talk. And song writers, why the city makes you come to a dead stop at every crossing with your car to keep you from running over a song writer working on a theme song."]

Beverly Hills, June 7, 1929

Congress passed a bill yesterday to redistribute some new Congressmen.

If you remember, this session of Congress was called "just to relieve the farmer." So, if you are a destitute farmer and can get enough other poor farmers to go in with you and sign the census rolls, why, they will relieve your stranded condition by giving you another Congressman.

The only relief I can see out of it is send a fat one so you can eat him.

Beverly Hills, June 11, 1929 [*The Rockefeller Foundation*]

The whole viewpoint of the people in regard to our rich men has been changed in the last few years. Now we judge a man's greatness on how he has spent his money. I guess there has never been a time in our history when as many fools are making money as now. Just to be rich and nothing else, is practically a disgrace nowadays.

June 22, 1929

A Thoroughbred race horse breeding establishment is more in line with royal marriages than anything I know of, only they are careful to never inbreed.

But as far as Love that's a lot of Hooey. They think it brings Nations closer to each other to have the heads marry to each other. Well it didn't do so much for Germany and England.

Santa Monica, June 24, 1929

Today's paper says the rattlesnakes are so bad at Mr. Hoover's

Virginia fishing grounds that they are getting razorbacks to exterminate 'em. A snake can't bite a razorback hog because he splits his tongue on his back. That adds another product to Virginia's other two. Now their slogan is, "Come to Virginia, home of hams, rattlesnakes and Presidents (but not lately)."

Mr. Henry Ford is going on talking on "how to enforce prohibition" till Mr. Hoover will get even with him by putting him at the head of enforcement.

Ford and his mass production is where the bootleggers got their ideas.

Beverly Hills, June 27, 1929

Viva Democracy! Viva Charley Dawes! Among all the diplomats gathered at King George's imperial court, Charley was the only one that didn't wear rompers. He would not bare his Chicago shins to the crowned heads of the British Empire. Among all the satin step-ins of the other males, his long and uncreased pants stood out like a diadem. It was not only a victory for modesty, but a godsend for the people who sell material by the yard. Even the women, they say, followed him. But not even an ankle would he reveal.

Long live Charles Dawes and longer live his long breeches!

Beverly Hills, July 2, 1929

See where this fellow Kemal Pasha, the head man of Turkey, is considering making us a visit.

They claim, people that have been over there, that he is the biggest man in the world today. He is Mussolini, Borah, Aimee McPherson and Charley Dawes combined.

He jerked the veils off the women, the fezzes off the men, rolled the flappers' stockings, made the people all learn to read and write a new language, put in a golf course, gave the farmers relief, discharged his Federal Reserve Board and whipped Greece — all in one week.

Santa Monica, August 29, 1929

President Hoover opened up a Xmas tree for the politicians

when he suggested that all government land be turned back to the State in which it was located.

Just announce that there is something going to be divided up and you get the whole nation interested in national affairs. Announce that there is something to pay and you get one hundred million anarchists on your hands, so Mr. Hoover is becoming a politician fast.

I don't know how bad the Federal Government manages the land, but as bad as they do it, it can only be one forty-eighth as bad as the States will do it.

September 7, 1929

England has been the Daddy of the Diplomat, the one with the smooth manners, but still be going after what he wants but always the Gentleman. You know that's one thing about an Englishman, he can insult you, but he can do it so slick and polite that he will have you guessing till away after he leaves you just whether he was a friend or foe.

It's hard to unite both classes over there. For a Gentleman in England is a man that disagrees with whatever the laboring Party wants. But if it means money, they all agree, and where there is money involved (coming in) you can generally interest what is humorously called the "better classes."

Santa Monica, September 12, 1929

See where they are forming in Europe a new organization called "The United States of Europe." Nobody knows just what it is or what its aims are, but we ought to be for it if only for one reason and that is, it's the first thing been formed since the war that we haven't been asked to go over and join.

If it's an economic boycott against our high Republican tariff I don't see why the Democrats wouldn't be allowed to join it.

I guess this epidemic of forming clubs and things, that we have just so disastrously passed through, is just hitting Europe.

Santa Monica, September 15, 1929

Ramsey MacDonald is coming over here. Watch him, Herbert.

Englishmen are the only race of people that never travel for just fun.

Personally I think he wants to show us the advantages of England retaining the largest navy. You won't be asked for any monetary consideration, Mr. Hoover; just do a little fancy ship sinking.

October 26, 1929

The Senatorial Investigation about finding out who is a Lobbyist and who is a Bootlegger in Washington has started now and that will be the best one of the bunch. There is no law against Lobbying any more than there is against a man going out and trying to get votes for the Senators when they are running for office. It is simply a case of trying to convince someone that this or that is the best thing under the circumstances.

But Washington is going to investigate them and see how they make this living. For it look like a terrible graft, and during the investigations will be brought out perhaps the finer points of Lobbying.

There will be no chance to get any legislation through Congress as all the Senators are on investigation Committees and they will never have a Quorum.

Santa Monica, October 27, 1929

The Carnegie Foundation got their answer about paid athletes yesterday. One half million people attended seven games where the athletes were subsidized. Less than half that many attended 50 games where the Athletes were pure, but not much Athletes.

The public don't care how you got to college. It's how you are going to get from the forty yard line to over the goal that they are worrying about.

We are a "get the dough" people, and our children are born in a commercial age.

Why if a babe in arms can cry loud enough to get paid for it we are tickled to death. Make 'em pay for talent whether its art, music, football, literature, radio announcing or flag pole sitting.

Any actors that can draw 88 thousand people in one day is worthy of their hire.

Don't let Wall Street get all the gravy.

Beverly Hills, October 29, 1929

What's the matter with this for a laugh, when the stock market goes down, Mr. Morgan, Lamont, Charley Mitchell and Mr. George Baker hold a meeting and let everybody see 'em in this huddle, then the market perks up?

I was just thinking what a great idea it would be if we could get these boys to room together for six months. There is no telling to what heights the market might go.

Just think what a calamity if they forgot where they were to meet some day to inspire confidence.

Beverly Hills, November 12, 1929

Instead of observing Armistice Day Monday, Wall Street decided to hold a little session for the boys that crave more action than ordinary peace affords, and everybody was jarred loose from a 5 to 50 point drop. That will make some of 'em remember that the day has some significance anyhow.

Beverly Hills, November 13, 1929

I guess this stock market drop is due to the fact that Rockefeller and all those big men who stabilized it a couple of weeks ago have about reached the limit of their margins and are being sold out. What the market needs now is another bunch of men that will stabilize it during its next 100-point drop.

November 14, 1929

Prosperity this Winter is going to be enjoyed by everybody that is fortunate enough to get into the poor farm.

[With the Stock Market spoiling "more appetites than bad cooking," Will told how he nearly took a flier himself. He held "out some dough on Mrs. Rogers out of the weekly stipend" and went to talk with Eddie Cantor who was "piling up a fortune that Rockefeller couldn't vault over." Will told him that he "wanted to get in on this skinning of Wall Street. Everybody was doing it" and he "wanted to be in at the killing." He then went on]:

I didn't have anything particular against Wall Street, but knowing the geographical and physical attributes of the Street, I knew that it was crooked. (You can stand at the head of it, and you can only see to the bend. It just won't let you see all of it at once as short as it is.) I just said to myself I would like to be with the bunch that has the credit of straightening this Alley out.

Well Eddie had just that day made fifty thousand according to closing odds on the last commodity. I says show me the fifty. He then explained to me that he hadn't the money, that that's what he could have made if he had sold. But he hadn't sold, as to-morrow he should make at least another fifty, or even if he only made 49 why it would help pay for burnt cork. Then he explained the stock market to me in a mighty sensible way. He didn't much want to take my money, knowing how hard I had worked for it, both from the Theatre Manager and Mrs. Rogers.

But I went on telling him I was 49 years old and had never in my life made a single dollar without having to chew some gum to get it. So he says, "Well I will buy you some of my bank stock. It's selling mighty high and with this little dab you got here you won't get much of it, but it's bound to go up, for banks make it whether the market goes up or down. Even if it stands still they are getting their interest while it's making up its mind what to do."

So he said I will get you some of this, you don't need to pay me for it, just let it go. Put it away and forget about it. Then some day when you want you can send me a check for it.

Well just think of that! Here I was going to break Wall Street on credit! Well I shook hands and told him that I had always known and said that he was the greatest Comedian on the stage but now I knew he was the best financier we had in our profession. Well I went back to my own dressing room at my Theatre and I

never was as funny in my life as I was that night. I had Wall
Street by the tail and a down hill run.

I stayed up the next night till the papers come out to see what
OUR Bank had closed at, and after reading it stayed up the rest
rest of the night wondering if Eddie could possibly be wrong.
Well one little drop brought on another, till one day I received
a letter from Eddie's broker saying that my check would come
in might handy and for me please remit undernamed amount.

Well in the meantime I had used most of the money celebrating
the fact that I had bought the stock. In fact I had really spent
most of it in advertising Eddie and his humanitarian qualities.
Each night I begin to get unfunnier and unfunnier. This strain
of being "In the Market" was telling on me. Eddie could laugh
at a loss and still remain Komical. But when there was minus
sign before my lone stock, I just was not unctious. I didn't want
to tell Eddie. But finally I sent for his personal Aide De Camp
and told him that on the morrow when the market opened,
among those desiring to dispose, I would be among those present.
I got out with a very moderate loss. Next day it went up big.
But the whole thing is no place for a weak hearted Comedian,
and from now on when Eddie wants to help me, he can just give
me some of his old jokes.

November 23, 1929

This Stock Market thing has kinder had the front page groggy
here lately. They thought we had the thing just about as low as
they could possibly get it, but here lately it's been getting still
worse.

Course all that's great for the rich, for they just sit around and
wait till somebody goes broke and then buy in. But the old
Margin Boy has got a mustard plaster on him all over. He can't
take any good stocks of his to protect the weak ones, for there is
no good ones, the good ones are the ones that are going down.
England says our Market is all cockeyed and that it will eventually
get so stabilized that if a thing pays around five percent it will
be worth right around 100, and that if it pays ten percent it will
be worth 200. That is everything will be based on just a fair

percentage of what it earns. Our Folks been buying without even having any idea what they were earning. We been buying just alphabetically, the nearer A you could get the more it seemed to be worth.

If the President of the concern was a good after dinner Speaker and made a good appearance, why his stock would go up to two or three hundred. Nothing determined the worth of the stock but the fact that it was going up, and it hadn't reached a thousand yet and there was no reason why it shouldn't keep going till it did.

CHAPTER EIGHT

"Restoring Confidence" — Republican Style

Toledo, Ohio, January 9, 1930

Just passed thru Chicago. The snow was so deep today the crooks could only hit a tall man.

To try and diminish crime they laid off six hundred cops. Chicago has no tax money. All their influential men are engaged in tax-exempt occupations.

What they got to do is to tax murder. Put such a stiff tax on it that only the higher class gangsters can afford it. It's the riff raff that makes any business disreputable.

January 11, 1930

The late Stock Market Crash was not only responsible for a lot of fine hard working conscientious fellows losing their hard earned money, but it has been responsible for developing two types of the biggest Liars since Golf started.

One is the fellow who tells you how many thousands he lost when you know the poor fellow never had a dime not only to lose but to eat on, and then the other fellow who says, "Everything I had was bought outright. Of course I had some paper losses, but the way I do is buy it, throw it away and forget it."

It's almost been worth this depression to find out how little our big men knew.

Maby this depression is just "normalcy" and we don't know it.

It's made a dumb guy as smart as a smart one.

Why don't everybody try to make a living out of the conditions we got instead of waiting to make it under conditions that

are supposed to come. Suppose "good times" don't never come?
Will these manufacturers still hold their stuff at the same price
till it does?

Depression used to be a state of mind. Now it's a state of
coma, now it's permanent.

Last year we said, "Things can't go on like this," and they
didn't, they got worse.

[Will was in New York in January to confer with Winfred
Sheehan and, finding that it would be several weeks before another picture would be started he decided to jump over to London to see the opening of the Disarmament Conference.

"When I was a little boy out in the old Indian Territory," he
wrote, "I remember seeing a Sheriff disarm some men one time
and it always fascinated me. When they told me they was going
to disarm whole nations over in London next week why I just
grabbed the fastest thing there is, the Bremen, and went."

Will had little hope. He had seen nothing of any value done
at the previous one at Geneva nor at the one at Washington
preceding that.

Two days later the Conference had become "synthetic" by
holding no more public meetings. From now on no one would
know what happened until they "read one of the delegate's
memoirs after the next war. If any American correspondent
sends any news home today," Will warned, "he has made it up."]

London, January 27, 1930

Boy, there is some tough babies here. Talk about taking boats
away from them. There is delegations here that wouldn't give
up an oar to see eternal salvation.

London, January 30, 1930

The Japs never say a word or miss a word. I met Admiral
Takhira out at Ambassador Dawes's last night, and on leaving,
I shook hands with him very warmly and said, "Admiral, I am
going right home to America and I want to say that I have shook
hands with the winner."

SS Ile de France, February 3, 1930

H. L. Mencken and I were going to Hyde Park, London (if rain hadn't spoiled it) where, if you have anything against the government or King, or even any one as lowdown as a Sir, why, jump up on a box and get it out of your system.

They sink the navy, impeach the Crown and cancel the debts, and when they finish they are just as happy as if it had been done. It's real democracy.

Over home you have to be elected to the Senate before you can do it.

I was going to enter Mencken. He says the system is still in vogue in Maryland, the only civilized State left.

SS Ile de France, February 4, 1930

I see by a delayed American paper that Mr. Coolidge is going to print the history of the United States on a single rock.

Well, I could print the history of the present results of this disarmament conference on the head of a pin and have room enough left for the chorus of "Yes, We Have No Bananas."

Lindy's lake kinder sobered up today and bunches of us began drawing dividends on our passage money by being directed to where the dining saloon was.

New York, February 9, 1930

Changing prohibition enforcement from the Treasury to the Department of Justice is just like a dog scratching his fleas from one part of his body over to another. He has relocated 'em, but as long as he is a dog they are going to be bothering him some place.

February 7, 1931

Nobody is going to disarm in the least. You know the men that every Nation that is gathered there are not the "Idealists" that think, "Oh, we can't have war, it's too terrible, we must not have war."

Well, that's wonderful, but these men know history too well. They know each other too well. They know that war is not only a Possibility but a probability. They know they can't go back home and tell their people that they have left them unprotected.

New York, February 14, 1930

If you can start arguing over something, and get enough publicity, and keep the argument going, you can divide our nation overnight as to whether spinach or broccoli are the most nutritious.

We can get hot and bothered quicker over nothing, and cool off faster than any nation in the world.

Beverly Hills, February 23, 1930

Radio is a great thing. I believe it's our greatest invention, far greater than the automobile, for it don't kill anybody. It don't cost us millions for roads. When we are too lazy or too old to do anything else, we can listen in.

Beverly Hills, February 27, 1930

Best way to make one of these "Red" meetings mad is to offer 'em work. Nancy Astor pulled the best one on them, she offered to pay the fare of any that would go back to Russia. Only three took her up, and they starved to death there waiting for their "comrades" to divide up with 'em.

Should have a place where they can get up and denounce anything from Washington's wig to Hoover's fish bait. They are likeable cusses and smart, and perfectly happy when they are talking. That's the only way they have of showing their education, by sound and not by accomplishment.

Beverly Hills, March 2, 1930

Not only the week's biggest laugh but the year's biggest guffaw come from the United States Senate during the oil lobby hearing.

They discovered that Senators were trading oil votes for sugar votes. They were surprised and practically dumbfounded that such a condition could exist.

Yes, just about as surprising to everybody that knows politics as it would be to discover that Herbert Hoover was born in the United States, was over 30 years old, and white.

Vote trading got 'em all in the Senate and kept them in there (if the trades were good enough).

March 4, 1930 [*At the Dedication of the Coolidge Dam on the Apache Reservation*]

You know as you saw all those Indians you couldn't help but think of the old days. Here was the old warlike Apaches that fought to hold all they had, and most of them wound up in jail, but there was a Washington that fought for his tribe against invaders and wound up with a flock of Statues and a Title of Father of his country. And yet I expect if the truth was known the old Apache Chiefs went through more and fought harder for their Country than George did. But George won. That's the whole answer to history. It's not what did you do but what did you get away with at the finish.

Is there any reason in the world why Japan should be all the power she is and China with its millions and resources, that go to the four corners of the earth, should be where she is? China has STOOD for so much from other Nations that they are not classed as one of the big shots. Why because they concentrated on peace and not war. So Japan is at London now, and China can't even make a Rotary Convention.

Spain discovered half the World, her ships were on every sea, but she let her Navy run down and wound up in the class Z League. Look at Holland, great Country, big as England, and they have Colonies, but do you ever hear of them when they talk of what the big powers want? No, you would think they were Rhode Island. Why? No Navy, and some of the rest of them the same.

We don't rate their culture, we don't rate their achievement, their Art, their Literature, their Integrity, their population, their size. In fact nothing but how big is their Navy? Why Brazil is bigger than all England, France, Italy and Japan, and has more natural resources than all of them combined. Yet she couldn't get to a Chamber of Commerce Membership rally. Same old answer, no Navy. They all know that.

So you can see why there won't be any tall sinking done by
any of these Babies that are up there on top now. It would be
a marvelous thing if all of them could see that there was to be
no more war and go ahead and do away with their arms of defense. But, unfortunately, they have all studied History and
they know that these ideas we are talking about now are not
new, they have all been gone over before, and they just can't
hardly bring themselves to believe that this is going to happen.

Beverly Hills, March 18, 1930
America's favorite "prodigal son," Scarface Al Capone, has
returned to us and in his honor we killed two fatted gangsters,
and met him with more publicity than we did the release of Mr.
Coolidge after his six years of solitary incarnation.

Capone goes free to take up his useful life's work, and on the
same front page Doheny, who developed a great industry and
has given high wages to thousands for years, is called "a menace
to society." We who lived neighbors to him know that if he is
convicted of "staking" all old mining days friends, he will serve
2000 years.

I joke about our prominent men, but at heart I believe in 'em.
I do think there is times when traces of "dumbness" crop up in
official life, but not of crookedness.

[In a blast on March 24, 1930, against what he called Grundy's
tariff bill, Will asked some pertinent questions and gave some
equally pertinent answers]:

"How many people is there in the U.S. that don't manufacture
anything?"
"Oh, roughly, I should say about 112,000,000."
"Who pays for the raise that the manufacturers receive under
the bill?"
"The same people who sent the men there that passed the
bill."
"Well, what's the answer to it all?"
"Brother, there is no answer. It's been going on like this for
150 years. If you take it serious you are cuckoo."

Beverly Hills, April 1, 1930

Each State is allowed two statues in the Capitol Hall of Fame. The old Keystone State put William Penn in there for what he took away from the Indians for Pennsylvania. Now Grundy gets the other statue for what he has taken away from the white people for Pennsylvania.

Beverly Hills, April 7, 1930

We can get all lathering at the time over some political campaign promise, or some conference pledge, but if the thing just drags along long enough we forget what it was that was originally promised.

The short memories of American voters is what keeps our politicians in office.

Beverly Hills, April 16, 1930

Just reading these late census reports and it shows that the small town is passing. We not only ought to regret it, we ought to do something to remedy it. It was the incubator that hatched all our big men, and that's why we haven't got as many big men today as we used to have.

Take every small-town-raised man out of business and you would have nobody left running it but vice presidents.

Beverly Hills, April 24, 1930

Brothers, we are riding mighty high in this country. Our most annoying problem is, "Which car will I use today?" "Isn't the static frightful?"

March 29, 1930

When Scarface Al Capone was smuggled through half the jails in Pennsylvania to avoid the crowds on his release, that really come under the heading of front page "Copy."

Then anywhere you go some Bird will get up and tell "How Our Civilization is advancing, and how primitive it all was a few years back." Honest there is times when it looks like we haven't got over two ideas above a Flea. Just give anything enough publicity, and we would pay admission to see folks Guillotined. I happened to be playing last Spring in a Theatre in Philadelphia when this estimiable Gentleman Capone was arrested there, that is he arranged for his arrest. An opposition Gang was just two Machine Gun lengths behind him and he was looking for a refuge, so he just had himself arrested, and put where the exponents of America's thriving Industry couldn't get at him. He looked all the Jails over and decided that the Pennsylvania ones were the hardest to break into. He told the Policemen that he was carrying a gun, and for them to arrest him on that charge. Can you imagine arresting a man in America for carrying a gun nowadays? Why in Chicago there is Pistol pockets put in your Pajamas. There is thousands there that are faultlessly dressed in artillery that haven't got underwear on.

Beverly Hills, May 18, 1930

Been reading these Frenchmen's books they leave after they are dead. It looks like some of 'em died just to start an argument. France awaits the death of each one to find out what he thought of the others. A "best seller" is the one that can dig up the most dirt. There ought to be a law in every country making a man read his autobiography out loud before his enemies and see what happens. As it is now a fellow can tell you anything he wants to, and make you still madder by dying before you can get at him.

Beverly Hills, May 19, 1930

President Hoover is reviewing our whole American fleet tomorrow. It looks awful unnecessary to see all those ships and not a war booked.

But, taxpayers, they are our spare tire. The countries that have no navys are standing by the roadside fixing a flat. England without her navy would be another Czecho-Slovakia.

America has a unique record. We never lost a boat in a battle, but we have had many a one shot from under us at a conference.

Did you ever figure it out? If we had never conferred we would not have to be conferring now to try and get parity.

Beverly Hills, June 3, 1930

Say, these miniature golf course have sure been a lifesaver for the towns with plenty of prominent vacant lots.

In the past if you had a vacant lot, you were stuck with it during Republican prosperity. Why, all you could do with it would be to build a drug store or filling station. But now you can get something permanent.

They try to get all kinds of odd hazards to shoot the ball by. Why don't they just leave the weeds and trash on it as it was? You couldn't bet better "bunkers" than them.

They are even buying costumes now to play this "demi-tasse" golf.

Boston, June 17, 1930

We been awful busy here today celebrating Bunker Hill. Daniel Webster made the most famous Bunker Hill address, so I was really pinch hitting for him. He spoke good English, too. The Websters wrote all their own. You give me a chance to write my own dictionary and make a word mean anything I want it to, and I will show you some English.

They are a broad-minded people up here. They celebrate a victory that the British won, and the monument is not on Bunker Hill — it's on Breed's Hill.

But one thing they have got, and that's the old fighting ship Constitution — the only ship that has withstood every disarmament conference.

Boston, June 18, 1930

I said yesterday Daniel Webster wrote the dictionary. Well, these Harvardites have been calling me up before daylight telling me it was Noah Webster and not Daniel.

How was I to know? I never read the book. I never could get interested in the thing.

Well, anyhow, the mistake will only be noticed in Boston.

Minneapolis, June 29, 30, 1930

The Senate just sits and waits till they find out what the President wants so they'll know how to vote against him.

Mr. Hoover has done lots of things, but he never trained circus animals before. Up to now, the animals have had him hemmed up and doing the tricks instead of them. Now, he is a man that is quick to learn anything new, and the minute he finds out they are cowardly, why he will grab that sharp pole and pistol, and he will have Congressional lions, and Senatorial hyenas jumping through more fire hoops and rolling more barrels than you ever heard of, and the audience will applaud and eat it up.

They will dog it if he takes after 'em. Roosevelt jumped 'em into the Potomac with their clothes on.

Sic 'em, Herb.

June 28, 1930

You know I have often said in answer to inquiries as to how I got away with kidding some of our public men, that it was because I liked all of them personally, and that if there was no malice in your heart there could be none in your "gags," and I have always said I never met a man I didn't like.

July 19, 1930

Mr. Coolidge had one in the other day that kinder jarred all of us, and made us wonder if he wasn't having a Ghost writer do some of his stuff. It advised the working man to spend his money, and buy everything that he could possibly afford, and in that way help out the whole economic thing, so that it would put more money into circulation, and make more jobs for those that had none.

Now that is absolutely going against all the laws we have been brought up to. We have always been taught to save and put by every dollar that we could, and not buy anything unless we absolutely needed it, and to spend no money for things that we could do without.

Now all at once we are advised by everybody to start spending, so it will help somebody else. Imagine telling the working man to spend, that if he don't put his money into circulation why he won't have a job very long. That is what Mr. Coolidge said.

Now that sounds so unlike him. Here is a man that the whole basis of his popularity is based on his economy and thrift, and all at once to help out a situation, why he says "Spend." So it's hard to tell what to believe nowadays.

July 24, 1930

Say did you know they arrested a Girl here in Hollywood the other day? She was driving down our main thoroughfare with nothing on but a heavy tan, not a stitch. A Modern Lady Godiva. She didn't even have the advantage of long hair. Course this is all hearsay. I *would* miss it!

I think she come clear, for it's awful hard to tell when a woman is nude nowadays and when she is fully clothed. If the worst comes to the worse she could always say it was an evening dress.

Santa Monica, August 6, 1930

What has the poor farmer done against the Almighty that he should deserve all this?

If it's not the heat, it's the deep snow. If it's not the drought, it's the floods. If it's not the boll weevil, it's the tariff. If it's not the cinch bugs, it's the Federal Reserve. If it's not relief he needs, why, it's rain.

But there is one pest that he is always free from — that's income tax.

Santa Monica, August 10, 1930

See where one of these young boy tree sitters has just passed his 500 hours sitting in a treetop.

There is a good deal of discussion as to what to do with a civilization that produces prodigies like that.

Why wouldn't it be a good idea to take their ladder away from them and leave 'em up there?

August 16, 1930

This conducting a column is considered a kind of low grade type of human endeavor. It's not classed among what might be called the Arts. It's just a kind of a stop gap to keep the Coyote from the doorstep, and as a dignified profession it's sorter null and void. It's just sorter in the papers to break your jump on the way over to the advertising pages. But while it does not bring home the Literary praise, it does fetch in some buck-wheat cakes accompanied by bacon. It can be sneered at till meal time, then it has its good points.

Tahoe Tavern, California, August 21, 1930

We are up here at this beautiful lake near Reno, Nevada, working on a picture, and today a fellow come up and wanted me to help get him into some soft job in the movies. I asked him what he was doing.

He said, "I am a house detective in the big hotel in Reno where all the divorcees live."

I said, "Brother, you must be hard to please. John Barrymore is not doing as well as you. Why you got a better job than Coolidge writing a gag a day."

I told him, "Go back to work, and don't even envy Hoover. But if you are going to give the job up, consult me. I'll change with you."

Tahoe Tavern, California, August 24, 1930

The Islam women in Jerusalem have asked their Government to take their veils off and allow the bride and bridegroom to see each other before marriage.

It won't do 'em any good. We don't use 'em over here, but you would think we did.

Tahoe Tavern, California, August 31, 1930

Just back from a rodeo over at a great little town called Winnemucca, Nevada. That's a great State. When you feel that the people around you are taking too much care of your private business, why move to Nevada. It's freedom's last stand in America.

Yet they don't do one thing that other states don't do. Only they leave the front door open.

You can get a divorce without lying, a drink without whispering and bet on a game of chance without breaking even a promise.

Camp Richardson, California, September 10, 1930

We got a funny situation here. We brought up about a dozen girls to play the "divorcees" in the Hotel scene in Lightning, and here every day watching us shoot is a hundred real "divorcees" from Reno, and around the lake here, all dying to get into pictures while they are serving their time.

If any woman is missing from your community and you don't know where she is, she is here.

The most popular charge here lately as grounds for divorce is snoring, and husbands staying out late playing miniature golf. They put in their spare time making their trosseau.

Camp Richardson, California, September 11, 1930

A fine old fellow about seventy-three years old, Luke Cosgrove, after reading Governor Roosevelt of New York Statement on prohibition in the paper this morning, said, "Will, Governor Roosevelt says he wants to bring back liquor, but not the old-time saloon. Why that was the only thing about the whole business that was worth having. We want to bring back the old-time saloons with five cent beer, and outlaw liquor."

September 13, 1930

I thought we was going to have some Farm Relief to report to you by this Sabbath day. But the commissions are just gathering data. They won't take the farmer's word for it that he is poor.

They hire men to find out how poor he is. If they took all the money they spend on finding out how he is, and give it to the Farmers he wouldn't need any more relief.

But soon as winter comes he will be O.K., soon as snow flies he can kill rabbits, that will be the biggest relief he has had so far.

October 18, 1930

That Russia is kicking up an awful lot of dust, and Germany is harboring a terrible lot of dissatisfaction. That Hitler has got 'em all stirred up over there. He made a speech last week in which he advocated the breaking of the Versailles Treaty. He said that it was made by a lot of old men who, most of them, were about ready to die, and now here was a lot of young men grown up and they had to carry all this burden, for which they were not directly to blame, and that it was only a matter of time till they just wouldn't do it. They would say, "Well, come on France, what are you going to do about it? We can't be any worse off if you come in and take over our Country than we are now."

Then those little Balkan Nations, they are like a little mess of stray Terriers anyhow. They just as well be fighting as like they are. This has been about the longest they have ever been between wars.

I see the other day where Russia was just on the verge of invading Roumania. They have always had it in for them and figured they only had to take a couple of days' rations and rounds of ammunition and go over and take that Country anyhow.

Russia and Poland are always on the verge of war. I remember when I was over in both countries in the summer of 1926, why they were growling at each other like a couple of Fat Prima Donnas on the same Opera bill.

Then Italy is ranting around down there trying to pick up some more country and outlet for their population. France is watching them with an Eagle eye all the time, and that's just what Mussolini wants. He had rather worry France than anything. France feels that she would have no trouble whipping them, but if she went down there to do it, Germany would take the opportunity to get at them and she just don't want to have to take the chance.

Then the Checko-Slovakians feel kinda hemmed in down their way, and of course the Turks, there is nothing that irks a Turk so much as peace.

Austria, they just been so bad off since the last war that they know there would be no way that war wouldn't be welcome to them. Bulgaria has started all the rest of them, her and Serbia, and they don't want to lose their reputations. They want to go down in history as having started all the big ones.

I try to read all that all those old World Diplomats write over there, and there is not a line of it that is not in regard to another war. They just can't write a prescription without predicting what will happen in the next great war. Their whole minds is on it, and from all that I read of them there is no two that seem to give anywhere near the same possible line-up. It's like the National and American League if when time come to play the World's Series they would just take all the players from all the clubs in their League and then choose up and play the other side. No one knows where the thing will start or with who, no one knows how the line-up will be, for they don't know who will be fighting who.

Some of them that hate Russia like poison will want to join her on account of her strength. They will all want to wait and see who looks like the winner. They did that in the last war. Quite a few staid out waiting for the best offer. Lots of pretty smart men think that is one of the biggest contributing factors to our present state of economic unrest, is that all big finance is afraid of what will happen in the near future, and they don't know where it will end up.

That's why everybody is hanging on to what they got. There is more in the wind than just our little local condition over here. We got as much as we ever had — there is just as much money, as much to eat, and as many to feed, as many to buy. But still our conditions are uncertain. Why?

Just because it's things outside our own land that is worrying 'em. They know that signs are not right all over the World. Look at South America. When during our lifetime has there been as many disturbances at one time? No, Sir, the whole thing is world wide. We are affected by it less than anyone.

If we keep our nose clean and don't start yapping about somebody else's honor, or what our moral obligations are, we might escape it. But it's going to take better Statesmanship than we have been favored with heretofore. But the way we are now we are mighty lucky to have nothing but a little business depression that is bothering us. Think what those other poor Devils are up against!

Beverly Hills, October 23, 1930

Say we got a great treat in store for us next Tuesday evening. Bernard Shaw is going to talk to us over the radio for forty minutes. He is the most interesting and entertaining man in the world today. He and Mussolini are pretty near a tie. You don't need to ask any questions when you meet either one of 'em. Just sit still and listen. Shaw told me that the United States and Russia are the most unique countries in the world today. Russia was trying a great experiment and was trying everything that come along, and that we were both in the experimental stage. England don't know yet whether Shaw is for 'em or against 'em.

Beverly Hills, October 27, 1930

Half the world is fighting mad and the other half is out of a job, and would as soon be fighting as starving. For that's one thing in favor of war. They do feed you during one.

Then, in the midst of all this, we start sinking our navy to save taxes. Saving taxes don't help the unemployed. They get nothing, are earning nothing, hence they pay nothing.

Beverly Hills, October, 29, 1930

This must have happened to thousands of school children all over our country. My three come dragging in last night from three different schools, and I immediately asked 'em if they had heard Bernard Shaw's great speech over the radio that afternoon.

They all said, "No, their teachers had 'em listening to 'em."
Now here was perhaps the most brilliant and wittiest speech of
our times, brought right to us by this great invention, yet teachers
gave their own lectures instead of Shaw's. Even the newspapers
only published extracts of it. But they published all their own
editorials. They were improving on Shaw too. So what good
does it do to have a brilliant man tell you something?

November 2, 1930

It looks like the Democrats will get in a bunch of new ones.
They always do mighty well on these off years. We get 'em in on
off years and get 'em out on Presidential years. But it gives some
people something to get worked up over, and get all excited over.
It don't mean anything. We been staggering along now about
155 years under every conceivable horse thief that could get
into office, and yet here we are, still going strong.

I doubt if Barnum's Circus, or Hagenbeck's wild animal circus
has housed as many different kinds of species as has been in our
Government employ during its existence. Yet as bad as they are
they can't spoil it, and as good as they are they can't help it.

We are just a river flowing along. We have a drought year,
and we have a flood year. They build dams to stop us, but we
just fill up and flow over 'em, so there is really nothing that can
be done about us. We are just flowing to the sea. Corruption
can't retard us, and reformers can't assist us, we are just flowing
along in spite of everything.

A good man can't do nothing in office because the System is
against him, and a bad one can't do anything for the same
reason. So bad as we are we are better off than any other Nation,
so what's the use to worry.

Beverly Hills, November 12, 1930

Celebrated twelve years of continuous peace yesterday, and we
looked about as bad off as we did twelve years ago when we celebrated the end of two years of wars.

Beverly Hills, November 21, 1930

I see where they say Wall Street is coming back. Yep, coming back for more. They figure people about had time to save up another little dab.

That's one good thing about the rascals though, they always give you warning when they are coming.

There ought to be some way figured out just what it takes to support that whole gang (in the manner in which they are accustomed) then charge everybody in the U.S. so much and deduct it from their salary.

That would eliminate all speculation, and everybody would know just where they stood.

Everybody is saying that the trouble with the country is that people are saving instead of spending. Well if that's a vice, then I am Einstein. Since when did saving become a National Calamity?

Beverly Hills, November 25, 1930

Every Government in the world today has more discontented people than usual, but I think there is less complaint by the subjects in Russia than anywhere else.

That is, they don't complain as long.

Hollywood, November 26, 1930

Some of the writers are having a little trouble scraping up a reason for Thanksgiving this year. Some think we ought to skip a year and put on a big one in 1931.

The original idea of the day was to give thanks for a "bountiful harvest." Well the "bountiful harvest" is the very thing that's the matter with us. Too much wheat, too much corn, too much cotton, too much beef, too much production of everything.

December, 1930 [Appeal for Relief for the Unemployed]

Now in a way I always hate to do this. I have never particularly liked the idea of someone getting up and telling someone else what to do with their money, and I don't believe you like it either.

I would like to hear a program where us usual spielers were made to sit and listen, and have people that are in actual need get up here and tell you what is needed. No one that's not in need can talk with the conviction of one who is in need.

That's the trouble, we all talk too much. If we gave as freely as we talk, there would be no needy.

I am in no way trying to detract from the splendid men who have made appeals here tonight. They are our most conscientious and highest type men. Some of our biggest people are the most unselfish, but a lot of us just send in our check to our Community Chest and get the idea that that ends the needs of the poor for the year.

We even kinder wonder if on account of the hard times, and everyone not making as much, if we can't kinder hedge, or cut down on our donation.

Donation? It should never be allowed to be called a donation, it's an obligation, an honest obligation. It's more important than our taxes.

This will keep people alive.

We find every excuse of cutting down on this year's amount. We can find an excuse for it everywhere but in our own conscience. You can't fool your conscience, and if we will actually give in proportion to what our own conscience tells us, we will help our unfortunates through the most trying winter in our existence.

Santa Monica, December 14, 1930

When somebody calls you "names" and there is no truth in it and you know that everybody knows there is no truth in it, why you naturally don't pay any attention to it. You just laugh it off. But if what they call you is hitting at the truth and kinder getting you in your weak spot, why you start hollering and denouncing at once.

Well last week Mr. Hoover said, "The boys in the Senate are playing Politics at human expense."

Did the boys laugh it off? Not quite.

So figure out the answer yourself.

Beverly Hills, December 16, 1930

There must be an awful lot of factories, and firms, and individuals that have always shown some kind of appreciation to their folks on Christmas, who perhaps this year on account of conditions are not able to do all they would like to, and are at a loss just what to do.

Wouldn't this be more welcome than a gift, send each one a note, and tell 'em that they are not going to be fired, that their position is secure? I believe that will be a mighty acceptable Christmas present to everybody that is on salary.

It will beat any present you can send, relieve their anxiety, and let them go out and do some shopping on their own, and thereby help everybody.

We are bad off, but the world ain't coming to an end yet.

Hollywood, December 21, 1930

One of the best indications that America is a mighty tough nation physically is the fact that they can live on nothing for over a year till their government finally votes funds to give 'em employment.

These folks were out of a job all of last year, and Congress was in session all that time. But it looked like they kept waiting along to see if the people would live through it, and they did and fooled the government.

CHAPTER NINE

"Commissions" to Find that Corner

[The year 1931 began with the outlook dreary indeed. It looked that if things kept getting worse, as Will said, that "by July fourth Ford and Rockefeller would be on the dole."

To make the situation more critical there was a drought in the Southwest.

But the current "rulers" at Washington did not know how to hear, had no way of "remembering." The very next day, January 7, 1931, Will reported]:

THE SENATE passed a bill appropriating 15 million for food but the House of Representatives (up to today) had not approved it. They said, "No," they seem to think that's a bad precedent, to appropriate money for food. It's too much like the "dole." They think it would encourage hunger.

The way things look, hunger don't need much encouragement. It's just around the corner naturally.

[With the situation worsening by the day Will went to Washington to see if he could stir up something. On the way he flew "all day over Oklahoma and the poor red clay hills of Missouri and Indiana" and "looked down on those dejected, desolate, anemic-looking houses" where people had no crops to sell and nothing to eat. He wrote sarcastically, "Yet you don't wonder how they eat. You wonder how they keep warm. If the Government thinks it's unsound to feed 'em, maby they would compromise with their conscience by giving 'em some coal."]

Washington, January 15, 1931

I am here for relief. You got to come and get it personally. You can't do it through your Senator or Congressman. They are worse off than we are. Times are so hard, they are allowing constituents into their private lunch rooms to buy their representatives meals.

Congress hasn't done anything in so long that even the lobbyists that work on commissions are starving and hollering for personal aid.

Congress yesterday turned down the 15 million food bill, and passed 15 millions "to improve entrances to national parks."

You can get a road anywhere you want to out of the government, but you can't get a sandwich.

Well in two years there won't be a poor farm that won't have a concrete road leading up to it.

I am staying all night with 'em tonight, but I am sleeping in my overcoat.

[Then what happened in all this crisis in Washington? "The Prohibition report is turned in. The only possible thing you could think of that we don't need right now outside the Einstein theory. If you could butter that report and put it between two loaves of bread it would be welcome now. What an aid to Arkansaw that report will be in this crisis?"

A Navy plane was loaned to Will and with Frank Hawks flying him, he set out on a speaking tour of the worst drought-ridden area to raise money for the Red Cross. For three weeks, from town to village, making two and three speeches a day to audiences that paid as much as they could, Will went over the country. When the weather was bad he went by automobile. He raised thousands of dollars, every cent of which was turned over to the local Red Cross chapters, and sparked a real effort on the part of communities to help the needy. His talk was direct and to the point.]

I am not a guy that hollers wolf. I like to look at 'em from their brighter side. But we are, honest we are, in for a hard few months, and if we don't give, and we don't help, we have no excuse for the consequences that may happen for every man in this country.

If you can't give him work, you must give he and his family food.

Remember, luck is a funny thing. It goes up and it goes down, so give according to your conscience and not your purse.

Fort Worth, February 1, 1931

Senate argued Saturday on prohibition, so there must have been some pretty important business before them. They never argue it only in the busiest times. Soldiers are trying to get a part cash payment on their Government compensation, but Mr. Mellon says that would upset the bond market and cause Government interest rates to raise.

You owe the Government something and see if they worry how much interest you got to pay them. Mr. Mellon is going to have that budget balanced if he has to join Al Capone's gang to do it.

Durant, Oklahoma, February 4, 1931

Mr. Hoover dispatched a flyer to Arkansaw and the stricken area to see how bad things were. He could have sent a blind man and found out. The Red Cross is feeding 70 counties in this state.

Santa Monica, February 13, 1931

Well here we are, back home, and what a trip we had our here in all this rain and fog.

Last night, during a forced stay in Albuquerque, they gave us a dinner, and Frank and I just to keep our hands in and not forget our little jokes, passed the hat for a thousand dollars to pay their Red Cross quota.

See where the Republican Party had cut down on the U.S. Navy and aeroplanes to balance their budget. They better give up a postoffice building and a concrete road.

[Back home again, Will almost immediately had to send out a warning in his daily wire. "The Government Saturday passed a bill to appropriate 20 million as a loan to farmers in the drouth

area, but it was to be loaned on security. Now the man and his
family that are hungry down there have no security. If he had
any security he wouldn't be hungry. He would have already put
it up." He then added, significantly]:

So this loan has not relieved the people that the Red Cross has
been feeding at all. They have got to go on being fed by the Red
Cross. So you towns that have been so slow in raising your quota
because you have been waiting on the Government to see what
they would do, now you see. So get busy and raise it.

[Will might have added that the bill could only possibly help
those that had been "slow" in giving, the richer and the absentee
farmers, a member of the group that the Republican Party always knew how to help through their government.]

Beverly Hills, February 19, 1931
You talk about this country being hard up, every place thinks
it's worse off than the other. The Red Cross, as usual, is doing
heroic work, but it's the people that they can't reach, people that
they never heard of, people that are so far back in the woods that
the rest of the world has almost forgotten 'em. Those are the
ones that I pity in all this depression. I am speaking of the Senate
and Congress of these United States.

I want to see a Red Cross relief formed that will go so far back
into the underbrush of the hinterland that it will reach this little
known but patriotic group.

Then can the Red Cross say, "We have performed our duty."

Beverly Hills, February 20, 1931
Well yesterday I had what I thought was a kinder "funny" gag.
I said the people the Red Cross really should reach was the ones
away back in the woods that no one ever heard of, the Senate
and Congress of the U.S.

Well I pick up the paper this morning and I find their sense of
humor didn't jibe with mine. They had added the word "not" to
the Senate and Congress, and made it so it not only didn't have
any humor but no sense.

What I am trying to get at (if I can get the papers to use it as I want it) is to have the Red Cross care for Congress and the Senate instead of having it done as a "dole" from the taxpayers, as it is now.

Beverly Hills, March 12, 1931

As there was more money spent on cold cream and cosmetics last year than on bacon and beans, why naturally there must be more people interested in beautifying themselves.

The International Beauty Congress met in New York yesterday and they had figured out that this rubbing something on your head to prevent baldness is really what causes it. They claim that you got to take stuff internally for it.

So now on if you see a baldheaded bird reach for his flask, don't ask him for a swig.

It's only irrigation juice for his roof.

Beverly Hills, March 18, 1931

Right in the midst of all this depression and starvation, why one old boy hasn't had it so bad. He has been measuring six thousand college girls. He compares 'em with co-eds fifty years ago. From what our elderly women led us to believe, we didn't think they would have allowed it.

Well this fellow finds that the present ones are higher, wider and thicker (he don't say if it's head or body).

These today, he says, have more lung capacity. Well we know that. Maby because of the strenuous life at a female college, the parents only pick out the big dumb ones.

Beverly Hills, March 20, 1931

Every state in the Union gambles as much as Nevada does, but they were smart enough to pass a law and get some tax money out of it. If Wall Street paid a tax on every "game" they run, we would get enough revenue to run the government on.

Beverly Hills, March 27, 1931

They claim business is getting better because fewer apples are being sold on the street.

Lord, that only means it's getting worse.

Beverly Hills, March 29, 1931

Mr. Hoover just got back from Porto Rico. He told 'em he would see that they had the same opportunities we enjoy here. So I guess he is having Charley Otis and Company, Stock Brokers, put in a branch down there. That will give them a leisure class, and the rest of 'em employment working for 'em.

March 28, 1931

It's funny how quick a College Boy can find out that the World is wrong. He might go out in the World from High School and live in it, and make a living in it for years and think it wasn't such a bad place, but let him go to College and he will be the first one down on the Square on May Day to shout down with the Government.

But as soon as they grow up and go out and if they happen to make anything, why they backslide.

Beverly Hills, April 1, 1931

It's very seldom you find any good that comes out of the war, but the only investment that has proven sound during all this mess is the Liberty Bond. So the old "three minute" speaker was telling the truth and didn't know it.

But the tough part about it is, everybody lost theirs by having to put 'em up as margins on things that was supposed to be sound. During the Coolidge Cuckoo days they were considered the lowest form of investment. When you look back on things now you wonder why anyone in America escaped the insane asylum during that time.

April 4, 1931

Say, did you read in the papers about a bunch of Women up in British Columbia as a protest against high taxes, sit out in the open naked, and they wouldn't put their clothes on?

The authorities finally turned Sprayers that you use on trees on 'em. That may lead into quite a thing. Woman comes into the tax office nude, saying, "I won't pay."

Well, they can't search her and get anything. It sounds great. How far is it to British Columbia?

[In April, 1931, when Nicaragua had a terrible earthquake that nearly destroyed Managua, Will flew down. He felt that we had done them enough damage with our Marines that we ought to help them out in this. He immediately began making pleas for help. "I have finally found somebody poorer than a Southern cotton renter farmer," he wired back. After telling everyone to send their money to the Red Cross (which thousands did) he then added]:

Here is some divine spark of relief for the anti-prohibitionists. Everything in town was destroyed but the brewery. Churches, schools, banks, stores all went. But it was an act of providence at that for the water works were destroyed and all they had to drink was beer. The commandant sent twenty marines to protect it and with the 100 that was already there why they were able to hold it. Even a quake has its good points. The Senate and Cabinet run out of town and haven't shown up since. What wouldn't Hoover give for the recipe!

Now they need money and help. The poor people just walk about dazed but in addition to money to help feed 'em and restore some sort of roof over their heads what I think is needed worse down here is Chick Sales.

Carlsbad, New Mexico, May 10, 1931

Celebrating "Mother's Day" by giving "Ma" Rogers a vacation. Picked her a white desert flower and walked her for seven miles through the celebrated Carlsbad Caverns.

I thought the biggest hole in the ground was when you was drilling for oil and struck a dry hole. But this is bigger even than that.

It's just the Grand Canyon with a roof over it.

Then when you get inside it's got all the cathedrals of the world in it with half of 'em hanging upside down.

If a "drunk" suddenly woke up in that great hall in there, he would think he had died and gone to Heaven, for that's the nearest thing to his imagination of the place.

Santa Monica, May 31, 1931

President Hoover, in his speech at Valley Forge, found somebody that was worse off than we are, but he had to go back 150
years in history to do it.

But Washington only had to worry about getting through the
Winter. We got to worry about getting through the Summer,
then the Winter, then another Summer before the Democrats can
possibly do anything for us.

Beverly Hills, June 23, 1931

We are living in an age of publicity. It used to be only saloons
and circuses that wanted their name in the paper, but now it's
corporations, churches, preachers, scientists, colleges and ceme-
teries.

Beverly Hills, June 24, 1931

Germany got a Moratorium, the Big International Bankers got
their guarantee, Taxpayers got another assessment, and the
Farmers got exactly what everybody had been predicting they
would get — two bits for their wheat.

Beverly Hills, July 24, 1931

Financial depression is so bad that American millionaire polo
players are having to play on American horses.

Beverly Hills, August 16, 1931

Farm Board destroying every third row of Cotton is the nub
of a great idea. What could give more relief than extinguishing
every third Senator, every third Congressman, every third Committee, every third stock broker, every third law.

Make a third of the Vice Presidents of concerns go back to
work. Turn the cows back into every third golf course, convict
every third gangster arrested.

Do away with one third of all millionaires that issue optimis-
tic reports from aboard yachts, too many banks, bump off a third.
Stop up every third oil well, and every third political speaker.
Destroy one half the newspaper columnists, and last, but the

main thing the matter with the whole world is there is too many people. Shoot every third one.

This whole plan is inexpensive and a surefire scheme back to prosperity.

Beverly Hills, August 31, 1931

Mr. Mellon is today's headliner. Borrowing one billion, one hundred million at three percent. Could have got it about one and a half, but wanted to give the boys a break.

This means they are going to finance by borrowing instead of increased taxes on those able to pay.

It's too close to election to antagonize the big boys.

September 20, 1931 [*To a Group of Stockmen*]

I am here tonight representing the Banks. Now I am not going to foreclose on you boys, for I would rather see you suffer than to have to suffer myself.

No, sir — a Banker ain't a Cowman — and neither is a cow owner a Cowman nowadays. Their ain't nobody nothing nowadays that he thought he was. Even the oil men are getting cock-eyed.

Now the question arises — what is the future of the cow-business? Well I can't see but one future to it. That's to plow under every third Cowman and castrate another third, so they will stop breeding any new ones.

Well you all don't look so bad. I don't believe we are going to lose over 5 percent of you this winter. That's not counting, of course, a lot of old Lumpies and Stags.

I think dude ranching would be a good thing to try out here. They eat a lot of things that white folks won't eat, and they breed like goats. You can handle a lot of 'em to the acre, if you put in a bar on the acre. One herder or Hazer can handle a big bunch of 'em. All you got to do is just to keep the males and females parted in the day time. You can give a hazer a good sheep dog and he can help bring 'em in at night.

Yes, there is a big future in dudes. You got to handle' em kinder like a Brahma. If one breaks out you don't take after him, or her, just let 'em alone. They will run their horse down and he will come dragging in before supper time.

Yuma, Arizona, September 29, 1931

They are trying to find a scheme to raise more money without hitting big incomes.

Republican's theory is that if you tax big incomes too much you will discourage him from making so much for himself.

Didn't discourage him during the war when income tax ran as high as seventy percent.

Some of the biggest fortunes were made at that rate of income tax.

Any guy that's been lucky enough to have a bucket of water during this two years' drought shouldn't kick at handing out a drink.

El Paso, Texas, October 2, 1931

These old big boys work fast and away ahead of time. Big Bankers are coming down from New York daily to show President Hoover that the "debt moratorium" should be extended maby a year, maby five years. They didn't know which, but they were sure they should be cancelled entirely.

In that way it would make it easier for them to collect the money that was owed them personally.

Mr. Hoover ought to told 'em, "Boys, I will cancel half they owe us if you will cancel half they owe you."

That would have checked their philantrophy.

Beverly Hills, October 9, 1931

Today there just ain't much to talk about but Mr. Hoover and his "relief for frozen assets." We had heard of all kinds of relief, drouth, grasshopper, and potato bug, but the general run of us didn't know that these frozen assets were in such bad shape till this plan come along. In fact we didn't know what a frozen asset was, but now everything is clear.

If you got a little frozen asset in your house why the Federal Reserve will take it over. Everything's "jake" now.

[President Hoover appointed "another" Commission, this one to do something about unemployment. "No matter how bad the depression gets and how short we become of the necessities of life," Will wrote, "we never seem to run out of material to put on a commission. Mr. Hoover just got ahold of a book called 'Who's Who For No Reason at All,' and appointed sixty men. That breaks his own record for quantity, if nothing else. He picked every bank President and Corporation Head who have handled their own affairs so ably in the last year and half that it is their stockholders that constitute the present needy."

Will went on the radio, at the invitation of this committee and made a plea to ask people to get behind an employment drive. "Mr. Hoover has done some splendid work for us lately," he said, "he rounded up the bankers and told 'em they better start letting out some dough without the security of a right eye and three ribs, if they wanted to continue to get 8 and 10% from the yokels. He told 'em to melt some frozen assets. A frozen asset is just a banker's mistake. Anyhow he sent 'em home renewing notes." He then said]:

We used to be told that depression was just a state of mind, but starvation has changed that impression, depression is a state of health, its moved from the mind to the stomach, and it ain't really depression either, its just a return to normalcy, we are just getting back to earth and it don't look natural to us anymore, we are back to twobit meals and cotton underwear, and off the $1.50 steaks and silk under rompers. The trouble with us is America is just muscle bound from holding a steering wheel, the only place we are callused from work is the bottom of our driving toe.

Now everybody has got a scheme to relieve unemployment, now there is just one way to do it and that's for everybody to go to work. *"Where"* why right where you are, look around you see a lot of things to do, weeds to be cut, fences to be fixed, lawns to be mowed, filling stations to be robbed, gangsters to be catered to. There is a million little odds and ends right under your eye that an idle man can turn his hand to every day. Course he won't get paid for it, but he won't get paid for not doing it. My theory is that it will keep him in practice in case something does show up, you can lay off so long that you can lose the habit, so keep practicing so work won't be a novelty when it does come. You eat just as much loafing as you do working, in fact more, you got more time.

The trouble with us today we are in such bad shape that it takes us all day to tell about it, we keep yawning and yapping for the good old days of '26, '27 and '28. Well we just as well wake up, for those "Cuckoo" times are not coming back anymore. How we all escaped a lunatic asylum during that time is more than we know now. We paid a dollar down on everything under the sun that anybody had to sell. I had a fifty cent equity in every lot in America.

Now don't wait for the Government to feed these people, the taxpayer is feeding now about one fourth of the people who are not doing anything much for 'em. I'll bet you that every town and city comes through. I have seen lots of audiences and heard lots of appeals, but I have yet to see one where the people knew the need, and the cause was there, that they dident come through, even Europe who hates us and thinks we are arrogant, bad mannered and everything else, but they will tell you that we are liberal, dog-gone it, our folks are liberal. I don't know anything about "America" being fundamentally sound and all that after dinner "Hooey," but I do know that America is "Fundamentally Generous."

[In November, 1931, Will determined to go to China to find out what was happening. "The Japanese and the Chinese haven't officially declared war yet," he wrote. "All this killing and fighting is just rehearsing in case war should be declared. If you get killed now it don't count."

On the SS *Empress of Russia* he ran onto his old friend, Floyd Gibbons, whom he had met in Warsaw, Poland, in 1926, on his way to Russia. Surprisingly, on this trip he wasn't seasick. However when they ran into a typhoon he cabled, "There ought to be a law against making an ocean this wide. That's something Congress can take up next session as they won't have anything to settle much outside of unemployment, two billion dollar deficit, arrange extra taxes where they will do the least harm next November, relieve Wall Street, and think up something new to promise the Farmer. Narrowing an ocean will be just a chore for this Congress."]

Aboard SS Empress of Russia, *December 4, 1931*

Now don't get me mixed up on this Oriental Pilgrimage with this fellow Floyd Gibbons. He is a war man and is over here to tell you about them. That ain't my business over here at all.

I am a peace man. I haven't got any use for wars and there is no more humor in 'em than there is reason for 'em. Get your war news from Gibbons and your Geisha Girl news from Rogers.

I am over here scouting for Ziegfeld's Follies, and I want to see where they train these Japanese diplomats that go to an international conference and bring home everything but the desk that the treaty was signed on.

Tokio, December 6, 1931

Well, sir, yesterday on the boat before we steamed into Yokohama I got first indication that the depression had really turned the corner. A professional Scotch Golf Player deliberately and with malice aforethought drove six golf balls from the deck away out into the ocean.

Tokio, December 7, 1931

After drinking at least two barrels of tea and wanting to be fair, here is about how Manchuria looks to me.

China owns the lot, Japan owns the House that's on it.

Now who should have the policeman?

China is trying to save its country, Japan is trying to save its investments, the League of Nations is trying to save its face.

Now, somebody has got to lose.

Kaijo, December 9, 1931

Well here we are in a different country, Korea, and this is the capitol. Flew down the inland passage from Kobe to Nagasaki and it was beautiful, then from Japan to the mainland of Asia

across the Sea of Japan about 150 miles. And, oh, say I found
people that have funnier hats than the Princess Eugenia kind
you are wearing back home. It's the Korean men, the peasants.
Its a sort of old black cab driver's derby but it's made of screen
netting like the thing we used to keep over cheese in the Claremore Grocery Store.

Dairen, December 10, 1931
Gibbons quit me and took the locomotive. These Japanese
pilots was flying too close to the tops of the rice fields to suit him.
Had a great flight in here, Dairen the most modern city and port
you ever saw, and spent the afternoon visiting historic old Port
Arthur of Russia-Japanese War fame, the birthplace of Japan and
the graveyard of old Russia.

If I can't find this present war I can find where some of the
others were fought. I am only two wars behind.

Mukden, December 11, 1931
This is the famous Mukden in Manchuria where all your war
news comes from. This Chinese army evacuated the city and the
American newspaper men moved in. They been here so long and
times are so tough that about half the banditry is committed by
them.

They got no American news until I mushed in over the snow
today. They did not know old General "Ma" Garner, with 220
Democrats, had marched on Washington.

Harbin, December 14, 1931
This is Harbin. It's 32 below. Horses wearing snowshoes.
Vodka is not a beverage but a necessity.

I got on a fur hat that looks like Daniel Boone and what do
you think I found? A War? A Revolution? No! Abie's Irish
Rose! Played by Russians and Chinese combined. What more
cause could there be for a war?

Mukden, December 15, 1931
League of Nations is sending here a commission to look over
the ground.

That's like a sheriff examining the stall after the horse has disappeared.

Now I am on the ground and can do that, and for half the money, and will send in the same report they will, only shorter.

America could hunt all over the world and not find a better fight to keep out of.

There is only two things certain out here, the Manchurian problem won't be settled this year or next. The second certainty is any commission that tries it will wind up in wrong with both sides.

We don't belong to the league, they are the ones that are refereeing it, and we have yet to referee a fight successfully.

But of course we will join 'em and get in wrong. It's too big an opportunity to lose.

Dairen, December 16, 1931

Plenty of excitement in these countries. Japan's cabinet resigned, China's resigned. It's funny we can't ever have any luck like that.

Human nature is about the same. Chinese have planted a new big crop of soya beans and they haven't sold the last two years' crop. Don't that sound exactly like the wheat and cotton farmers at home? Yet we call these heathen, yeah?

Peiping, December 22, 1931

Vice President Marshall found what America needed. I can tell you what the Orient needs.

Don't bring a lot of clothes. You can get anything here — toilet articles, cigarettes, shoes, Scotch and all of the American Standard equipment.

But, for mercy sakes, bring a pillow, one with feathers in it. These out here are stuffed with rice which wouldn't be so bad if they had cooked it first.

Peiping, December 23, 1931

The American missionaries have taught the Chinese to not fight but rely on the Lord, and the Chinese diplomats have taught the people to rely on the League, but now they feel that both have fallen down on 'em.

This is a time in the history of the world when you better be pretty well prepared or you won't get anywhere.

Peiping, China, December 24, 1931

Get a lot of British news over here in the papers. She may be off the gold standard but she has got a navy that will make the other nations think a long time before they start throwing rocks at her.

When a British warship steams into these ports she anchors just close enough to give the local Congress and Senate a real view of what a dreadnaught is. When you see those guns pointing at you, you don't ask whether they are on a gold, silver, waste paper, or zinc basis. With that navy Nicaragua could go on a banana basis and still be a cock of the walk. Merry Xmas, Will.

Shanghai, December 25, 1931

I didn't know that Christmas did mean so much till you have to spend one away off like this from home. I don't know when these Chinese have Christmas but it wasn't on the twenty fifth.

Course Shanghai where I am now is supposed to be the livest town east of Suez but all the false whoopee in the world don't make up for the old Christmas tree at home, and there is thousands of 'em out here feel the same way.

Shanghai, December 28, 1931

When these Japanese run a war they run it on schedule. This new part they are taking is as big as Oklahoma. This washes up your League of Nations, this slapped them right in the face.

Shanghai, December 30, 1931

Trouble with me, I have been in China too long. If I had only stayed a couple of days, I would have had a better idea of China. The more folks you talk to the more you see and the less you know.

Always dodge the "expert who has lived in China and knows

China." The last man that knew was Confucius and he died feeling that he was becoming a little confused about it.

Aboard SS President Taft, *January 1, 1932*

Shanghai was a knockout. It's Brooklyn gone English. Say, where did they get this Chinese chop suey stuff? I have run the legs off every ricksha motorman in China and nobody ever any more heard of it than Nevada did Volstead.

Another hoax was that a Chinaman's word was as good as his bond. Well that goes with the chop suey. That might have been in the old days but not since the missionaries and businessmen come in. Chinese are just as human as anybody now.

Aboard SS President Taft, *January 3, 1932*

I just found out who China is like. It's the Democrats at home. Individually they are smart, likeable and efficient, but let two get together and they both want to be President.

Formed a new government at Nanking yesterday and nobody would let the other be head man, so they called it a Committee Government. Now everybody is President. There's a new idea for you Democrats.

Penang, January 8, 1932

The gold standard is all Greek to me. But if you want to sell any goods anywhere outside of home you better either cut your prices down to where they would be if you were off the gold or get off.

Our salesmen say they haven't sold anything out here since other nation's stuff went off the gold and got cheaper.

Salesmen are even smoking their own cigarettes and burning up their own gas they can't sell.

Athens, January 18, 1932

This is the longest aeroplane route in the world from Java to Amsterdam, ten thousand miles with the same pilot, same crew, same plane all the way. Holland line tomorrow from Athens to Rome in eleven hours. Old Plato and Caesar would have liked to have prowled that fast.

Paris, January 20, 1932

Flew over Corsica Island today. No wonder Napoleon left there.

Now here is a warning. All Europe is looking for us to do all the debt cancelling, so don't send delegates with hardened arteries, as usual, but get some with hardened hearts, for these people are rehearsing their crying now.

[The next day Will reported that the President had signed another bill for 125 million for land banks. "You can tell this is election year from the way these appropriation bills are passing," he said. "It will take the taxpayers fifty years to pay for the votes in this election. Our only solution of relief seems to be to fix it so people who are in a hole through borrowing can borrow some more. If no individual or country could borrow a dime for five years that would be the greatest five year plan ever invented. But what would Morgan and Co. do? That would be discriminating against them, wouldn't it? Well, we won't do it then. Just let it go."]

London, January 26, 1932

I would like to stay in Europe long enough to find some country that don't blame America for everything in the world that's happened to 'em in the last fifteen years.

Debts, depression, disarmament, disease, fog, famine or frostbite. If the dog had two pups and they were expecting more they will show in some way where the debt settlement was directly responsible for the canine delinquency.

But the other day was the best one. They had a prison mutiny and so every paper said it was American Movies and American influence that give their prisoners this unusual idea.

The birth rate is falling off, so I am going to get out of here before we get blamed.

Paris, January 30, 1932

I would like to tell you a little story. It took place at the American Club in Paris, where once a week all the Americans, lots of Frenchmen that speak English, and both French and American newspaper men meet.

The reason I want to tell you this it's about the debts, told to them right on their homegrounds, and it was the best received and most favorably commented on speech I ever made.

I have so many flops, you will pardon me for bragging on one that didn't. I wasn't the speaker. Some nut just happened to call on me.

I had been to Japan, Manchuria and China, and had just flown into Paris from Singapore, Malay Straights, a nine thousand mile flight across Siam, India, Persia, Mesopotamia, Egypt, Greece, Italy and into Paris on my way to the disarmament conference at Geneva. Mr. Frank Symonds, the very fine American writer on international affairs, had just told them that sentiment in America was against cancellation of the debt, and he gave lots of splendid reasons.

But here was my reason. I have always felt it, and I told 'em so, and it's only one thing. It's lack of appreciation. Americans don't feel that they won the war, but they do feel that they contributed something. Then we loaned you money, cut the amount to be paid in half, cut the interest in half, give you 65 years to pay. We was called boastful, greedy, called "Uncle Shylock," we got no German colonies, we got no reparations, yet we was called selfish. So it's not that you haven't paid us, it's not that perhaps you won't pay us, it's just that we feel you haven't appreciated what we did do.

If Americans felt in their own hearts that you nations over here really appreciated what they did for you, you would get your debt voluntarily cancelled tomorrow. It's human nature to help the fellow that looks like he really appreciates help.

No, you folks don't know America. You scolded when you should have been bragging on us. You can take a stick of candy and toll America right into the ocean. But you can't cuss and drive 'em in there.

No, if there was a nation in Europe today that we felt appreciated us, they could get the key to our treasury. That's my idea on the subject and I will stick to it.

[Will attended the Disarmament Convention at Geneva. Of course, to him, the Japanese Delegation, with a war going on in China — a war of aggression — was the real laugh. "Disarmament Conference was held up for one hour while we all went to the League of Nations meeting to demand of Japan that she quit shooting while the opening session was in conference. That meeting was much more dramatic of the two." Then he announced, "The Conference is off to a flying start. There is nothing to prevent their succeeding now but human nature."

After a few days of amused watching Will set off again to Cuckooland where he also saw and heard much to amuse him. "I went clear around the world to keep from coming back across the Pacific," he moaned, "and here this ocean is worse than the Pacific was."

Will arrived in New York on February 9, 1932, glad to get his feet on American soil "even if it has got a second mortgage on it." This had been a great trip, the greatest of his life, and he believed "if everybody made it" they might come back poorer, "but better off in the feeling toward our country." He felt that "if we can just let other people alone and do their own fighting" we would be in good shape and if we did not, "when you get into trouble five thousand miles away from home you've got to have been looking for it."

Of course one of Will's first moves was to go to Washington to see how the boys there were doing. "Appropriations were just flying every which a way today here in Congress," he reported.]

Beverly Hills, February 25, 1932

Mr. Whitney the man in charge of all the "Faro and Roulette Tables" of the New York Stock Exchange throwed a scare into Mr. Hoover and some Congressmen yesterday by telling 'em if they stopped speculators selling something "they haven't got," why it would stop the Stock Exchange, and people with stocks would have to sell 'em like folks with horses, or cows, or wheat, for just what they are worth.

Now if you can just imagine the terrible consequences of that exchange being closed. Why it would be terrible. At least 115

million out of the 120 million would put on a celebration that
would make Armistice Day's look like a wake.

Beverly Hills, February 29, 1932

Every time Congress starts to tax some particular industry, it
rushes down with its main men and they scare 'em out of it.
About the only way I see for 'em to do, so it would be fair to
everybody, would be for Congress to go into secret session, allow
no telephones, no telegrams, no visitors, so no outside lobbyists
can get at 'em. Then tax everything they want to, and should
tax. Then announce, "Boys, it's all over. There is no use shooting at us now."

As it is now we are taxing everybody that don't have a lobby.

Beverly Hills, March 21, 1932

The good old U.S.A. holds one international record: our
international bankers have loaned more of other people's money
to foreign countries, on less security, than was ever loaned before,
even on security. Now there is a record we want to see beat, but
no other bankers are dumb enough to beat it.

New York, March 23, 1932

Congress knocked the rich in the creek with a seventy-two
percent income tax. Then somebody must have told 'em, "Yes,
Congress, you got 'em while they are living, but what if they
die on you to keep from paying it?"

Congress says, "Well, never thought of that, so we will frame
one that will get 'em, alive or living, dead or deceased."

Now they got such a high inheritance tax on 'em that you
won't catch these old rich boys dying promiscuously like they did.
This bill makes patriots out of everybody. You sure do die for
your country, if you die from now on.

Beverly Hills, March 30, 1932

Wait a minute here now, it's all right for Jack Garner's re-
formed Congress to pour it onto the rich with income taxes, to
fine a man for dying, to put a tax on malt till they make it cost

like beer even if it don't taste like it, to refuse to pass a sales tax, then turn around and tax everything that is sold, to put a tax on matches, and drive the U.S. to the insane asylum trying to make cigar lighters work — all these fool things come under the heading of Congressional employment, but when they put a tax on chewing gum, the only thing left for a poor man to chew, that's going too far.

Beverly Hills, April 5, 1932

Congress yesterday gave forty minutes to Philippine independence, gave forty minutes but no indepedence. Democrats all voted for it. They are in about the same fix the Philippines are.

Sugar and immigration were the things they were voting on. The freedom of a race of people never entered into it. We better give 'em their freedom while we got 'em. The only reason we ever held 'em this long was because Japan didn't use sugar in their tea, but they are liable to start using it any day.

Beverly Hills, April 11, 1932

After Wall Street had been dead for a couple of years, and everybody that had so generously contributed to the funeral was just about to go to work and forget it, why now the U.S. Senate, who investigates everything after it's dead, is going to dig up the body and hold an autopsy.

They will find out exactly what everyone else already knows, "Deceased died from overgorging while the gorging was gorgeous."

Beverly Hills, April 12, 1932

The Senate Grand Jury which is in session now couldn't get much nourishment yesterday out of this fellow Whitney that's head of the "Wall Street Gang."

There is one kind of a noble thing about our modern racketeers, they will go to the electric chair before they will give away any of the workings of their organization.

At first we thought when they had this investigation we was

going to get the names of our "Big Men" who were betting the country would never amount to anything. Oh! Yeah!

Hollywood, April 22, 1932

Did you read that Senate Wall Street investigation? The Senate sent out and got a fellow named Gray, well he didn't ask the usual Senate questions, Gray knew where the body was buried, and poor Mr. Whitney who had had a cinch on the stand up to then, why it looked like he was going to break down and confess. Twenty four thousand patriotic Americans, and some splendid friends from France, was all betting against the country and we used to arrest men for just saying something against it.

That lawyer Gray for the Senate must have lost some dough on the Street, and he's out to locate the guy that got away with it.

Beverly Hills, May 4, 1932

Wall Street is being investigated, but they are not asleep while it's being done. You see where the Senate took that tax off the sales of stocks didn't you? Saved 'em 48 million dollars. Now why don't somebody investigate the Senate and see who got them to get that tax removed? That would be a real investigation.

[The Republicans nominated Herbert Hoover and the Democrats nominated Franklin D. Roosevelt as their Presidential candidates. The contest against "rugged individualism" and for more humanity in government was on.]

July, 1932

[When Florenz Ziegfeld died Will was asked to say a word, in lieu of a religious service, at his funeral services. Here is what he said]:

We stand before our Lord to give back all that is mortal of our friend. I am not ordained, or have any ecclesiastical credentials. I am not an accredited witness, neither am I an innocent bystander.

I AM SIMPLY ONE OF OUR PROFESSION PAYING A LAST AND SMALL
TRIBUTE TO A MASTER OF OUR CRAFT.

Among us gathered here, our religious beliefs are many, but
one belief is universal with all, and that is that there is some
divine higher than earthly. We can speak to Him in many devious
ways, in many languages, but He sees us all in the same light, and
judges us according to our actions, as we judge the actions of
our children different because we know they are each different.

Among all our earthly accomplishments, the greatest is to
beautify, for beauty speaks no language, beauty appeals to every
eye that is put into the human head.

Well, certainly our Divine Being above welcomes back into
His fold a man who has been on earth and given to it beauty.

[In August, 1932, the Republicans put on a stock market rally
that sort of "rattled" in its chest. "Now they are just buying and
selling among themselves," Will wrote, "in stocks that haven't
shown a cent of increased power. That shows the thing is
'cockeyed.' The earnings should come first and then the raise
in price of the stock. But don't forget the original idea of it
was to beat the poor old Democrats, who never did anybody any
harm in their lives."]

San Salvador, October 10, 1932

I am leaving for everything south of the equator. Revolutions
are thicker down there than Roosevelt Republicans. Am flying
down the west coast by Chile, then to Argentina for a week, and up
the east coast by Brazil. I will see more in a week than a New
York gossip artist can see in five years of keyholes. South America
is our coming country, so it's good to know where it's at.

I want to get back just before election. Not to vote, but just
to see the show. I think people would like to read something in
the papers beside "Hoover said this" and "Roosevelt says that." I
think it's a good time to go. In fact, I am gone.

[Will had an enjoyable trip through South America, flying the
Andes, playing polo in Argentina, marvelling at the size of

Brazil. But he had a great disappointment. He thought the
election would be on November 4 but it was on November 7 instead. He arrived back "in the midst of the most collossal Rodeo
of Applesauce in the history of our national pastime." Mournfully he said, "from now on you will never catch me without a
calendar."

Will then went on to advise them, "instead of calling each
other names till next Tuesday, why you can do everybody a big
favor by going fishing, and you will be surprised but the old
United States will keep right on running while you boys are
sitting on the bank. Then come back next Wednesday and we
will let you know which one is the lesser of the two evils to us."

The next day Will asked mournfully, "Don't you all kinder
wish that the President of our country wouldn't have to run
around all over the land getting up on a soap box to shout his
merits like a backwoods congressman running for reelection?
That's why a President's term should be for six years, no reelection. And be retired for life on half salary. Then he serves with
dignity right up to the finish."

From now on, politically, the country was to sit back and wait
until the following March Fourth for the new President to come
in. During this entire time Will wrote about the harmful result
of such a condition, even suggesting that Hoover and the defeated
Congressmen and Senators get out and let their successors take
over at once.]

Beverly Hills, January 19, 1933
[Still harping on the foolishness of discredited government
officials holding office — simply because when the government
was organized with transportation systems then in operation it
took four months to get things under way — Will gave a homely
example of actually what was happening — that we had a President in office who was no longer President, and a President-elect
who was the choice of the people]:

Here is how this two-headed President thing works out. We
have a President that's in, but has no authority. A President

that's out, but has no authority. A Senate that's in, but has no leader; a house that's in, but's been voted out. A budget that both sides are afraid to try to balance. Debts that are owed us that will never be paid, debts that we owe which we keep adding to. We are sore at Japan because they took Manchuria. Sore at the world because they won't disarm. In fact, we are just sore at ourselves because we muddled everything up.

And in the midst of it all we tell the Philippines "what constitutes liberty."

Oakland, California, January 22, 1933

Another big bank failure.

Suppose the fire department was run like a bank? A fire examiner finds a small fire, goes back from time to time to see it getting bigger. Then just as there is nothing left but the chimney he notifies the Department, "We better see what we can save for the people."

[Will was able to report, in the way of progress, that "this is not only the lamest lame duck Congress, but it's our last lame duck Congress. States stayed up all night in order to be able to ratify it, and here it was turned down by Congress six years in a row."]

CHAPTER TEN

*"The Year of the Big Switch,
From Worse to Better . . ."*

[Franklin D. Roosevelt was inaugerated as President of the United States on March 4, 1933 and almost before he had reached the White House had declared a bank holiday. Things began to pop.]

March 11, 1933

These moratoriums they are having all over the country are mighty good things. We thought of 'em for Europe three or four years ago, but nobody ever thought of 'em for us. We said, let's fix it so Europe don't have to pay their debt. Then it took us three years to think of, Let's fix it so we don't have to pay ours. We are just naturally a fast thinking people. We had thought of everything to relieve the farmer, but to keep him from losing his farm, and the funny part about it the Banker didn't want it.

But we just thought, well we always have foreclosed, why do anything different? Giving him some more years to pay in never entered any one's mind. Now we are all sitting pretty. If we owe anybody we just wave to 'em and holler, "Moratorium, happy moratorium to you!"

You see the fellow that loaned the money is always better able to lose it than the fellow that borrowed it. The fellow that borrows it blows it in and never uses it for the cause that he borrowed it, but the fellow that loaned it, he never loaned all that he had, he only loaned what he could spare, so if he could spare that much, why he didn't need this that he loaned.

So you see the moratorium didn't hurt anybody, and then it's an awful word anyhow. It's like propaganda, and a lot of new things that we have scared up since the war.

We used to call it just spreading bad news, and they generally just did it out of pure devilment, but now that it's called propaganda and they get paid to spread it, why it's legitimate.

The difference between doing a thing for money and doing it for nothing makes it legal. So half the enjoyment now is folks paid to spread some lie that will aid somebody, and the whole country is clogged with propaganda, where it used to only be clogged with house flies, measels and cramp colic.

But all in all it's a great country, it's the best and worst one I ever lived in, and I been living in countrys for 54 years next November Fourth.

I was born on Election Day, but never was able to get elected to anything. I am going to jump out some day and be indefinite enough about everything that they will call me a politician, then run on a platform of question marks, and be elected unanimously, then reach in the treasury and bring back my district a new bridge, or tunnel, or Dam, and I will be a statesman.

As I say all I got to do is get muddled up enough on public affairs, and I am slowly becoming that way. I wouldn't bet you ten cents that this is the month of March, everything is so cockeyed. So look out, Rogers is becoming a politician.

Santa Monica, March 13, 1933

Mr. Roosevelt stepped to the microphone last night and pointed a lesson to all radio announcers and public speakers what to do with a big vocabulary.

Leave it at home in the dictionary.

Some people spend a lifetime juggling with words, with not an idea in a carload.

Our President took such a dry subject as banking (and when I say "dry" I mean dry, for if it had been liquid, he wouldn't have to speak on it at all) and made everybody understand it, even the bankers.

Santa Monica, March 14, 1933

I don't know what additional authority Roosevelt may ask

but give it to him, even if it's to drown all the boy babies, for the way the grown up ones have acted, he will be perfectly justified in drowning any new ones.

So viva Roosevelt, and banzai everything.

It just shows what a country can do when you take their affairs out of the hands of Congress.

Beverly Hills, March 16, 1933

Beer is coming back, wine is coming back, Greta is coming back, Sister Aimee is coming back. Senators' salaries cut 15%, that's fair, movie salaries cut 50% (not so hot), newspaper columnists' salaries cut (that ain't fair), but if Roosevelt says it is, why it's O.K.

March 18, 1933

When you read some blab about somebody telling how overpaid Movie stars are, in the first place our salaries are always overestimated. But they don't stop to think that a movie star is one person that can't be overpaid, that is not for long. There is no other business in the world where the company you work for knows just to a penny just what you are worth to them.

Is there any way checking up on a bank president, or vice-president to see what he can actually by his own efforts draw into his bank? Is there any other business you can think of outside of stage or screen where they know just exactly how good you are to them in dollars and cents?

Greta Garbo don't get that dough because she is a long tall Swede, she drags it into a box office and they know just how much she dragged in. They can tell you to a dime what Dietrich with her breeches on or off can draw into a box office. So they are all worth what they can get, and they can only get what they can draw.

Don't begrudge the movie folks that are lucky enough to get some money for a little while. It's not a business where you can charge off depreciation for your buildings or equipment every year, no matter what age might be doing to talent. There is many an ex-star broke today, that have in their short careers paid the government more money than a half dozen successful business men will in a life time. Mind you this is not a wail about taking it away from any of us, but make the thing fair, take it away from all alike.

March 18, 1933

A financier receiving interest from tax exempt government bonds don't pay a cent to the upkeep of his government. Now think that over a bit and wonder what is the matter with the country. It's tax exempt bonds, is the the biggest thing in the world the matter with the country.

They ought to call in and pay off hundreds of millions of these and stop that interest on 'em. Put 'em back out with no interest. People would still buy 'em, for it's not interest they are looking for today; it's security. It's certainly a queer critter that is looking for interest on his money today.

It's the most unjust and unequal law we have in this country. Everyone of you that own or make anything pay some sort of tax on it. Yet there is a way that a very rich man could draw millions from our government and never pay a cent of it out in taxes. Nothing in our country should be tax exempt. They yell about hoarding. There is where the hoarding is.

Beverly Hills, March 28, 1933

Our country may be short of work, short of ready cash, but, by golly, depression has bred real patriots.

Right here in Beverly Hills (the heart of art) in the exclusive Beverly Wilshire Hotel some friend of the common people sneaked in and stole six saxaphones, four clarinets, a bull fiddle, and base drum. Our town constable is looking for him to prosecute him.

The people are looking for him to reward him.

Beverly Hills, March 30, 1933

Glad to see that re-forestration and employment bill pass. We got to have a lot more forests and trees, otherwise these cigarette smokers won't have anything to burn up.

April 1, 1933

Say this guy Hitler has grabbed off the spotlight from all the Dictators. He is a Dictator to end all Dictators. When I was in Europe a year ago this January I made arrangements from London to go to Munich to see this Hitler for an interview, then some newspaper guys talked me out of it, saying "Why he is only a flash in the pan. Before you get your interview published he will be through."

Dog-gone it I wish now I had gone. I would like to see what kind of a bird he is. I don't know but what I will prance over yet and take a look at him. But he is so big now I guess I couldn't get an interview. If I did I would sure make it a nice one (all in his favor) till I got out of Germany anyhow. For that old boy runs that Country like a warden.

There must be an awful lot doing over in Europe now. Things are stirring around, kinder smells like another war. You know those Nations over there are just like a lot of so-called society women in a small town. The minute two of 'em get their heads together, it starts all the others wondering. Each one don't know which other one to hook up with. They are so busy scheming and fenagling around that it's no wonder they don't get anything done at home.

France has been kinder lining up for the forthcoming festivities, signing up what Nations she could. She has Poland under contract. Mr. Woodrow Wilson fought hard to get Poland some freedom, but she is about sick and tired of it, and is about ready to go to war to end the whole thing. She is about as big as the lower half of the King Ranch in Texas, but has the biggest standing army in Europe. Poland don't hardly know who to jump on till France makes up her mind for her.

Then, Roumania signed up with France for the duration of the next war, and one or two of those little nations that France loaned enough money for the King to get him some new uniforms. I guess we are about the dumbest nation in the world in that respect. We have loaned more money to foreign nations than anyone, but we never was smart enough to make 'em sign that they would help us out in case Mexico or Canada or some other bully jumped on us.

So the old war will be on again pretty soon, but this time with different line ups, and we will all say "Ain't it a terrible thing!" And here we will kill more on a nice Sunday afternoon on our roads than they will in the first year of war. Well if we get in the next one I will vote my first Republican ticket.

April 8, 1933

Most buffet suppers, or dinners either, are a kind of an excuse for not having much to eat. There is something about a "buffet" that suggests that it's only going to be a couple of sandwitches and some potato salad.

No nations ever had two better friends than we have, you know who they are? Well, they are the Atlantic and Pacific Ocean. There is a couple of boys that will stand by you, and you can depend on 'em, three thousand miles wide and a mile deep.

Give me a couple of good oceans between me and my enemies and I will sink a battleship and do away with a couple of companys of cavalry, but you take old France bedded right in there next to Germany, with nothing in the world between them but a boundary line of two hundred years of hatred, and I am going to tell you, brother, I would look out for France. And I don't blame 'em for looking out for France.

What we forget is that every nation has to look at things from their own angle, not our angle. You must always remember America can get altruistic, but remember we got the two oceans, our pals.

Winslow, Arizona, April 20, 1933

The papers say we are off the gold. The best way to tell when each of us went off the gold is to figure back how many years it was since we had any. The last I remember getting my clutches on was in Johannesburg, South Africa, some five dollar English gold pieces that we carried in a belt around our waist. I used the last one to pay a third class passage to Australia, so I went off gold in 1902. So this move strikes me as no great novelty or calamity.

New York, April 23, 1933

My old friend Arthur Brisbane accuses me good naturedly of

being worried over this "inflation." I wasn't worried, I was just "confused."

There is quite a difference. When you are worried you know what you are worried about, but when you are "confused", it's when you don't know enough about a thing to be worried.

But Arthur even my confusion is all over now. Everybody that I meet has explained this whole "inflation" thing so clearly that now I am going around explaining it myself.

You see Medical science has developed two ways of actually tracing insanity, one is if the patient cuts out paper dolls or works at a jig saw puzzle, and the other is if the patient says, "I will tell you what this economic business really means."

Beverly Hills, April 27, 1933

Governments are having the same trouble now that individuals have been having for three years, that is trying to find out the actual value of what they have. You don't know the value of your land, your stocks, your house, or anything. Now England and America and France have met to find out what the dollar is worth, and what the pound sterling is worth, what silver is worth. Everything is jumping up and down now like an international banker at a Senatorial investigation.

Nations are like a lot of women with their babies, each thinks that theirs is the best.

New York, May 1, 1933

Everybody is happy here in New York tonight, the market went up today. Spirits here just go up or down according to that day's market. They think the whole U.S. just depends on what pocket the little white ball rolled into on the Exchange roulette table that day. But our country has got so that each one of us has to live by a "racket" of some kind, and none of us must be too critical of the other fellow's "racket."

When you figure it right down, none of us are in a really essential business but the farmer. And he raises so much that even his business is partly non-essential.

New York, May 3, 1933

[Will Rogers signed up to do seven coast-to-coast broadcasts over NBC sponsored by the Gulf Refining Company. In a letter to the two organizations, the Red Cross and the Salvation Army, he notified them that all of the proceeds were to be turned over to them]:

Here is how this rough and tumble broadcastin' thing come about. The Gulf Oil Company kept wantin' me to litter up the microphone with some Oklahoma grammar. Now Amos 'n' Andy, Jack Pearl, Wynn, Vallee or Cantor have never had any cause to be jealous of me in their industry, but I did want to make a contribution to a couple of good causes that had done such fine work durin' our earthquake and I didn't have the dough to do it with, so Mrs. Rogers figgered it out, as she does most of the other things. She says "You got the wind to do it," so she figgered out how I could do it with just talk, which I would be doin' for nothin' anyhow to anybody I could hem up and make listen to me, so I am to preach for seven Sundays, and the Gulf Company is to take all the money and send half of it to the Red Cross and the other half to the Salvation Army, both to be used for Unemployment Relief. So I got nothin' in the transaction but my voice and I never lost it yet. The only one I see can lose is the Gulf Company, that is if they don't sell enough gas to pay for the gas they bought from me. So soon as I get through they will mail your check. Don't thank me, thank the Gulf Company or better still thank the listeners. They will be the sufferers.

New York, May 7, 1933 [*Gulf Oil Program*]

I generally follow these big men because they always have a lot of logic and theories and everything, and somebody has to come along and offset them with facts.

But not with Mr. Roosevelt. There is a plain spoken man. He is a fellow that doesn't mess around with a lot of big words.

[Will went on in his inimitable way to explain inflation and other knotty problems that were confusing the people.

The White House telephoned Richard C. Patterson, Jr., executive vice president of the NBC, at the Company's studios a few minutes after Will had concluded his broadcast and requested a copy of the cowboy humorist's talk. The transcript was read over the long distance telephone and taken down at the White House by shorthand. It was explained that President Roosevelt wished to see the text of Rogers' talk before making his own radio talk over combined NBC network.]

Tulsa, Oklahoma, May 12, 1933

Oklahoma wants to vote on the beer thing but they have no money to pay for the election so Missouri offers to pay for Oklahoma's election provided Oklahoma will guarantee to vote dry and let them have the sales privilege as they do now.

Corn is forty and fifty cents a bushel but no farmer has any. He sold last fall and winter at fifteen cents. They thought Roosevelt was just another President.

May 13, 1933

Washington is really a Merry-go-Round. They never saw such excitement. But, after all, nothing really definite has really been done. All these things are just bills that give the President authority to do them, and the whole thing sums itself down into trusting the President to carry the thing through. And almost all of them thinks he will do it the very best way. The people trusted him by electing him, and we hollered for action. Well, brother, we are getting it, so now the whole thing is up to him.

Washington, May 24, 1933

[J. P. Morgan was called before a Senatorial Investigation Committee to explain some stock manipulations that looked a bit shady. It seemed that there was "a preferred list" that got advance information so that their gambling in stocks might be a sure thing.]

Back in here to see the "Morgan Follies." You know he has made himself a mighty pleasant and agreeable witness. This "preferred list" that they read today, everybody that's not on it is knocking it. Some think the whole trial won't do much good. But anytime one half learn how the other half live why it does us all good. You see there is a lot of things these old boys have done that are within the law. But it's so near the edge that you couldn't slip a safety razor blade between their acts and prosecution.

New York, May 25, 1933

Just flew in from Washington from the Morgan investigation. I have always said I never met a man I didn't like. Well I liked this Morgan. You would like him. You couldn't help it. I am not speaking of his "racket." I am speaking of the man. These Senators will be banking with him before this thing ends. When I met him I started to hand him what little I had right there.

Now these Senators started out to prosecute him. I want to save him. I can see the makings in him of a regular guy. He has the money, he has the brains, and above all he has the personality. If he will devote (we will say just the afternoons) of his life to public service, or philanthropy of some sort, he will die happy and loved.

Funny thing about this so-called preferred list that Morgan Co. put out. All of 'em held the stock too long and it died on their hands. So it was really a "sucker" list.

May 26, 1933 [Gulf Oil Broadcast]

[Will and Betty spent the night as guests of the President at the White House. He made a report of it to the radio audience]:

You wonder how this man, under this tremendous strain, is taking this. I have not been in a home since 1929 where it really looked like there was joy and happiness and good spirit. I don't mean that he is unmindful of all of those out of work.

But, by golly, he is not sitting down moping over it. He has a grin on his face. This man absolutely believes, he knows that he is going to help these people. It is not conceit, it is absolute confidence. I believe Roosevelt would absolutely bet you that he could pull you out of your predicament, I don't care who you are. That is the way he feels about it, because he knows that everything is in the country that ever was in it, and he knows simply by manipulating it around and doing certain things — It is like a clock; it has a hundred different parts. He knows if he winds the right thing, the whole thing will get going.

The unemployment is a thing that worries him the most; it is not Europe. Europe is a side issue with him.

The things he is doing is really bearing fruit. I never saw a man as frank as he is. He would sit at the table — I don't believe in disarmament. I don't believe they will get anywhere. I would ask him about it, and he would come back and explain it to me. You know, after I heard what he said about it, maybe he will get away with it. I don't know.

You know, this fellow, he has got some kind of a feeling — I believe that he has some kind of a divine feeling — I don't know how to express it. He knows that things is going to be all right.

Humor and laughs — My goodness, I didn't get nowhere with my little jokes.

At dinner, he wanted another helping of fish. He told us (there was about 12 of us there) "the hardest thing, the biggest hardship I have had in the White House is to get a second helping of anything."

I said to him, "Well, Mr. President, why don't you put it in the platform the next time — a second helping for all Presidents."

The next morning — Mr. Roosevelt sits in his bedroom. I think he has breakfast in bed. He had the awfulest sweater over his pajamas I ever saw. Maybe I shouldn't tell that. He sees people that come in there. He doesn't go to the office until about eleven o'clock. He is in there.

Imagine a guy like that! When I came in, I said to Mrs. Roosevelt, "Where is the President?"

She said, "Wherever you hear the laugh."

So, I went in there, and there he was. He said, "Now, Will, sit down here a minute and you will see what everybody wants as they come in and out."

I said, "No; I can't do that. It is about ten o'clock, and the Morgan investigation was on at ten o'clock. I have got to go. Lord, I can see a President any time, but I never did see Morgan in my life. I am not going to monkey — "

So he told me, "Will, I don't blame you — I am like you. I wish I could see him, too. I wouldn't mind looking at him, too."

Santa Monica, May 30, 1933

Knowing I had been to the Morgan investigation, everybody asked me on the way out, "What's it going to lead to, and will it do any good?"

Yes, it's going to be very educational, not only of the Morgan investigation but of all business.

It's going to show us just how "Big Business" got big. It got big according to law, but not according to Hoyle.

Beverly Hills, June 1, 1933

"Farm prices have advanced seventeen percent in the last month" — Now that's better news than a speech on "Good Relations" by Mussolini and Hitler combined.

Santa Monica, June 3, 1933

[When Will finished making the Movie, *State Fair,* the studio gave him the hog, Blue Boy, that was used in it.]

I had to go home to see Blue Boy. More people interested in Blue Boy than Garbo, and he is just as tempermental. When he didn't want to work, he wouldn't. Even Will Hayes couldn't make him. He is billed in Iowa as "Iowa's Own Star, Assisted by Eight Others from Hollywood."

He is a great pig and when better pigs are born they will call him "Papa."

See where bicycling is the rage in Hollywood. Will Hayes says,

"Keep riding, you can't be immoral on a bicycle if you keep going."

I asked Garner, who drank more, House or Senate? "Well," he said, "it's almost a tie, but I believe the House drinks more, not much, but a little more. You see there is 531 in there and only 96 in the Senate. If the Senate had about two more members they would go ahead of 'em."

Roosevelt's middle name is "Delano." It could be Hitler and he'd still carry the Bronx in New York.

Only trouble with the Democrats is there is just so many of 'em that the Government can't give 'em all jobs. In the old days they didn't have many, and if they did get in it meant work for all of 'em.

If they'll just move J. P. Morgan's trial to Chicago the Fair will sell out.

Most all the Congressmen here have signed up for the off season with the re-forestation army.

The Republicans have turned Democrats so fast that some of 'em forgot to wash their hands.

In this one Week Roosevelt did these things:

Monday, he relieved the Farmer, re-inflated the dollar and made silver jingle again.

Tuesday, he heard Hitler was going to speak Wednesday, so he beat him to it. He lectured England and France and spanked Hitler.

Wednesday, sent a copy of his scenario to Russia who up to then had been the "forgotten man" among Nations. He also took care of Mussel Shoals and the Tennessee River.

Thursday, he relieved the Bankers again, relieved Russia of her plans and used 'em himself.

Friday, reviewed the Bonus Army parade, sent a Bill to Congress to fix the oil situation.

Saturday, Bankers needed relief again.

That Bill just passed was to cancel the debts and pay them for all the expense and trouble they had been put to.

This Bill the Clerk just whispered to me was to sink the navy and take all the Sam Brown belts off the army.

That Bill was to recognize Russia and Wisconsin, give Japan Honolulu and the Philippines and all have a two week's vacation.

Beverly Hills, June 19, 1933

There ain't but one way for these foreign princes (or so-called titled birds) to prove it to Americans, and that is for one of 'em to marry a poor girl. Then we will know he is a prince. For in all our story book reading the Prince always married the poor girl.

Beverly Hills, June 22, 1933

There is one line of bunk that this country falls for, and always has. "We are looking to America for leadership during the conference. She has a great moral responsibility."

And we, like a big simp, just eat it up. Our delegates swell out their chests, and really believe that the world is just hanging by a thread and the American delegates control the thread.

Why they didn't discover us until 1492, and the world had had 1492 wars, 1492 peace and economic conferences, all before we was ever heard of.

England controls all the oceans, half the land, over half the world's international commerce. France is no babe in arms. Japan and Russia are of age.

Yet it's America they kid into thinking she is the whole cheese.

Beverly Hills, June 29, 1933

There has been millions and millions of dollars made out of wheat in the last month, but not a cent made by anybody that ever raised any. Or anybody that ever really owned any.

No wonder the people in so many states voted for legal betting on horse racing. You could never get a penny in of this.

Santa Monica, July 18, 1933

Mr. Roosevelt, most of your plans are working, recovery is slow but is fairly sure in most all lines. But one gang beat the barrier, it recovered entirely. I don't think I need remind you what "industry" this is. I think a signal sign saying "slow" on a street called Wall (Placed there by you personally in order to let 500 essential industries catch up to them) would be appreciated by all other traffic headed for recovery. It woulden't be so bad, but these are the same traffic violators who got too far ahead and gummed up our last parade.

Santa Monica, July 17, 1933

If Nevada could build up their marriage industry like their divorces what would be the matter with guaranteeing everybody a wife, or husband, after six weeks residence?

Washington, D.C., August 18, 1933

I been working day and night since almost yesterday with this fellow Johnson on a code for comedians. He claims that Senators and Congressmen come under our code. I claim theirs is a separate union, that they are professionals, and in a class by themselves, and that us amateur comedians should not be classed with 'em. I hate to defy this N.R.A. but I am going to carry my fight to the country, because according to his code, it would give work to more Senators and Congressmen, and I claim that's the only thing we don't want any more of. So it looks like I am really the first one to lock horns with this tough guy, Johnson. But I believe I got the people with me.

Chicago, August 20, 1933

All the big oil men of course were in Washington, and that of course meant a big poker game.

Anytime two oil men meet, they don't open a filling station, they open a poker game. Then an oil man never travels without his big lawyer. Then in another room the lawyers have a crap game. In the poker game for the first time it was all cash on the the table, no checks, they didn't trust each other. That's their new code. The lawyers used their same old code, of cash, they had never trusted each other.

[On August 27, 1933, Will went on the radio in a plea to try to line up the country back of the N.R.A. He started out by

telling them that on the surface the idea sounded "nutty," perhaps
it was, and that those that had tried it, by hiring another man,
hadn't yet seen any good come of it. Will then told them that,
after all, Santa Claus did not come for four months yet, and
that "it is going to take a few months for all these thousands and
millions of small pay checks to reach your business," and that in
the meantime, it was going to be hard to keep up the extra expense. "The government helped the banks out," he said. "and
they got to help the people. And," he begged, "please don't run
in and raid some little fellow's store because he has no eagle
painted on his chest. Talk to him and see his angle, find out and
see what's the matter with him." He then added, "it's going to
take money and it's going to take a little patriotism before this
whole thing works out. This thing sounds goofy but it's absolutely sound. We don't have to know much economy to know
that if everybody is working we would have prosperity."]

Beverly Hills, August 29, 1933
  So Germany has barred Schumann-Heink. Say, if my own wife
barred Schumann-Heink from anything, I would be with Schu-
mann. A grand liberal-minded soul.

Beverly Hills, September, 11, 1933
  Talking to Oscar Lawler yesterday. He's California's most
capable and common sense lawyer.
  He says that the N.R.A. is nothing but a code of fair ethics of
people doing business with each other. And thinks it was rather
a slam against a nation that we have to be forced by government
control and patriotic persuasion to do what's right.
  I never thought of it in that light, but that's all it is. It looks
like they are trying to get a little more conscience on the market,
and a little less preferred stock.
  It's just decency by government control.

Santa Monica, October 15, 1933
  So Germany left the League. Well we can't criticize. We never
even went in. The poor old League never had a chance, for it
      (over)

had no power. It tried to keep everybody good by having 'em sign a pledge (but there was nothing they could do to you if you broke the pledge). They didn't need guns to make the League a real success. An economic boycott against any nation by all the others would have done the trick. Let the world quit trading with Japan and China will have Manchuria back by breakfast time. Nations will give up their lives (even cheer about it), they will give up their money in order to give up their lives, but to ask one to give up their trade to prevent a war, well that has never been done.

Beverly Hills, November 17, 1933

The Senate went investigating, some went East, some went West and some went over the cuckoos' nest.

The Washington bunch and the California committee who were looking into receiverships, and fake stock sales schemes (which are one and the same), they found out Californians will buy anything in the way of stock if it's phoney enough.

Santa Monica, November 19, 1933

This country is gradually getting democratic at that. See where J. P. Morgan had tea for the first time in the White House. Of course he took his own tea, but it was nice of him to drop into the old frame hut at that. I tell you big men are changing.

November 20, 1933

Mr. Roosevelt was rather undecided exactly what to do on the stabilization of the dollar till the U.S. Chamber of Commerce come out and told him what to do.

Then he knew exactly what to do. Do what the Chamber said not to do.

Mr. Roosevelt knows he is right now, before he was in doubt.

Beverly Hills, November 24, 1933

Big headlines in today's papers say that the big bankers to show Roosevelt his financial scheme don't suit them, they are unloading Government bonds and securities by the bushel. He won't play their way so they are going to sell their ball and bat and get out.

I can't just recall, but as well as I remember, wasn't they the fellows that the Government was helping so much not long ago? They ought to pray every night, "God, Bless Mama and Papa, and all my family, and interest, and Roosevelt."

I want to apologize to the President for putting interest ahead of him, but interest has been helping 'em out longer than he has.

Beverly Hills, December 1, 1933

Now France is on the gold and are cuckoo. She reads every morning how many millions in gold was shipped out the day before, (just like we used to do before we went off the gold) and it's gradually driving them "nuts." So it looks like everybody has either got to be on it, or off of it. You can't play solo.

Santa Monica, December 10, 1933

Many a thing in our Sunday papers today that showed a great picking up of things, and it was not ballyhoo, and not all Government paid works either.

This thing of, "We can't go ahead till we know exactly what our dollar is worth," is all hooey.

Your bankers and your financiers marry with no gold clause. The preacher just guarantees you, she is a wife. How long you can keep her, what she is worth to you, is all up to you.

Roosevelt, like the preacher, says, "Here is a dollar, it can always be used for a dollar."

Beverly Hills, December 13, 1933

These gold dollar arguments are dying down. Used to pick up a paper and all you could see was what Mr. "Got His" had to say about money, but now you don't hear a peep.

Everybody seems to be trying to get ahold of any kind. This would be an awful good time to pass off some Confederate money.

Beverly Hills, December 18, 1933

I see where Jesse Jones, and his R.F.C. (Redistribution Finance

Corporation) are not satisfied with the way the banks are just sitting counting their money. So to make the banks ashamed of themselves, the R.F.C. is going to make loans to industries. The banks will about be so humiliated that they will be the first ones to borrow all that Jesse has. Jesse, you been a banker yourself, you ought to know you can't shame a banker, especially a big one.

Beverly Hills, December 31, 1933

A few hours from the time I am penning you these lines, the old year will be going out, and it looks like she is going out without a single mourner, and at that, it hasn't been a bad old year (as years have been going lately).

CHAPTER ELEVEN

Wheeling and Dealing

Beverly Hills, January 5, 1934

There has been many who has had to say, "Mister, can you spare a dime," but President Roosevelt is the first man in the history of the world who looked a nation right in the face and said, "Mister, can you spare ten billion dollars?" Well Congress and the American people considered it such a compliment to be asked for that much that they really liked it.

Beverly Hills, January 7, 1934

Poor old France and Japan are about in the same fix. France don't know whether it would be better to jump on Germany and lick 'em now while they can, or "Will I sit here and wait till they are ready to pounce on me." Japan is on the same spot. They feel they can lick Russia now, or will she wait till Russia is able to come pounce on them.

This thing of living in an ambitious nation is not what it's cracked up to be. We are certainly glad Mr. Roosevelt announced that we had about all the country we wanted. In fact he suggested that if we could get a decent offer he would let some of it go.

Riverside, California, January 9, 1934

The Republican national Committee come out strongly yesterday against Roosevelt's economic policy. Just two days ago the deficit of the Republican National Committee had been published. It was the biggest on record. There ain't nothing like one broke man telling another one how to run his business.

January 13, 1934

I been watching Congress like a cat at a rat hole, and, you know, considering everything, they have been acting pretty nice.

Mr. Roosevelt made 'em an awful pretty speech when the play opened. Biggest applause was when he said little Finland had paid us every cent they owed of. Course it was only about two dollars and six bits, but the spirit of the thing was worth more than that.

He said he was going to have something to say on the debts later on. If he waits till we are paid anything before he says anything about 'em, it will be later on. He had a little sly dig in there at La Belle France, but I tell you it takes more than digs to make France dig. She has been dunned by better nations than us.

He also had a kind of another little sly crack in there on Morgan, if I haven't got my Geography mixed. He told of the big men evading the tax, "if not the law itself, or the letter of it, but they sure evaded the spirit of it."

There is one thing about this fellow Roosevelt. He don't play any favorites. Now they don't come much bigger than France and J. P. Morgan, but he dives for their ankles, I don't care how big they are. This fellow is really trying to get a readjustment of some of our ills. While he hasn't exactly got it in for big moneyed interests, he has got it in for some of their modes of doing business. And he is making Christians out of some of 'em, too. Here a little while back they was raring up and defying him, but he has got 'em wagging their tails and looking up at him longingly now.

Beverly Hills, January 15, 1934

I never thought the time would come when I thought I would be able to advise colleges how to run their business. But in California Sunday we saw our first real professional football played, and twenty five thousand come away raving about it. Especially the rules under which they play where you can pass from anywhere, anytime. Now as football is not only the backbone but the gravy of college existence, you fellows better open up your game, for this pro game was just made for an audience. No penalty every minute to keep an audience sore, nobody getting hurt every play, referees not in the way of players.

Colleges have developed the yelling, but the pros have developed the game.

Now you colleges wake up. I don't want to see you have to close your doors.

Santa Monica, January 21, 1934

By the way this depression and the fall of the big man has kinder knocked the props out of all those success storys we used to get fed up on. This is just an age of being a good Democrat and holding an office. That's all there is to success now.

Santa Monica, January 22, 1934

If this administration never did another thing, the New Deal toward all our neighbors to the South has gained us many friends. And the best friend anyone can have is their neighbors. Give the Philippines their freedom, and take that godfather clause out of our Cuban treaty, and the first thing you know we would be called "Brother," and not "Big Brother."

Beverly Hills, January 23, 1934

Good deal of Japanese news last day or so. One day our eyes are turned to Europe (to see if the boys have any token payment). The next day it's Japan that draws our attention. We are going to have a crooked neck from trying to look both ways at once.

Washington, January 29, 1934

Since the big money stabilization bill passed Saturday everybody here is in fine cheer and great optimism.

Senators all practicing dancing for the Big Ball. Our President is going to have a wonderful birthday, but many a lady's feet is going to suffer for their loyalty.

Santa Monica, February 5, 1934

Well, I am glad to get back here in California among you

orange squeezers, and speaking of oranges, the juice in a big hotel is fifty cents a glass. That runs about $150 a barrel. You can have it or champagne, both cost the same.

Out here, or in Florida (have to put their name in or I will get a lot of letters) you can buy a ten cent orange squeezer and two bits worth of oranges and mix you up a wash tub full.

A steak is two dollars to two and a half back there. My wife and I had one each, and I could have gone home to Oklahoma and bought a good off-colored dry cow for that.

That's what Mr. Roosevelt is after with some of these schemes of his. He feels it's too far from the raiser to the eater.

I have often wondered why the stuff we all eat is not about half spoiled. It passes through so many hands, part of 'em with no gloves on. He is trying to fix it so everybody can live, but not off each other.

I was in Washington last week when the complaining season of N.R.A. opened. Now the N.R.A. is this way, if you have gotten a job, or sold something under it, it's O.K. If you haven't, it's wrong. It had one mistake, trying to make people be honest and fair in business by law. But it's done more good than harm. The big guys have kicked on it more than the little ones, so that shows it has merit.

New York, February 20, 1934

It was so cold today that for one hour this morning they didn't roll the dice on the New York Stock Exchange. When those crap shooters hands can't roll 'em it's cold.

New York, February 23, 1934

Just flew up from Washington late this evening. Senate or the House neither one was operating, but they was awful busy investigating. They was investigating sugar.

We have more arguments over sugar than we do over all the things combined that sugar goes on or in.

Another room they was investigating Wall Street. That was a real sugar investigation. Corporations loaned 20 billions to Wall Street in 1929. So Mr. Roosevelt didn't invent the word billion.

New York, February 25, 1934

Clark Gable is back here appearing on the stage, and I am here trying to help keep the women off him.

The big brokers of Wall Street are all moving down to Washington, for all their big clients are on the stand there all the time. They are putting tickers in the investigating rooms now.

New York, February 26, 1934

Hurry up planes and start leaving here. I can't walk in these snow shoes. Been run over by two sleighs today. Taxicabs are being pulled by dog teams, and the weather man says there will be a blizzard tonight. And to add to the gloom of this city is the death of John McGraw. N.Y. owes much to him. He was responsible for bringing more people to New York to see his Giants in World Series and league games than any man New York ever had. Typified the spirit of his day and time, and was a sweet character and a fine friend.

New York, February 28, 1934

Landing in Newark from Washington today. The pilot put us in the back end of the plane so it would keep her tail down when the wheels hit the deep snow. Give you an idea how many thousand men clearing the streets in New York. They have missplaced 51 thousand and can't find 'em.

Seven below zero in Washington this morning, and snow a foot deep. Lobbyists standing frozen to death outside of Congressmen's homes. A lobbyist has nothing to keep him warm but his brief case. The hotels of Washington should erect a monument to General Hugh Johnson. They been coming on pilgrimages by the thousands since last July to make a code, change a code, or cuss a code.

New York, March 1, 1934

Japan coronated the new emperor of Manchuria. They would have had the coronation earlier but they didn't have any armored car to haul him to the festivities in.

Washington got liquor today. Must have been a big novelty. About like a baby being continued on milk.

Santa Monica, March 4, 1934

Did you know that we got ten dry States, 11 part dry, and the other 27 can have anything they want, the same as these 21 do.

Beverly Hills, March 6, 1934

Statistics is about the poorest form of reading that we have to listen to, but I believe these that President Roosevelt used ought to be drummed into our heads. "Ninety percent of our people live on salary or wages, ten percent on profits alone. People in this country whose income is less than two thousand a year buy more than two thirds of all the goods sold."

His talk come at a mighty opportune time, for lots of folks had figured, "Ah well, the N.R.A. has died out, why have to abide by it?"

This will put new life in it and incidentally throw a scare into some of the boys.

Santa Monica, March 7, 1934

They can't seem to agree on the Wall Street control bill (Fletcher-Rayburn Bill). What they ought to do with Wall Street is like with the farmers, say, "How much gambling did you do last year?" "Your honor, I bet a hundred thousand dollars." "Well, this year we want you to cut it down to 75 thousand, and we will pay you thirty thousand for not betting the other twenty five."

Beverly Hills, March 12, 1934

Trouble with American transportation is that you can get somewhere quicker than you can think of a reason for going there. What we need now is a new excuse to go somewhere.

Hollywood, March 15, 1934

I was just thinking, if it really is religion with these nudists colonies, they sure must turn atheists in the winter time.

Hollywood, March 16, 1934

I can't imagine any punishment worse than not being able to

return to your own country, no matter what country it is.
You can't legislate intelligence and common sense into people.

Hollywood, March 22, 1934

You would love Nevada. It's the West without dressing up to
look the part. A herd of cows, and a hole in the ground made
it a unique State, and a long riata, and a pick keep it a unique
state.

Hollywood, March 27, 1934

Funniest thing in this controversy over a bill to regulate Wall
Street. Wall Street now wants to write their own bill. They are
pleading guilty, but want the privilege of pronouncing their own
sentence.

Pasadena, California, March 30, 1934

Here is something I think will bear repeating, two kid brothers
one 14 the other 12 hiking in the mountains out here, the young
kid bit by a rattlesnake, the 14 year old one cut the wound all
up with a knife, and they took turns sucking the poisoned blood
out, the younger one finally fainted, the other carried him up the
mountain two miles on his back, and he has saved him. We are
not so bad off. These kids are Daniel Boones and Davey Crocketts
in any age.

Beverly Hills, April 3, 1934

See where the President is prolonging his fishing trip. It's going to be pretty tame for him when he gets back. He has been
used to fishing for real game fish, like the broadbill, and the
swordfish, then come home and have to bait his hook with some
little post office worms, and fish for mudcat Congressmen, and
eel Senators.

Beverly Hills, April 4, 1934

Investigations start out so sensationally, and peter out so
quietly. Investigations are held just for photographers.

Hollywood, April 6, 1934

New York Stock Exchange is having their own investigation. They are investigating 14 different stocks that have been acting so funny that Wall Street itself didn't know what they were doing. In other words you can fool the public, but you mustn't fool the members of the lodge.

The high income tax come pretty near passing in the Senate. Well there is millions and millions that are not making it, that would be glad to give up ninety-nine percent if you would let 'em earn a hundred thousand or more.

Santa Monica, April 8, 1934

I will say one thing about a Democratic President fishing, maby he hasn't caught anything but we don't have to look at pictures in the papers of him dragging some poor little trained perch in. The Republicans would get a camera man before they did their bait. One summer here one poor little fish got so he would get his picture taken and then take the hook out of his own mouth and go back and wait for the President the next day with a new photographer.

Santa Monica, April 16, 1934

Woman died at Savannah, Georgia, age 123. She had smoked a pipe for 112 years, while cigarette smokers figure they are passing out daily at the ripe old age of thirty and forty. I think it's the fatigue from tapping 'em on the cigarette case that wears 'em down so early.

Santa Monica, April 17, 1934

Baseball is our national game. We become a great nation under baseball and commenced to flop the minute we started to take up a lot of poor substitutes. Golf is played for conversational purposes. Polo is played by us lazy ones because the horse does all the work, and we love to just go for the ride, but you have to play baseball for itself alone. There is no clubhouse to talk it over in after the game. From an old first baseman of the Oolagah, Okla., Giants.

Santa Monica, April 18, 1934

You know there is two places where what a person says should not be held against 'em in a court of law, one is at a dinner, and the other on the witness stand of a Washington investigation. Both affairs are purely social, and should be covered only by the society editor.

April 24, 1934

Don't worry about the movies. We will be in the ash can before you could get a code ready.

Two bad pictures in a row, and then the public will make our code, and it will be, "Oh, Lizzie Bean, they say her picture is terrible." There is your code without anybody making it.

The Presidents of Cuba are coming in and going out just about as fast as these intellectuals and writers come and go out here to fix the movies.

The Sante Fe Railroad payed dividends for years just on folks that were going to make the Movies more intelligent.

I been out here working in 'em now for 15 years, off and on, and the Pictures are about the same, and the people that look at 'em are about the same.

Somebody will make a highbrow one that will play to about 1.80 cents, then some plain old country picture will come along and gross a couple of millions. Maby it will be just about what was made in the Silent 18 years ago, with the exception of having noise in it, and, too, the off-colored or risqué pictures haven't been going so good as they used to.

It wasn't that tastes were improving, it was that there just wasn't nothing new they could shock folks with, and then they tried out of series of things that were supposed to be sophisticated. That's where there is a lot of bright talk about nothing in the world.

Well, they never got over for they were always about people that the audience didn't care if they lived or died at the end.

I saw a list of Movie Stars salaries. I can only speak for myself, but I wish I was doing that well. Had me up with Miss Garbo and Chevalier. The salary I was drawing you would think I was a "furriner."

I thank 'em for making the mistake in my favor, but I also want to thank the income tax people for knowing what I really get.

Santa Monica, April 26, 1934

Japan, you got to admire 'em, they are so ambitious, and they just got everything that all the other nations have, but a sense of humor. Their papers took great satisfaction and glee, and screamed it in headlines, "The American fleet can't get through Panama Canal in 24 hours." They never figured that the size of the fleet might have something to do with it.

May, 1934

Say did you notice I been gabbing here for quite a little bit and I haven't dragged in any jokes about the Senate.

Did you see where they sent that fellow to jail for ten days the other day for defying the Senate? I didn't know they could do a thing like that. I guess he didn't either, but he does now.

You won't hear me telling any jokes about those babies tonight. There is a fine body of men. No, sir, I never will get through complimenting the Senate from now on.

You know, you used to think the Senate was just a place where men met and talked into a record, and then the record was mailed out free to people who wasn't able to take a newspaper.

You see New York has what they call "night clubs," but the Senate is just like 'em only you called 'em a "day club." As I say that's what I used to think the Senate was, but not since they sent this fellow to jail. I tell you it's a great deliberative body, 96 fine men, and I am for 'em.

May, 1934

If ever a nation lived in the wrong place it's Austria. I believe if I was Austria I would just disband till things picked up. I was down there years ago, I thought they had the prettiest uniforms on their officers, and the best beer I ever saw in my life.

But she is a country that's too close to her neighbors. They can write awful pretty waltzes down there, but a country just can't live on waltzes (I don't know though, we got along mighty pretty for a long time with "Over the Waves" didn't we?).

But those Austrian officers always looked to me like they would look more at home with their chins resting on a violin than on a musket. This little Dolphus, that little Dictator they got, he is a little bit of a fellow. He just about comes up to May West's ankle.

A country used to think they only had two ways to go — liberal or conservative. Even our Republican or Democratic form compared to that. But now, Lord, you can go Nazi, fascist, communist, royalist, rugged individualist, or New Deal.

From the looks of the various investigations in Washington, rugged individualism got a little too rugged and was caught by the umpire.

San Francisco, May 15, 1934

It looks like every time you get one of the notorious criminals, you get about two women to each man. Looks like about all the police would have to do is arrest every man that has more than one woman along.

Times do change. The old time outlaw never mixed his women and business.

Hollister, California, May 17, 1934

Sure had a good time today. Been out to a calf branding at the "Quien Sabe" Ranch. Forty thousand acres and one of the prettiest in California.

Didn't mind all the men beating me roping but when a girl did it looks like golf will be coming on me pretty soon.

This is a real old cowtown, but prunes, and easterners are getting a hold in here and they are both hard to eradicate.

There is not a better day in the world to be spent than with a lot of wise old cow men around — barbecued beef, black coffee and good "free holy" beans. Cattle men have lost more in the last few years than anybody and say less about it.

When you ever have any doubt as to what might happen in

these U.S. go to the country and talk with cow men and you will come back reassured.

Beverly Hills, May 21, 1934

Poor old N.R.A., if we all had spent as much time observing it as we have arguing over it, it would have worked right or wrong. There is great good in it, and evidently great ills in it. Now if both sides are not broadminded enough to see and admit it, then let the argument continue, but charge admission for it.

Beverly Hills, May 22, 1934

Senator Norris wanted to abolish the electoral college. This is a bad time to try and do away with anything connected with "college." He will have to wait till the lowbrows get in. Well, he is not a man to get discouraged. He was years trying to get them to abolish the "lame duck" session.

When you get down to common sense and level headedness, and answerable to nobody but his own conscience, you just about got the definition of that quiet fighting old Senator.

Beverly Hills, May 23, 1934

Not long ago ex-ambassador to Germany, Jimmie Gerard said there was fifty men running the country. Now they say they have let 49 of 'em go, so naturally we have those 49 ex-country-runners all on our hands and dissatisfied.

You can't let people out, no matter for what good reason, and have 'em go away bragging on you. I don't suppose there is any business with as many unemployed as the "advising" business. What gets these big fellows goat is, Roosevelt listens to 'em all, but they can't tell whether he is paying any attention or not.

Beverly Hills, May 28, 1934

Secretary of Agriculture has got a tough job. It's by far the toughest job in the cabinet. Sec. of the Navy only has to deal with an Admiral, Sec. of the Army with the Generals, Postmaster General with the Politicians, but when you deal with the farmer, you are dealing with a man who is a dealer himself.

June 10, 1934 [*Gulf Oil Broadcast*]

It's hard to think of something new to talk to you about, but I am going to speak about something that hasn't been brought up in public in years. I would like to say a few words for the Republican Party — For those not familiar it's spelled — R-e-p-u-b-l-i-c-a-n.

Your father and grandfathers will remember the name. The reason I know it's not been spoken of is that you can't speak of something unless you think of it, and you can't think of it unless something happens to bring the name up. I got to thinking of the Johnstown flood, the Galveston tidal wave, and the Chicago fire, and my thought naturally drifted to the Republicans, not that they were responsible for the above events, but there has been lots of people always been awful suspicious.

Now where has that party gone? Such extermination of an entire race has never before been recorded.

Now the Democrats are spending all of this money and the Republicans are asking who is going to pay for all this.

Now who do you suppose is going to pay for it? If two men are eating dinner and one has no money and the other has, why who is going to pay?

But how will they know that the Republican has got the money? Why, by the way he is acting. If you hear him kicking about how much all this all is going to cost, why that means he has the money. And if he joins the "Save the Constitution" or "Liberty Society" why then you will know that he has lots of money.

Be a good joke on the big men if Roosevelt was able to bring about recovery without 'em, wouldn't it?

I am out here tonight to explain what the Democratic Party is trying to accomplish. What they are trying to get at, they are trying to get at what few Republicans there are left. So a lot of you that have been in doubt all this time as to just what the Democrats were driving at, why that's it.

The Republicans have got the money, they all went South with an awful bank roll while they were in there. I don't mean the office holders, they never get anything, only a moderate salary. But they kinder turn their heads and let "the Boys" get theirs.

June, 1934

We never was living in a more secure time. If you are hungry Roosevelt is certainly going to feed you (we know that, he has proved it) and if you are rich he is going to take about half of it away from you in taxes to do it on. So what's the shooting about?

You will find that most of it is from the old boy that don't want to give up the half.

Why, didn't the Republicans have their big meeting the other day and couldn't decide themselves what their issue would be? — Of course the issue was, that the Democrats were taking the dough away from the Republicans — but the Republicans couldn't just come out and say that. So the Republicans are trying to arrange some kind of a slogan that will make it look like they want to do right by the people that are down and out (and they do) but they don't want it to cost 'em anything to do it.

It's just as I say, there are two schools of thought, the HAS-es and the HASN'TS, and as there are more hasn'ts than there is has-es, it looks like they are going to jar the has-es loose from something. So it looks to me like the better nature the has-es take it, why the better it will be.

Then, anyhow, the Democrats won't be in but a few more years, and the Republicans will get back in and get it all back again. So there is no harm done.

We just lope around in a circle anyhow.

Roosevelt is such a charming man personally that it's almost a pleasure to hand him over 50 or 60 percent of what you make.

He ought to hold a thing like the King in England does. That is where he and Mrs. Roosevelt would receive at court and all the big taxpayers' daughters and wives would be received. The ones that paid the most, the daughter could bow the longest and the lowest.

Why, Lord, the rich would just fall over each other to see who could pay the most taxes. They would pay in enough money that the poor would get foundered.

We are living in a great time. Just think what we got to be thankful for. Every nation in the world can't go to sleep at night for fear its neighbor will pounce on 'em before morning. And here we set with two of the finest neighbors in the world. We can't possibly get a war without going from three to seven thousand miles to find it. And when you have to go that far to fight, it just ain't worth the trip.

No nation in the world was ever as secure, no nation in the world was ever so blessed by Geography.

We haven't got a thing in the world to do but set down here and take care of our own business, have every military and naval and air protection against any possible foreign invasion. Then just set and read the war news from other countries.

If any man can tell me any good reason why we should fight Japan I will give him an introduction to Mae West. If any man can tell me any good reason why, if Russia and Japan got in a war, we should get in too, I will see that he has a date with Garbo.

June, 1934 [At a Stock Show]

I don't want to take anything away from judges, but I don't believe you can look at one of these animals and tell which one is the best. I think you got to eat him to tell.

Right here at this table is the only place to judge beef, and I claim I am as good a judge as any professor in the world.

When cattlemen can afford a banquet, why that looks like the cow business is looking up. Course they are doing it on government relief money.

The Government bought all their old poor cows. Imagine a government buying all your poor cows, then some of 'em voted the Republican ticket. Then they wonder why they ain't a success in the cow business. The Government give more for the poor ones than the Los Angeles market give for the fat ones.

Hollywood, June 17, 1934

China (by far the smartest nation in the world) has a word that I don't know how in the world we live without it. It's called "Face," saving face. We have it just as much as China does and call it by a hundred other things. But it all gets back to the same thing, "Face." "How can I do nothing, and still make it look like I did something?"

Hollywood, June 19, 1934

We was all setting around on the Moving Picture "set" this afternoon. Irvin Cobb entertaining us 100 percent as usual.

"Irvin," I said, "I got to write my daily mess. What's something Komical in the day's news?"

"Well, Will, you couldn't get anything much funnier than England and France wanting us to use our influence with Germany to get them to pay France and England. I wouldn't be surprised if they don't try to show where we was on the note, and they will be suing us."

Hollywood, June 21, 1934

The President kinder held up for his brain trust, said he would take brains anytime in preference to politics. He just as good as admitted you couldn't get both in the same body.

Beverly Hills, June 29, 1934

Headline says, "13 Bankers in Detroit indited." You would think Detroit was a bigger town than that.

Mr. Roosevelt's speech seemed to satisfy all but those that had made up their minds in advance that they wouldn't like it, no matter what he said.

Santa Monica, July 4, 1934

I said yesterday that the Republicans made their campaign speech when the whole U.S. was tuned in on Germany, and that nobody heard it. But by Golly I was wrong. From some of the criticism I read of it from the Democrats, they must have all been listening. I had no idea they were even paying any attention to the Republicans.

Get these Democrats on the defense, and they are not so hot.

A Democrat is a better fault finder than he is an explainer. So there is liable to be some excitement at this Fall's election.

Beverly Hills, July 5, 1934

A statesman is a man that can do what the politicians would like to do, but can't, because he is afraid of not being elected.

Santa Monica, July 8, 1934

See by the papers Hitler took a vacation. Most people doing the same thing would have took one too. The Judge would have said, "Now you take a nice rest for about 60 days, and some morning at daylight the warden will call you, and from then on you can rest again."

July 10, 1934

Retroactive means as you were before you got like you are.

Did you ever notice there is more bad ideas that will work than there is good ones.

The "smart" in "right smart" means numbers and does not refer to the smartness.

Well, we get pretty excited over politics, and pretty soon it's all over, and we settle down to cussing the guy we just elected. It just seems like we can't get a man that can take care of all of us after he gets in office. There just ain't enough favors to go round. The bigger majority a man gets elected by, the more enemies he makes, for that means that many more to turn down.

Well it's going to be a big year. In the minds of the candidates the country is always "on the brink." And your decision on November 4th will be the deciding factor on whether it goes on over the brink, or, if you will wisely vote for me, I will grab it just as it's going over and pull it back for you.

"Poor old Brink!" I don't know of anything we been on more of than we have of it. We have tottered on the brink so long and so much, that I think the "old Brink" has got hand holts on it. I am beginning to believe we wouldn't go over it on a bet. We are what you call "Brink" conscious. So don't let the boys scare you about this "brink" bugaboo. It's away overestimated.

Claremore, Oklahoma, July 11, 1934

I never get through the thrill of coming back home, seeing kin folks and old friends. Nature has been rough with the ranch-men and farmers here. The drouth wilted the corn just as it was starting to "roastin ear."

I asked about the wheat and oats, and some other Republican scourge had fallen on them. No grass for the cattle, but they did have an awful nice radish crop.

I never saw redder radishes.

Washington, D.C., July 12, 1934

They are finally starting something that should have been started a year ago, and that's this house building and repairing. The local bank, or local organization loans the money, up to two thousand dollars. The Government don't spend anything, it only guarantees twenty percent of it in case of loss. And these loans are made almost entirely on a man's name alone. Well just the idea of a man being trusted again is going to make the whole thing 100 percent honest. It's the best of all the plans.

July 21, 1934

Up in Alberta, Canada, there is only six on the Jury, and they tried their Premier of that Province for an affair with his Secre-tary. These foreigner's courts do have some of the most Puritan notions. The jury convicted him, but the judge said the Jury was haywire. So now they don't know which one to try, the judge or the jury.

CHAPTER TWELVE

Settling the Affairs of the World In His Own Way

[In the summer of 1934, accompanied by his wife and two boys, Will again went around the world, west to east, but this time across Siberia and Russia by train.

An interesting sidelight of the trip is that spurred on by his wife, Will started out with "a dozen of everything" but left a trail of shirts, suits, underwear, shoes and various sundry items of clothing behind him ("I just slipped one gripful to a bellboy in Honolulu") and ended up back in New York "with the little red bag, the old blue serge, and the typewriter." Will's method was to throw away clothes as they got dirty and to buy new ones on the theory that it was both handier and, with excess baggage to pay on airlines, cheaper.]

July 27, 1934
[Will just "happened" to arrive at Honolulu at the same time that President Roosevelt did.]

It is a kind of a freak place. By that I mean that there is nothing just like it anywhere. While it might at first suggest nothing but sunburn and surf boarding, ukeleles and cocoanuts, when you really get ashore you find folks working.

When you pull up to the dock they start giving you those beautiful things around your neck, pronounced lays, but I don't know how it's spelled. Then the wonderful Hawaian band plays a great welcome to each steamer as they come in.

I got to my hotel and I had twenty-eight of those things around my neck, and they were all of a different and wonderful fragrant breed of flowers. And you look out of your windows right down onto the beautiful ocean and Waikiki Beach. And guys coming in on surf boards as easy as a politician can stand up on a Fourth of July speaker's stand.

I didn't get mixed up in the ocean during the whole trip. Guess I am the only person ever went to Honolulu and didn't take a whirl at the ocean. But I couldn't ride one of those ironing boards with my stirrups hobbled.

Honolulu, July 28, 1934 [Speech]

The President is the only Harvard man that ever come out here that didn't get something. He come with a fishing line and didn't get a bite. The other old Harvard boys come with a Bible years ago and got an island. So we can't say that the intelligence of the Harvard graduate has advanced any. Here we go and elect him President and it looks like he is the least far-sighted of any of them.

We can't let Honolulu go. We got nowhere else for our army and navy to go for vacation. You sweeten our coffee and sour our musical ears.

There ain't a thing I know of to do with you folks unless it is to have the R.F.C. furnish the money and move you nearer the land.

I am bringing over the new quota on sugar.

Mr. Hoover did away with the Mayflower. We thought that was the scheme of having a yacht and not having the taxpapers pay for it.

But this one had Vincent Astor get one and he made him master of the yacht. Vincent had been messing around waiting to do something, but hardly knowing what, so Mr. Roosevelt says, "Vincent, go get a yacht and that will put you to some use and save the taxpayers paying for one." So now Vincent goes as a guest on the Roosevelt yacht, and he never has had to do anything for Vincent. There ain't much you can do for Vincent. Now if we can just keep him from going to Europe to try and settle any of these troubles. Poor Mr. Wilson, I told him the day he sailed, he better do his ocean traveling up and down the Mississippi.

I am bringing news of the Brain Trust but I had to carry it in someone else's brain.

I just left General Johnson over in Frisco. He sent Mr. Roosevelt word what to do.

Mr. Roosevelt is the first President that ever left home this long or ever set foot on the island. Well he can do it, he can go away and feel sure that nobody is trying to take his job. He can do it for Jack Garner is the only Vice President I ever heard of that didn't want to be President. Mr. Roosevelt is the only President that didn't have to learn to fish after he got in office. The others thought it was in the ritual that they sign when they went in. Coolidge used to fish but God how he hated it. The darn fish were too talkative.

Mr. Hoover fished because he wanted to follow out the Coolidge policy. And none of 'em liked the sea. Mr. Coolidge use to get on the Mayflower, but he saw that it didn't get out of the Potomac.

I don't know what Roosevelt is over here for, but I am here to try and give you back to Spain. I haven't been here in 33 years. You look just the same. I am on the track of the fellow that invented the steel playing guitar, the Musical Society of America has offered a bounty on him.

Here is the place where tourists used to come two thousand miles to be shocked by girls dancing in buckwheat skirts. Now they stay home and watch them dance in the raw — nude.

There is one way I could have outdrew President Roosevelt and that is if I had brought Postmaster Jim Farley with me. He is the one that hands out the jobs. We would have had all Honolulu here.

Here is the position we are in with you birds. We don't want you, but on the other hand we can't afford to let anybody else have you. You are our bear that we have by the tail.

Now about the missionaries. Now everybody told me, "Will, don't go over there pulling anything about the missionaries." Well, I just believe the Missionaries are good fellows, and can take it. In fact I know they can take it. They have always been able to take it. Gentlemen, the boat sails in the morning.

No, I have met the biggest part of 'em and they are the most regular folks I ever saw. Here is a side of it you must look at. The Missionaries had to be on their feet or the sailing boat captains would have taken their Bibles.

There was a bunch that was fast workers. They did well at sea but they did better on land. So you see there was the two factions. They didn't have it in for the Hawaiians. They liked them. It was just that they were trying to protect each other.

Now what has been the consequence due to those hardy old pioneers. You got a bunch of people in here that have grown to second and third and fourth generations. They are shrewd, they are hard workers, they have made money, but every cent they have ever made, they have put back into this country. And today you are the envy and the astonishment of every other set of islands in the world. Look at some of these other islands down in the South Seas. Every time they saw a Missionary coming they commenced to build a fire around the pot. Instead of asking the missionary to dinner like you hospitable .folks did, they asked 'em FOR dinner.

Now look at 'em. They are still climbing trees dropping coconuts on each other. While here you are driving around in a Ford. I think it is a great combination you got between you. There is only one suggestion I might offer, and I think that is being carried out by most of your patriotic islanders, and that is, all things being equal, they should give you the chance to work and make a good living, for after all you have just a ALLOAH — HELLOAH — that's a combination of the two languages.

Now lets get this thing straight. What am I doing here tonight? Well, outside of trying to help a splendid charity I am also here to take up and make clear a few of the things which Mr. Roosevelt just kinder skimmed over. Mr. Garfield, Mr. Poindexter, and Mr. Roosevelt all get up here and expound a lot of theories. Well I am here to offset 'em with facts. I want it distinctly understood this is no good will tour or talk. Through Americans running around the world, "good willing," we are in wrong with more nations than any other nation on the globe. So this talk tonight and this world's hurried tour of mine is called "charity to none and malice to all."

Now the President come here bragging on you. Well that's fine. That's what he does everywhere. He bragged on the Virgin Islands. You ever been at the Virgin Islands? Well, I have been there, flew through there twice on two flights around South America, and it's a pretty sorry looking lay out. It's even misnamed. So you can't believe all even a President tells you.

Now before we get right down into the heart of this sugar argument, I got a few other things to take up with you. I, here like Paul Revere, I rush out to tell President Roosevelt the dam had broke and the Republicans was washing down the valley, and you see he picked right up and hurried home. You see the Republicans can get themselves all heated up, and the President can go on the radio, and with one talk can drive 'em into their holes like prairie dogs.

I brought the President some fish from the mainland. He couldn't catch any out here. You folks should have had the Kanakas dive down and put one on his hook.

They call you the Sandwitch Island because you are stuck in between the Republican and Democratic Parties and have nothing to say about what bread goes on top or bottom.

Tokio, August 16, 1934

Well, Japan won't have her world supremacy in business long. I saw a lot of golf courses being put in. That's the beginning of a nation's commercial decline. When we traded a spade for a putter that's the way we started in the red.

Novosibirsk, August 24, 1934

These folks got an entirely different alphabet and it's only in a few towns where there is telegraph operators that can send messages in English.

We are still in Siberia. If you think it's not big we been for days and haven't made a dent in it.

Irkutsk, Siberia, August 26, 1934

They just passed a law in Manchukuo that you mustn't mention the Emperor's name, but you got to call him his majesty.

It's just like if they should pass a law in Kansas that you'd get your head cut off if you ever mention Bill White by name. You'd have to call him His Honor instead.

I reckon that's one way to beat the depression, but you got to be born east of Claremore to understand it.

Moscow, August 30, 1934

These Russians sure believe in mass production. Just come from the race meet and they had 36 races. They run the Soviet derby today. All the horses belong to the government but are raised and entered by different parts of the army and collective farms. Half of 'em running and half trotting races.

When the trotters come out old David Harum wanted to come down and take over the ribbons.

Tomorrow I am trying out Russia's commercial aviation. Flying down through the Ukraine and Caucasus to the Black Sea.

August 31, 1934

I met a guy today that could remember back to the time when there was a Czar in Russia, Trotzky was pressing pants in New York, and Upton Sinclair was away uptown, Texas steers had longhorns and Governments paid their debts. Flying South through Soviet Russia and the oil wells smell like regular capitalistic oil.

Odessa, September 2, 1934

Say, these old Russhians can really fly. We had about a 65 to 70 foot ceiling today and they stuck right under it. That's what the Japanese are more afraid of than any other thing, is that these guys will outfly 'em. Commercial aviation not hot but military, and it looks like they got 'em by the thousands. Who hasn't pictured Odessa on the Black Sea?

Russia and Turkey been fighting over this for a thousand years. Do you remember it in the Russian picture Potemkin? That long row of steps from the ocean to the hill. Well they are right into this hotel.

Helsinki, September 4, 1934

This is Finland, integrities last stand. They told our minister, "You loaned us the money when we needed it and we are going to pay you back."

Them's mighty scarce words. I tell you they got just about the most stable government right now of any of them.

It's a beautiful little city and clean. When these Finns aren't running a twenty-five mile race they are scrubbing something.

Vienna, September 11, 1934

This is Vienna — Europe's hot box. If a war starts, this is supposed to be the place that it starts. It's a beautiful city. Flying on to Bucharest tomorrow. Got to see Queen Marie's country.

Bucharest, Rumania, September 12, 1934

This Rumania is a real place. This is a beautiful city of eight hundred thousand. The king is in the mountains and Queen Marie is at the seashore.

Here is some political scandal. Saw Senator Joe Robinson at the Opera in Vienna last night. Democrats are going Boushwa.

Budapest, September 13, 1934

I am going to keep flying up and down this Danube River till I find a place where it's blue.

London, September 14, 1934

Budapest for breakfast and London for dinner. I have reached in my pocket for my passport in so many different countries today that I am all in. Crossed Hungary, Czecho-Slovakia, Austria, France, Belgium and England.

There is twenty countries over here in a bunch all thinking of some trick to pull on the others. They do love each other.

London, September 17, 1934

They are talking about holding an ammunition-selling investigation over here now. Ammunition is about the only export now. Wars ought to be awful equal for they all use the same guns and ammunition.

Best show in London is a colored show from Harlem.

Edinburgh, September 18, 1934

I been coming over since 1906 when I first worked on the stage in London and do you know I had never been to Scotland before and I want to apologize for being so dumb. It sho is pretty.

You got these Scotchmen wrong. Why they are the most liberal and hospitable people you ever saw. Course I have to carry an interpreter to tell me what they say, but they are awfully friendly.

Grouse is Scotland's principal export. You got to rent a castle, then rent some drivers to drive the grouse by the castle. Then the grouse been shot at so much they know just about who can hit 'em and who can't. It's a racket and the grouse and the Scotchmen work together and the Americans and the Englishmen pay the bill.

September 19, 1934 [A Simulated Long Distance Telephone Call from London]

Hello . . . Hello . . . Is that you America? Who is this on the line? Well, it don't sound like America. Your voice don't sound natural. You sound sad.

Who is this I am talking to anyhow in America? Oh, it's Mr. A., one of the fellows with money. I thought it was somebody that was awful blue and dejected.

This is Will over in London. Will . . . the prodigal son. It's two-fifteen in the morning here and I just couldn't sleep. I got to thinking about how you all was at home and got up and put in this call for you. You see, I got nothing but the worst news about you all everywhere I been. There ain't but one thing that seems to worry everybody and that was they was afraid America *would* come back.

Oh, things are terrible, are they?

Well, quit crying, Mr. Man-with-money, and I can hear you better. Yes, I know Sinclair was nominated. I heard that in Siberia . . . Siberia, that's the place where they send the rich

people to in Russia. Yes, I know we send 'em to the Senate. It's
about the same.

Do you live in California? Oh, you don't. Well, don't take it
too hard. I live there. Wait a minute while I cry.

I wouldn't worry so about it. No elected man is ever as good or
as bad as we think he will be.

And the market's gone to . . . What? Spell it. H as in Huey,
the third letter in Huey, L as in Long and another L as in Long.
But there is only one L in Long. Oh, I haven't seen him lately?

So the market's gone? And the country's gone to the dogs?
Well, do the 119 million people that don't buy or sell stocks, do
they know about the country going to the dogs? Well, if I was
you I would tell 'em.

Do you know what the old stock exchange in Leningrad is
now? The building is a rest room. No, not a pest room. You
are thinking of ours. Theirs is a rest room.

How about the A.L.L. — The American Liberty League? There
was headlines in Russia about that. It said the capitalists were
forming a League to give 'em liberty. Oh, it's blowed up already,
has it?

Well, what are you rich fellows kicking about anyhow? Oh,
you got nowhere to invest your money? That's what you are
crying about? So the principal problem in America is, "What can
I do with my money?"

Well, that is unique among world problems. I have been in
many a country since I left home and they have thousands of
problems. But America's problem as to "where to invest my
money?" is unique. The whole world would give their right leg
to be bothered with that problem.

Well, I wouldn't take it so hard, Mr. Man-with-Money. Maby
the President will figure out a way for you to invest some of it.

Wait a minute. I can't stand this wailing. Put me on somebody
else over there will you, Operator, just some old ordinary fellow
that's around there with or without a job. Are you a man without
money? Well, this is Will, everybody over here is afraid America
might come back. Now just how bad are we off anyhow?

Not so bad? You mean we are getting along pretty good? Well, by golly, what do you know about that? I just talked to a rich fellow over there and he said things were terrible.

Say, by the way, just look for some fellow that's crying and ask him if he knows what England's income tax rate is? It's the highest there is and they are the first country to recover.

They are the ones that used to give the dole to the unemployed and we said England was ruined forever. And we said that was the end of her. Well, she is sitting on top of the world now.

But here is something you want to remember. All her "big" men had confidence in her all the time. They bet on England to win. Over home they are betting on us to lose.

SS Ile de France, *September 23, 1934*

You know the American business man or traveler from home is a queer duck. All over Europe and a couple of days ago on the boat: "I tell you I am afraid of things at home. It don't look good to me." Well, for the last couple of days the market has picked up and today's news said the strikers went back to work. Now they are returning around the boat grinning like a possum.

Imagine people who's whole idea of our country is gained from what it does every day in a stock market!

Hempstead, New York, *September 26, 1934*

Boy it's great to get back into a country where something happens. Talk about Japan, Russia and Europe, why even a society reporter could cover their news.

With us something is cracking every minute. Hugh Johnson's retirement, why that's like Hitler stepping out. Hugh had never put any men to death, but he has certainly scared some of our biggest industrialists half to death. He has cussed 'em all collectively and individually.

You told many big guy the truth that had never been told before. Good luck to you, Hugh.

Washington, *September 27, 1934*

Flew in here this afternoon. Lobby of Hotel full of badges and found out it's the Police Chiefs from everywhere. Getting their code.

The President by tomorrow is picking five men to replace Johnson and run the N.R.A. I think that's what these police chiefs are all doing here. They are going to help him arrest the man that he appoints, for nobody would take a job like that voluntarily.

Washington, September 28, 1934

Just been helping on a new N.R.A. board. Mr. Richberg is the head of it. Three executives and two college professors take Hugh Johnson's place, in addition to an "Exec" Committee composed of the Cabinet and the President himself.

October 7, 1934 [Gulf Oil Broadcast]

Lord, it's good to get back. As I look out into this sea of intelligent faces — well I may be wrong about that, but they are honest faces anyhow, most of 'em — well, I been around the world since I saw you last.

I attended the Writer's Congress in Moscow, and they never did find out I was there. They don't recognize you unless you are a Bolsheviki writer. They hold this Soviet Writer's Convention, and the question is, "What will we hand the folks this year?"

They have only got one line to hand 'em, and it takes a pretty smooth writer to juggle that around and make it look new.

You talk about everybody being equal. There is a guy over there named Maxim Gorky that has sold 19 million books in the last five years. His income last year they said was seven million rubles. Then they say in a communistic country everybody shares alike. That guy has made all of that just writing about how terrible you rich are. Certainly taught me a lesson. I am going to open up and start telling what I know about you all. Maby I can jump my sales up. Trouble with me I have been lenient with you folks.

Yes, sir, the writers are the aristocracy over there. They waited outside the Congress Hall where they met, like they would in America to see Shirley Temple. Gorky is bigger in Russia than

Snozzle Durante is here. And he has got every cent of it out of panning the rich. I am working on a novel now called, "They Ought to be Ashamed of Themselves, or Ain't the rich got a heart?" Now you talk about funny looking guys, you should see the Communist writers that attend one of those Conferences. They come from all those countries over there. You know any group of writers are funny looking. But a Boushwa writer don't start in with a proletariat writer. One old big fat guy there with an Alpine suit on, feather in hat, bare knees, they said was a great communistic poet. I could just see him up in the Alps yodeling a "Brother Share with me" roundelay.

They was the only ones I saw with whiskers. They allowed em to keep 'em for a mosquito hedge.

About the way the Russians looked at you. They don't envy you. Well of course they wouldn't ever envy the way I dress, but Mrs. Rogers was kinder the Mae West of Siberia. But it didn't mean a thing to them. She just as well been Polly Moran.

They just look at you and say, "Capitalist, you made it out of somebody's else's labor." I wanted to tell, "Wait a minute, Brother, I am a real Bolsheviki. I made mine by telling jokes. I never had a nickle I didn't tell a gag for. So I ought to be one of you boys. I gotta ranch and a farm, but honest its never paid. I wish you Bolshevicks would take it over and run it."

Their marriage and divorce laws are patterned exactly after Hollywood and Park Avenue. Only they eliminate the lawyer. So it gives the poor a chance to get a divorce that over here would only be obtainable by the rich. We visited the marriage and divorce place. A guy walked in with a brief case. Sit down for a couple of minutes and signed his name and went out. I asked the Russian girl guide with us, what he was doing and she said he was getting divorced and was evidently on his way to work. I says, "Does the wife know this?" She says, "Well she will probably find it out when she receives a card informing her of the fact." On marriage you both got to be there and register. They can't mail you a card and tell you that you are married to Alexandrovich Slovolsky. They will have that soon however, for its an awful lot of trouble to have you drag your wife along when you are marrying. It's better to drop some beautiful girl a card and tell 'em you have married them. It's not like over home in one respect. You can't work that divorce and marriage too often. They look up your record and say, "Wait a minute. You gone far enough around this town. We got a lot of other men want to marry. You are not going to do all of it. This is a communist country and every man is supposed to have his share. You can't buy all the tickets to this lottery. You go back home and see if you can't hang onto the old wife. Otherwise you are going to be wifeless around here."

The main thing they marry a girl for in Russia is to get a room. In America it's no trouble for 'em to marry if they got a job. But rooms are the scarcest things there are in Russia. A fellow with a room to himself is the local young Astor. Rooms are divided off in square feet or meters. Your room might consist of six square feet in the corner of a room where there was three or four other families.

A wall in Russia is not necessarily a wooden partition. It's more apt to be a sheet hanging up.

They are building thousands of apartment houses for the people. They are four, five and six stories high. Yet I never saw a fire escape in Russia. I asked 'em how they was going to get down, and they said, they never thought of that. No elevators either in the apartment houses. They are just plain old long ugly buildings, all alike, no sign of a decoration. Looks like they are constructed pretty cheaply. Well they are in such a hurry to get 'em up and care for the people, that they just throw 'em together the best they can.

Moscow is a city now of over three and a half million and no one knows what it will be for they are flocking in there by the thousands. Russians are great people to be traveling some place. You see that is one of the things that looks to me like it mitigates against the system. No one owns their home, no one has a single thing to tie them down. If they hear of some other place where the feed is better, off they go, and the railroads stations are just literally packed with people with sacks and bags and children trying to get to some other place. Some of them wait at stations for days trying to get trains. They have no idea when there will be room for them on any train.

Los Angeles, October 14, 1934 [*Gulf Oil Broadcast*]

There is nothing new about Russia. Everybody has been there this summer. Russia is a country that you can answer anybody's question just like they want it to be answered. Do you want to hear that it's terrible? Well it is. Do you want to hear that they are all working and making some sort of living? Well they are. Do you want to hear that it may exist? Well it may. Do you want to hear that it won't? Well maby it won't. You can get any kind of answer in Russia that you want to.

The last time I was there I come home and wrote a little book about it, called "There is Not a Bathing Suit in Russia." Well that started a flow of tourists there. And what do you think those cuckoo Russians did? They got on suits now. Why when I was there and wrote that book I was the only tourist there. They do everything cockeyed.

Russia's a country that used to have three principal products, well, in fact, four. They had dukes, grand dukes, princesses and whiskers. Well, the Revolution has stamped out the dukes, and the grander they were the quicker it stamped them out. And the princesses — they all come to America to lecture. And the International Harvesting Company has mowed down the whiskers. There ain't a grand duke or a whisker in Russia. That's no kidding. Nobody's got any whiskers. There's one mustache and that belongs to Stalin. Of course, him being the Dictator he's allowed certain extensive privileges, and he runs the country.

There's been nothing comparable in all history to this man Stalin's power — up to the time Huey Long took over Louisiana. And Huey is a clean-shaven man. Boy, if Huey had a mustache he'd annex Mississippi.

Now to get any kind of idea of Russia, everything in the world we do, every viewpoint we have, every matter of fact way of looking at anything is entirely different in Russia. I was surprised they didn't walk on their hands instead of their feet, just to be different from capitalistic nations.

In the first place, the government owns everything. Well, that ain't so different than it is over here. The banks own it over here. Went to a race meeting one day. All the race horses belong to the government. The government pays the jockeys, the government runs the mutuel betting. Any time the government needs a little extra money, all they have to do is say, "Comrade, for the good of the Soviet Bolshevik system, you'd better pull that old hound you're on there and run about third. And if you don't, your next race is liable to be ridden in Siberia."

Now that may be exaggerated a bit, but it would be possible. They own the opera, they own all the shows, the actors and singers all work for the government. It owns all the making of the movies. I saw several new ones they'd made that hadn't been released. And they're all made in Russia, and they're all on propaganda.

The hotels are very good. The hotel in Moscow is good. Most of them are hangovers from the old Czarists days. But Moscow is building a thousand room new hotel there now.

Every sixth day in Russia is called the day of rest. They work five days — eight hours a day — and then rest on the sixth day. They observe no Sundays at all.

Well, you have to work in Russia or you don't eat. For when you go to buy your food you have to have a card. That shows where you work and all.

Now the main question everybody asks me is — are they happy? That's a tough one to answer. There are millions of people in Russia, I couldn't talk their language, so I couldn't ask them, are you happy? It's awful hard to look at a person and tell just how happy they are. Some of you look awful curious to me. Now we looked at 'em for eight days at hundreds of stations crossing the Trans-Siberian railway. We'd see the people come down to the trains and just stand there. They'd just be standing at the station with a dull, blank expression on their faces — no joy, no smile. They just looked like they didn't know what the future held in store for 'em. But I've sit in the gallery of the Senate, and in the gallery of the House of Representatives in Washington and I've seen the same dull, blank expression. I've seen that same blank, dull expression not knowing what the next election held in store for them.

Then, too, it's not just what you'd call a good year for happiness in any part of the world, anyhow. It's what you might call an off year for happiness. And then, too, here's what everybody tells me, the Russians are naturally a sad people. That they don't feel good until something's really the matter with them. In other words a Russian ain't happy till he's hurt. He thrives on pain.

So to answer the question "is Russia happy?" I should answer, yes, for they've certainly got enough the matter with them to make them happy.

Well, Russians I don't think would ever be as happy as we are anyhow, for they haven't got as much to laugh at as we have here. Perhaps we're not the most humorous people in the world, but the provocations to humor is greater in this country than anywhere else in the world. There's not a minute that there's not some of us doing something seriously that brings smiles to everybody else over here.

I'm only glad that some Russian didn't rush up to me and ask, Is America happy? I'd have to say, yes, and no. The fellow that's broke is happy, but the men that's got the money is mighty sad over here. He's unhappy here, brother. If you want to find the unhappy ones, it's the guy with the dough now.

Beverly Hills, October 18, 1934

There must not be such a thing in this country as what you would call an "amateur crook." Every person that is caught in some terrible crime, you find where he has been "paroled, pardoned, and pampered," by every jail, or insane asylum in the country. Some of these criminals' records and the places they have been freed from, it sounds like the tour of a "one night theatrical troop." It must be awfully monotinous belonging to one of these state pardon boards. There is days and days when they just have to sit around waiting for new criminals to be caught, so they can pardon 'em.

Sonora, California, October 24, 1934

Tonight Mr. Roosevelt is to speak to the bankers. That shows a mighty broad-minded spirit on his part, for there has been times that we all thought he never would speak to 'em again. I hope he treats with mercy and "don't shoot for the poor devils are licked."

Angel's Camp, California, October 25, 1934

This is in Angel's Camp, that original home of Mark Twain's high leaping frog.

Every old gold town that you have read about in Twain's or Bret Harte's stories is right around in this country. The adventure and romance of half a continent is in these very hills. Good roads, good hotels and great people and history to burn, so come in and see 'em mining gold on these original grounds and with descendants of the original cast.

P.S. Read President's speech. The bankers are still in the doghouse.

Sonora, California, October 26, 1934

The bankers finally made up with Mr. Roosevelt when they give up hope of him making up with them. They thanked him for coming over and doing an act for 'em at their banquet.

Beverly Hills, October 29, 1934

Well, sir, there was an awful heart-rendering little item of news in the papers this morning. It's just as well you maby didn't see it. The New York Stock Exchange lost $287,986 last year, according to their own press sheet. They state that it's the first time in the history of the "racket" that they have ever published their winnings or losings (well, in fact they haven't printed any of their winnings yet). But it's encouraging to the bread lines to have such a prominent new member join 'em.

Beverly Hills, November 14, 1934

Well we was just feeling fine, and we thought we had listened to our last campaign speech out here for two more years when who comes in here for a barnstorming tour but John J. Rascob, Irenne Du pont, and Edward F. Hutton, three hundred million dollars worth of talent. They got a plan called (no, not Epic) "Liberty

League. They feel that under the New Deal, that the U.S. Constitution is the "Forgotten Man." So they are doing a modern Paul Revere, and are going down the valleys in three private railway cars arousing the people. "Block that kick! Block that kick! The Democrats are kicking our constitution around." They are all three mighty fine estimable men, and if they happen to play your town, get all the bigwigs out. They are darn nice fellows and got the best show on the road this season.

November 18, 1934

With all the "haywire" ideas we have, ever once in a while we hit on a good one, like old age pensions, which is sure to come at the next Congress.

Beverly Hills, November 25, 1934

Just sitting here reading in all parts of the papers where "So and So" "Appealed to the President." Is there nothing that anybody in our country can do themselves anymore? If a strike is on, if a strike is even threatened, away goes the "appeal to the President." The American Chamber of Commerce sends about three appeals a week. "Can you guarantee our members so and so?"

We have a hard time finding good stories in the movies. I suppose we ought to "appeal to the President." And the Movie Companies ought to appeal to him for a guarantee as to what conditions will be by the time the picture is out. If you must appeal to somebody, appeal to the Supreme Court.

Beverly Hills, November 28, 1934

Thanksgiving Day. In the days of its founders, they were willing to give thanks for mighty little (for mighty little was all they expected), but now neither Government or nature can give enough but what we think it's too little.

Those old boys in the Fall of the year, if they could gather in a few pumpkins, potatoes and some corn for the winter, they was in a thanking mood.

But if we can't gather in a new Buick, a new radio, a tuxedo, and some Government relief, why we feel like the world is agin us.

[The Republicans who all during the year had confidently and hopefully predicted that the Roosevelt "honeymoon" was over had found out at the off-year election that the opposite was true. In his radio broadcast of November 28, 1934, Will made his famous speech in which he preached a "funeral" sermon on the demise of the party. "A friend passed away," he said, "and when you have heard of somebody since childhood, and then as you grew up and met him, and become to know him, and to like him, and to see him almost become a tradition, then see him pass right when it should have been the useful years of his life, well I don't know, it kinder gets you."

Will went on to state that "he had been ill but he was feeling more hopeful, but Tuesday morning, three weeks ago, about seven he started having acute pains, and as the day went on they got worse. By nightfall, just as the sun was setting, he breathed his last. This gallant old figure that had been loved by many, feared by many, had gone to where there is no returning. All that was mortal of The Republican Party had left this earth, had passed away because he wanted to live like a pioneer. He couldn't change with modern civilization."

And, as Will pointed out, it came just when he was at the height of his career, just when things looked the brightest for him, just when he was bragging on being, "Oh, so rugged." He had been warned but "not by any of his own doctors, or close friends" but by outsiders that "he was living too high." But he scoffed at them. "What do they know about me, and my health? They are just jealous of my ruddy condition. They can't match my power and they are envious. Why I will keep on living like this forever. I have solved the problem of power. It's mass energy. It's power everlasting, and we have solved it."

And then came the dawn.]

But you must give the old boy credit. When the blow hit him on that bright shiny October day of 1929, with no climatic warning, he lived up to all political tradition. What did he do? He said it wasn't his fault, and it wasn't his fault. It was everybody's fault. It was your fault, it was my fault, it was the Lord's fault. He just stepped in and said, "Wait a minute. How long has this been going on? This living on a dog eat dog basis. We will stop this thing right now and give you folks a chance to reorganize and redeem yourselves."

Now here is where the mistake was made. Had the Republicans held a clinic at that very moment and decided, "Boys, our patient is sick. He has got acute appendicitis. Now of course an operation is going to cost us all something. We are all going to have to chip in. It will take part of what we have, but it may save us in the long run. There is a change coming in our lives and we can't do the things we have always done. We can no more ask for the same conditions to continue than we can to ask for our youth to continue."

Now had that been done this obituary notice that was posted on every crossroad last Tuesday night might not have happened. But instead they decided at the clinic that it wasn't really appendicitis, that it was cramp colic, and that a strong healthy man like he was could throw it off. That he had always been healthy, and there was no reason he should be sick. And the only thing to do was just to let Nature take it's course, that they had always come out of the cramp colics without having to give up anything, and there was no reason why this one should be different. That was, as I say, from October 1929 to November 4, 1932.

On November 3, 1932 "nature took its course again." The patient had another stroke. They still said they wouldn't have to operate. They rushed with the ice bags again. But not with the knife. They still contended that they were right and the disease was wrong. Well, in an argument with a disease, be it physical or economic, you better at least let it have a hearing.

But in spite of his pain, in spite of his groans, his doctors, and his whole family maintained that he was "fundamentally sound," that he had never been operated on in his life, and had lived this long, and that they could see no reason to think that his same life's program and schedule should not go on as it always had.

So he had his third and last stroke last Tuesday, and he went to his maker, a physical wreck — but "fundamentally sound," and on his tombstone it says, "Here lies a rugged indivdual, but he wasn't rugged enough to compete with a Democrat."

Now we come to that great question of reincarnation — Does the soul return in another body? I believe it will. I don't know what animal he will come back in, it won't be as big as an elephant, it will be something with much more humility, it will be a very domestic animal, an animal more in the nature of a dog. It will have faith, it's whole soul will be consecrated to service.

And will this animal be needed?

He certainly will, for the Democrats by that time will have passed out through too much power. The Democrats could never stand power as long as the Republicans did. They are not used to it. They are getting "cocky" already and they only been in overnight. So the Republicans being the first to die, will be the first to come back. So let's say a good word for the deceased, and ask him to be ready to move over in his grave. The Democrats will be crawling in there with him pretty soon.

Beverly Hills, November 30, 1934

I once heard Lady Astor say, "Only two things get the House of Lords excited, a tax on liquor, and a tax on landed estates, then the old Lords really come to life."

Well about the only time you can get our "Big Houses of Finance" interested is to start talking about cutting that dollar up into little ones. The big fellows say, "Mr. Roosevelt, we think you mean well, but your ideas are wrong. We are not going to play with you."

He can say, "I am sorry, Gentlemen. Love to have you with me. In fact I think you are still playing with me. It's a game called heavy, heavy, hangs over your head, and it's not the axe. It's just a printing press which stops all government interest. Don't slam the door as you go out."

Beverly Hills, December 6, 1934

The investigation season opened earlier than usual this season. The "ammunition" investigating Committee had an awful exciting session yesterday. That Committee has got a job for life. The ammunition concerns sell it faster than the Committee can investigate it.

No nation will buy anything to eat, or anything to wear from you, but if you got a gun they will buy it, and more than likely shoot it back at you.

Looks to me like if every nation made their own ammunitions it would relieve their unemployment. Well there ain't no use arguing about it, nothing is going to be stopped anywhere that there is any money in.

Hollywood, December 10, 1934

One of New York's very very leading bankers was visiting our studio (and, incidentally, his studio) and he accused me of being an inflationist. I told him I wasn't an inflationist, that to be honest with him I didn't know anything about it. But that the thing that I felt was that if industrialists and business men didn't start investing, and helping the President, and not keep hollering for a guarantee of the value of their money, they would force the President to do the very thing that they kept hollering and asking him not to do.

This fellow had an economist with him. Pretty near everybody's got one, either that or a police dog, and the more wealthy have got both.

Beverly Hills, December 20, 1934

See where the doctors say, "President Roosevelt is in great physical shape and ready to face Congress on January third."

Well that being the case from one training camp, I would like to report from the other training camp. I have examined Congress and they are in great shape physically (I said physically). Mentally the boys are befuddled, but they are in the "pink." (That's what the fellows with the dough are afraid of, there is too many of 'em in the "pink".)

Remember the date, and tune in on the biggest show on earth, bar none.

Pasadena, December 25, 1934

Beautiful afternoon, marvelous race track, magnificent, staunch and sleepy old mountains in the background.

Some of the coyotes that I was persuaded to make a small wager on are as staunch and sleepy as the mountains.

Actors and actresses are thick here today, but they just as well be bankers as far as being noticed. Female screen stars are just some more women. Madam and Senor horse is king. Hollywood just as well be Skiatook, Oklahoma. The curry comb has replaced the lip rouge. Even Garbo would have to ride "Twenty Grand" to get a look in. It's the old oat eater's day and suckers. And it's proof positive that there is plenty of money to feed and clothe everybody.

It's only a rumor that everybody has been taxed to death.

CHAPTER THIRTEEN

"Sic 'em, Tige. Sic 'em"

January 6, 1935 [Gulf Oil Broadcast]

Mr. Roosevelt delivered his message the other day and he says, "The plan which I propose is going to take years. We're going to spend lots of money . . . "

The Republicans groaned. You know what I mean. "My Lord, is the guy going to stay in that long." Well, that wasn't very encouraging to them.

The Republicans — they have been accused of not having a plan — issued a plan, a twenty point plan. They've been accused of just denouncing. They meet and denounce and never suggest anything — just denounce. And they sometimes denounced when they didn't meet. In this twenty point plan they settled everything. The soldier's bonus is one of the biggest things coming before Congress and they — the Republicans — settled that right off. They didn't straddle it. No maby, or we propose to pay the soldiers, or we'll do this or that. They just come right out and said, "We favor being liberal with the soldiers." They didn't say how liberal. Get 'em another war or something, you know. Well, that was lovely.

Santa Monica, January 10, 1935

Dispatch in paper today, "Ford employs ten thousand more men, highest since the peak of 1929." And the auto show here and in N.Y. was booming. Now how does it come that auto industry don't just sit still and holler. "We could recover if the government would just lay off us awhile." No industry is restricted and taxed more than autos, so the government certainly ain't "laying off them."

January 9, 1935

Never a time in our lifetimes was money as scared as it is now. Even during the war when folks were asked to shovel it out they didn't hesitate, but then they felt that they were able to keep on making it. But now there is a doubt, and they want to hang onto it as long as they can.

We are getting two fairly well-defined schools of thought on what is one's obligation to another. Mr. Roosevelt has a very liberal idea on the subject. He thinks that there has to be a more generous feeling toward those who are in need, and if it can't be arrived at by persuasion, he will arrange some other way of making each meet their share. He has done a lot in his attitude to offset a Communistic feeling, for if he did happen to lean to the more conservative element, there would be some justification of hollering for a more equal division. But with his doing all he can, and still keeping within the bounds of fairness to all, why he offsets the old Red.

It's going to be an interesting session of Congress. The question will be who is going to break over the traces. The Republicans are naturally going to dig in, and do all they can to save their old principles and theorys. Then there will be the plum locoed ones among the Democrats who will claim that Roosevelt has gone too far to the right. There will be a dozen factions, and there will be things where enough of 'em can unite to offset any of the President's plans. He is not going to have any cinch. There is three or four hundred Democrats in there but there is two or three hundred kinds of 'em.

I am hoping to get back and see some of the games. I love to sit up there in that old Senate Gallery and watch 'em down there on that ten yard line fighting to hold those seats.

Well we are living in a great age, ain't we? I think we are in for quite a few changes. I think you will see lots of folks offering to play ball and glad of it, that now think it's their ball, so why should they have to furnish it?

January 5, 1935

Well Christmas has passed. I was just thinking if there was some way to make the Christmas spirit continue during the other days of the year, why we would be the most happy and wonderful Nation on Earth. Gosh, if all of us that was able would just feed and do things for folks without waiting till Christmas. I think we mean well, but we just sorter got in our heads that about one day a year pays our obligations off, then we swell up and hide our Conscience till the next gift day.

With all of our fact finding departments in our Government, and all our statistics gatherers, I believe you could increase generosity 100 to 1000 fold if there was some way of finding out just exactly the people that were in actual need.

You know that Conscience thing, it's one of the most individual things we have. It's not like human nature where they say "It's all the same." We got some mighty fine Consciences in this Country. They prompt the owners and the owner acts. Then we got some other Consciences. While they are supposed to be Consciences, they are almost invisible. They may urge their owners, but they don't seem to have any authority. So it's those Consciences that need to be helped.

Our Civilization is not so hot. Poor Mr. Roosevelt has tried to right some of it. He couldn't do it by persuasion, and he can't do it by law, so he may just have to give it up and say, Boys I have tried to bring a little social justice to you all, but even the Constitution is against me, so back to the old times, "sic 'em, Tige."

Memphis, February 4, 1935

Law is complications, and complications are law, if everything was just plain, there wouldn't be any lawyers.

Beverly Hills, February 7, 1935

There is a lot to be said for, and against the recognition of Russia, but I never talked to a well-informed man in the Far East who didn't tell me that it absolutely prevented a Russia-Japanese war.

Santa Monica, February 10, 1935

These old boys that's claimed they been dead and then come back to life, they seem to be getting all the play in the papers. The fellow in England claimed he got to Heaven and that it was great, and he is sorry they revived him. Well it's not much trouble to get dead again, a little street crossing without being alert will do the job.

Then we got an old boy out here in Hollywood that claimed he was dead for 22 minutes, and he says he was glad to get back alive again. Sounds like a Chamber of Commerce ad for Hollywood to me. Course, coming from where he does, he might have got in the wrong place. That's very probable. Anyhow they both lying, but it helps kill time till the Supreme Court acts.

Chicago, February 19, 1935

The Supreme Court, by a 5 to 4 decision, upheld the New Deal laws regarding the cutting of the gold content in the dollar.

Papers full of the gold decision. Folks couldn't be more excited if they had had any gold. Quite a few of the editorials have shown what the court ought to have done.

I have told a lot of alleged little jokes about the court splitting 5 to 4 on everything including the weather. So I have been vindicated in this decision. But regardless of that, I think they are a mighty trusty pillar for our country to lean on. But I do think there was just a slight warning in that decision to the Democrats to not try any more monkey business.

Beverly Hills, March 7, 1935

It's the usual custom for a writer or speaker to tell how much better England or France or Zululand, have handled their money than the U.S. Well in today's paper France is prohibiting the shipment of gold out of their country, and still they say they are not going off the gold, no but they are not letting the gold go off them either, then last week England had to put up millions of pounds to stabilize their money. So I guess over there they are pointing to the excellent way our system is working. Your own country always looks like they are the only one doing the wrong thing.

Beverly Hills, March 19, 1935

It ought to feel awful good to us, (even as bad off as we think we are) to be away off over here and not have to send a protest because Germany has decided to put on some extra help.

Those nations over there just get up every morning and start writing protests. If Mussolini ain't deviling the life out of 'em why Hitler is, whether you got a man in the army before the war starts or after it starts don't make much difference. He is going to be in there if it does start anyhow.

The trouble with the Versailles Peace Treaty is that the men that made it are dead, and the ones living say, "we didn't sign that mortgage." So it looks like our worries are mostly all tax worries.

March 31, 1935 [Gulf Oil Broadcast]

Excuse me for keeping my hat on, but I'm getting just a little gray, and I don't want it to show over the radio. Just one or two hairs in there that got mixed in.

Well, sir, I've been off the air for about seven weeks. I went off purposely to see if I couldn't give the country a chance to pick up a little, but it doesn't take much looking to see that it ain't done much since I've been gone. So I decided to come back on again, and see if I can't get it started up again.

Not only has the whole civilized world degenerated but also the Democratic Party.

When I had my head turned and wasn't looking on the radio Hitler broke out on me. I thought I had him covered. He tore up the Versailles treaty. It wasn't a good treaty, but it was the only one they had. They was years making it and he tore it up in about a minute.

That was last week. England sent its delegation over to talk with Mr. Hitler, and see if they couldn't get some other understanding with him. But England didn't get to say a word. Hitler talked all day and England didn't know any more when they went home than they did when they got there.

Another man named Eden has gone to talk to Russia. Then
France is going to talk to Russia. No nation likes Russia, and
they don't like Communism and all that, but they would use them
in case of war coming around.

That's one good thing about European nations. They can't
hate you so badly they wouldn't use you. Well, they're up there
and they've told Russia, "Now, you're Communistic, and you
believe in dividing up everything. Now ordinarily, we don't believe in it. But it looks like we're going to have a war over here
and we would like to split it with you boys." So they're going to
let Russia in on a good thing in case it shows up.

Well now they'll be coming over here pretty soon. You see,
they're rushing around now trying to sign up. Just like a baseball team, you know. They don't know who's going to be part-
ners in the next one, so everybody's rushing around to get some
new signatures on the thing. They're rushing around and saying,
"Who'll help out?" And they'll be coming over here with a propaganda pretty soon. There'll be delegations come and say, "We
didn't come to persuade you, or anything, but in case civilization
is attacked, why, where do you boys stand?"

Well, we better say, "If civilization hasn't done any more than
it has since the last war, why we're agin it." So we'll just stay with
the side that's against civilization.

Mussolini — I hadn't more than turned my head than he
jumped on Ethiopia. Seems that the allies right along during
the Versailles conference said, "Now Italy, don't you claim nothing, and then if you ever want anything in Africa our heads will
be turned." So he remembered that.

I don't believe I'm betraying any confidence when I tell you
that Senator Nye told me that they're going to introduce a new
bill that will take the profits out of war. And he assured me that
they was getting it ready, and that they were going to have it
ready in a few days. And, so he said, they're gonna put in a bill
where in case there is a war nobody will be allowed to make any
profits from it. And I think that's a great idea, and know everybody does. I think it would be still a better idea and would keep
us out of a lot of wars if they put in the bill there that not only
couldn't we make any out of our own wars, but we couldn't make

any out of anybody's wars. If we knew we couldn't sell anything
to any other nation while they was at war, we'd never get in it.
That's just a little idea of mine. That ain't in the bill. Too
much sense to that to ever get in the bill.

Somebody asked me, "Will, how long is this going on — this
spending all this money and everything?" I said, "Well, it will go
on just as long as the Republicans has got any money. That's all
I know about it."

Santa Monica, April 3, 1935

Talking to a cattle man in Claremore yesterday, he had just
shipped a bunch of steers to Kansas City and netted 128 dollars
a head, three months ago he tried to sell 'em for 30 dollars, these
just show you how quick your business can change. Now a sheep
man wires me that mutton hasn't gone up, now I don't want to be
caught helping out a sheep man, but it sounded like he may be
right.

April 7, 1935

Legislatures are kinder like animals in a zoo. You can't do anything about 'em. All you can do is just stand and watch 'em.

But man is still the main animal. You put a bunch of 'em in
the legislature and he can think of more funny tricks to do than
the same amount of monkeys in a cage will. He is still preeminent.
We cuss the lawmakers, but I notice we are always perfectly willing to share in any of these vast sums of money that they spend.
We say it's wrong, and unsound but we dont refuse to take it. We
say the government is nutty and throwing away money, but anytime any is thrown our way we have never dodged it. The general contention is that nobody is spending any money but the
government. Well, an awful lot of businesses are doing better
than they have for the last three or four years, newspaper advertising has leaped, subscriptions have gone up. Yet the editorials
all say Roosevelt is a — DUD. That the thing can't go on, that
the government is spending all the money. But they are doing
better than they have in years on the Government money. It
shows the absolute honesty of the press. It shows that the edi-

torial policy of the papers are not influenced by the man who is responsible for bringing 'em in all the business!

You know you figure it out and it's a peculiar state of affairs. Everybody that is doing better or making money has got it in for Roosevelt. But they don't seem to realize that they are doing better on the money that Roosevelt is spending.

[Will went on to say that all of us knew that the government was spending too much money but when no one else was doing any thing about it, what could be done? "Course one remedy would be for the people that have money to start spending it instead of the government. But that seems to be just about as unpopular as the Roosevelt idea. In fact worse."

Will then said that if a law was passed stopping the government from spending but forcing those that had the money to spend it, then a real scream and wail would go up. "Well, if the government is throwing this money away," he said, since the other method was out, "the only thing I see is for the ones that they are throwing it to (outside of those that absolutely need it) why have them refuse to take it. Just say, 'No, it's government money and it's tainted, and I don't believe in the government spending all this money and hence I don't take any part of it."

Will then went on and gave examples of how this would work. A man would come into a bank to pay a note with government money and the banker would say, "No, that is government money. I'll just carry the loan myself." Or a picture show operator would, if it was government money, just let the man with it in free.] He then said:

But you haven't heard that, have you? There is not a person in America that has received a dollar no matter where it come from that hasn't grabbed it. It might have been paid out to relieve a starving child. But if it reached us we were the starving child. So the only thing I see is for the fellow that don't believe in all this spending, is to not participate in the receiving of any of it.

I can't very well legitimately criticise a fellow for spending money, if I receive some of it without any criticism at all. So this five billion dollars that they are starting in to spend, we all know that that's too much money to just take and give away, but until we refuse some of it that comes our way, we haven't got much right to holler.

Now that brings us to the taxes — oh, boy — where is all the money coming from that the government is throwing away? Well, it just sorter looks like it might come from the ones that have got it. There is one good thing about our American form of government — the fellow that's got nothing pays nothing, and too lots of times the fellow has got something, but nothing to pay with. Well, he can at least let 'em have the property and break even. But the big yell comes nowadays from the taxpayers. I guess when the pilgrims landed on Plymouth Rock, and they had the whole of the American continent, and all they had to do to get an extra 160 acres was to shoot another Indian, I bet you anything they kicked on the price of the ammunition. I bet they said, "What's this country coming to that we have to spend a nickle for powder." Of course they got the lead back after they dissected the Indian. No matter what you pay for taxes, high or low, medium, the yell is always the same, 100 percent.

Course we know our government is costing us more than its worth. But do you know of anybody that has a cheaper one? You can try Russia — there is no income tax there but there is no income. Hitler hasn't got a sales tax but he is not selling anything. There is no poll tax in Italy, in order to vote, but there is no vote. So it just looks like we can't have everything like we want to.

Now the whole question is, how can we make such a holler on what the government wants to collect back from us, when they are the ones that paid it to us (admitting, as everyone seems to do, that they are the only ones that are spending anything). It looks like an endless chain to me. Only when it reaches our link, we don't want to cut any back into the kitty.

April 15, 1935

We can talk all the politics we want, but business rises above politics in this Country. The South has gone Republican, and the North has gone Democratic. Why? Both have done it because it looked like there was money in it.

Let Roosevelt start showing some results with this new money, and it will have a lot of outside dough join it.

There is not a Country in the World that can change our outlook as quick as we can. Just a dollar in our pocket makes a different man out of us.

So let's don't put thumbs down on this thing till we see, and the minute any of that dough commences reaching us, we are going to think it's a pretty good plan.

Beverly Hills, April 16, 1935

Got a wire today from an old boy in Parsons Kansas, and he wanted me to enter in a hog calling contest, you know I used to be an awful good hog caller when hogs were cheap, but the way hogs have gone up in price it's changed the whole system of calling 'em. It would take Henry Ford hollering with his check book to get one to come to you nowadays. I hollered all morning just for three slices of bacon and it didn't come, so there ain't much use of me howling my head off to try and get a whole hog to come.

Beverly Hills, April 23, 1935

Here is the latest racket if you are so rich you don't know what to do with your money. They are putting it in annuities in England, they feel it's safer there.

Then they wonder how it is that England recovers, it recovers because you couldn't in a hundred years get an Englishman to do what these folks here are doing. England will bet you on England to their last penny. In England they invest most of their money in income tax, read what their rate is.

With this money invested over there it's not hard to see where all the influence comes from to get us to keep joining something over there.

[In his Gulf Oil Broadcast for April 21, 1935, Will suggested, in lieu of the Republican plan ("Now, boys, my head is turned, just get it while you can") and the Democratic scheme (Now Mr. Roosevelt, he dragged more he-school names out of little red school houses, and they had more plans than they had shirts) , the

Rogers plan. "Now, my plan is a plan to end all plans. This country has been planned to death, the same as it was sloganed to death during the war." He summarized it up]:

Now the Republicans have a plan. Their plan is to do nothing and then Roosevelt can't either. The Democrats have got a plan — well, they got millions of them. Couldn't hardly mention all of theirs, but the Democrat's plan is "hold the postoffices, boys. They shall not pass."

Now big business — we're always hearing about big business — big business has got a plan. Their's they talked with Mr. Roosevelt. "Quit trying to reform us, and give us a chance to recover." That's what business says. "Quit trying to reform us, and give us a chance to recover." Roosevelt says, "Can't you reform and recover, too?" Well, that looks kind of hard there. But big business answers, "No, we can't do anything with a cop on every corner watching everything we do. Give us a chance, and honest when we're able we'll reform." And then they say, "Mr. Roosevelt, we never know what you're going to do next." Roosevelt says, "Neither do I." Big business says, "Look how England has recovered, for they're being let alone. Nobody is bothering them." Roosevelt says, "Yes, and if you pay as big an income tax as England does, then we'll recover, too."

So it just seems that all these plans, none of 'em please anybody. But my plan which is still in the nut shell is when a Senator, or Congressman, or even a man of great ability (we must quit joking about those boys, because they're great guys) comes to Washington with a plan is to send 'em to Russia. Yes, sir, send 'em to Russia with the plan. That's the home of plans, you know. Russia, they sleep and drink plans there. That's why there's starvation there, because you just can't digest a plan. It don't eat right. Everything in Russia is run by plans. Everything here is run by accident.

My plan is don't plan. Whatever you do, don't do it perfectly. Live haphazardly. Well, even more than we do now. There is nothing in the world more common as an idea, and there's nothing in the world as hard to carry out as an idea. So let's all kinder call a moratorium on plans. If the Republicans were to forget their main plan, which is to get into the White House, and if the Democrats were to forget their own plan, to stay there, and if these various third parties would just look at their history which shows that none of them ever did get in there, why we'd all recover over night.

So if you hear a man expressing a plan over the radio — run — don't walk — to the nearest dial and tune him right into the ground. And the plan will go right back into the nut shell where it belongs.

Santa Monica, April 28, 1935

This is dispatched just before the President goes on the air tonight, I am anxious to hear the comments in the Press. Even if it's good there is plenty of 'em won't like it, he can speak on the Lord's Supper and he will get editorials against it. Never in our history was we willing to blame somebody else for our troubles, America is just like an insane asylum, there is not a soul in it will admit they are crazy. Roosevelt being the warden at the present time, us inmates know he is the one that's — cuckoo.

Beverly Hills, May 2, 1935

The papers said today, "The President breaks with U.S. Chamber of Commerce." That's the oldest news I have seen in a long time, through habit of the last few administrations the U.S. Chamber of Commerce is supposed to be wedded (in an advisory capacity) to each President, but this particular union never consumated, it was an unhappy alliance on both sides from the start. And the break didn't come in the last day or so, incompatibility developed as early as March 4th, 1933. Both are headstrong and used to running things their own way, and it will be a divorce well worth reading about. Up to now Roosevelt is ahead, for he is collecting five billion temporary alimony.

Beverly Hills, California, May 3, 1935

I don't know which one was the littlest in the U.S. Chamber of Commerce versus Roosevelt argument, the President he got sore, and the "leading industrialists" they got sore. And it ended in a tie, that brought no glory on either one. Mr. Roosevelt should have kidded 'em. For they left a great opening.

Hollywood, May 27, 1935

Poor old "New Deal" she went to bat three times today with the Supreme Court pitching and she struck out each time. There was a bill called the Frazier Lempke bill (where a farmer didn't have to pay his mortgage for five years). The court said Frazier and Lempke were both wrong. Then come the N.R.A. and they washed that up. And to make it a Republican holiday, they decided that a Mr. Humphrey that used to work for the Federal Trade Commission, should be working there yet, even if he was a Republican, so the Supreme Court just stole the spotlight.

Hollywood, May 29, 1935

We are a funny people. Business men have howled from every luncheon table the evils of the whole N.R.A., then all at once the Supreme Court says, "The bridle is off boys, from this day on every man for himself." Now the same men are rushing back to the banquet tables and unoccupied microphones and shouting. "Wages must be maintained." "Cut throat competition must be curbed," "Child labor is wrong," "The sweat shop must not return." You just can't please some people.
P.S. Then the Stock Market went down six points.

Hollywood, May 31, 1935

Say just talk to some small merchants, or druggists, get them to tell you what's going on now in the price cutting, chiseling, and conniving line. It's terrible to have a law telling you you got to do something. But you ain't going to do it unless there is.

Hollywood, June 3, 1935

These Bacchalaurate addresses given to graduates, don't offer 'em much encouragement, outside of advising 'em to vote the straight Republican ticket.

Hollywood, June 4, 1935

Looks to me like Washington always asks the wrong man when they want to know something. Now today they called in all the big Democratic leaders to see *what they "think" can* be done. Well why didn't they just quietly ask the Supreme Court what "could" be done. Now if nothing can't be done under the present constitution, why they better just forget it, for I bet you a span of old grey mules that you ain't going to get folks to change that constitution. That's like asking an old man to change the brand of his chewing tobacco.

Hollywood, June 5, 1935

They going to try to retain the best features of the N.R.A. by persuasion. Hours, and wages.

You got to admit Roosevelt is trying to get a semblance of fairness. But they wouldn't even do it by law, so this scheme looks doubtful.

Hollywood, June 7, 1935

To read what all these critics of our country write, you would naturally think that everybody else was just sitting pretty. But France has offered their Premiership to everybody over there but Chevalier, and they know he is too smart to take it. England just today traded horses right in the middle of Thames River. Half of Italy has gone to Africa with a gun on their shoulder. Japan is just looking over Chinese maps, to see where to send their army. Russia must be in some devilment we never hear of 'em any more. So you see there's none of 'em that we can point with pride to. It's just a bad time to be in the government running business anywhere.

Beverly Hills, June 11, 1935

Well I got a kick out of that bunch of unemployed old timers, who call themselves the "Grass Root Boys." They just met and "denounced" and "re-denounced," give a prize to the fellow that called the President the most names.

But they all do it, when Mr. Hoover was in why the other side

did the same thing. In fact I think it's the same names, they call
him, for neither side has ever been original enough to think of
new ones. That's what makes politics such a high class gentle-
manly game, prize fighters meet and fight, and then are considered low brows, for saying, "Well the best man won."

Hollywood, June 20, 1935

All the big influential papers this morning are full of the "sock
the rich." And you can tell from the tone of their voices they
have been "socked." But as the scheme is mostly on the inheritance he don't really hit 'em good till they die, so I would call
that the nearest to a painless tax that could be invented, you
don't pay it till you die and then you don't know it.

Beverly Hills, June 24, 1935

See there is bill in Congress to do away with tax exempt bonds,
that's the best bill of all of 'em. The way it is a man could have
a million dollar income from tax free bonds, own no property
or nothing else, and not pay one cent of tax. And it's all lawful.
If they can make all these bonds pay tax they will be doing one
of the most fair share the wealth plans there is. It was put in so
that a town or a state, or the government could sell more bonds
than it ought to.

July 5, 1935

Mussolini sent his Army down into Africa, for a training trip,
hoping to annex some loose territory in route. That's your next
war.

England has strong remonstrate with Italy and told them of the
text in the Bible where it says (I think it's third chapter, third
verse of the Book of Dutyronimy) which reads, "Thou shall not
covet thy neighbor's territory, nor thy neighbor's prospective
oil wells, or thy neighbor's natural resources."

That's what England told Mussolini, and Mussolini broke out
laughing, and England's representative didn't know what Mussolini was laughing at, and he finally asked him, and Mussolini said,
"Where was the third verse of the third chapter of Dutyronimy

when you boys was coveting India, South Africa, Hong Kong and all points East and West?"

Well, for a minute, there wasn't any reply. The El Duce had the Englishman stuck, but not for long, for the Englishman replied, "Well, I guess that's in the New Testament and it wasn't written when we grabbed Ghandiland, and those other little Knick Knacks."

You see Mussolini is just native shrewd enough to know that about all the big Nations of this globe live in glass houses, and when they start throwing stones of criticism about coveting some outside range, why it's liable to catch 'em on the rebound, even as moral old Christian Nation as "The Land of the Free and the Home of the Brave" has gnawed off a little here and there during its short span of life. Grabbing off the Philippines was not exactly by popular demand of all concerned.

Course we are going to give 'em up, but not till just about two jumps ahead of when somebody would take 'em away from us anyhow. We are really dropping the candy just because we see a big bully coming around the corner to take it away from us.

Had we got out the day we got in, we would never have been humiliated. We did it pretty good with Cuba, only we never did really get plum out. We always had some sort of a bill where we was still to be the "big brother" as long as the sugar lasted.

We both individually and nationally we are just living in a time when none of us are in any shape to be telling somebody else what to do.

That's why your League of Nations won't hold water is because the big ones run it, and the little ones know that the big ones have only turned moral since they got all they can hold. I can come in with a full stomach and advise the rest of the gang not to rob the fruit stand. That ain't right.

The big ones would like to sorter stick together. They say it's to protect the little ones, but it's to protect themselves. There is no Nation laying awake at night worrying about a little Nation, unless that little Nation is one where somebody can march across to get to them.

It's not what you are doing to the little Nations; it's what you are going to do for us after you get through the little Nation. It would be a wonderful thing if it did. But brotherly love has never crossed a boundary line yet. Yes, sir, geography has more to do with brotherly love than civilization and Christianity combined.

Santa Monica, July 12, 1935

England wants Italy to lay off Abyssynian territory, yet look at the map. They control three sides of Abyssynia themselves. They have already got theirs, so you see there is two sides to every argument, and it's all a matter of "Who's dog is bit."

Beverly Hills, July 16, 1935

Went down and spoke at some lawyers meeting last night, they didn't think much of my little squib yesterday about driving the shysters out of their profession, they seemed to kinder doubt just who would have to leave.

Santa Monica, July 18, 1935

American Bar Association yesterday came out very strong against unethical and shysters lawyers, looks like I been vindicated. It seemed to be the unanimous opinion of the convention, that the management of the U.S. should be entirely in the hands of lawyer judges, and that elected representatives of the people didn't know what they was doing.

Santa Monica, July 30, 1935

Aimee Semple McPherson's daughter is in-the-Ozarks, and the Arkansawyers notified her, that she was welcome but that they didn't want to be "Redeemed," "Saved, or liquidated." That's right too, there is pretty strong characters down there, you can't redeem 'em, you just join 'em, that's what I had to do about 27 years ago with one of 'em, Joe Robinson is another one. Leader of 96 picked men of the whole U.S. who are in the Senate, anytime you tangle with an Arkansaw Hillbilly, or Hillbilyese, you are going to run second.

Santa Monica, July 31, 1935

Here is your headlines in the papers every day, "Jim Doakes

delivers blistering attack on Roosevelt," "Woodruff Republican of Michigan denounces heartily New Deal in its entirety," "Col. William A. Bohunk says unless country returned to good old Republican rule Moscow will annex us," "Dr. Jasbo the well known infantile paralysis specialist, a man of great means and a life long Republican says, there is something about the affliction and its after effects, that delusions the patient to want to bring equality, it's purely a mental disease and should be kept out of office." Now it's 16 months till election. You think they going to feed people on that for 16 long months. No, the boys started their race too early, the time to make your plea to the jury is just before they go out, you can't lecture a jury for a year and four months.

[Will's blast at lawyers was answered by a columnist, O. Z. Ide, in the *Legal Record* of Detroit who remarked that the contention had been made that the "dominant question" before the American Bar Association's meeting had been to clean up the profession. Will snapped right back and said that this was an error, that what he had said was that this should be, not was, the dominant question. He then went on to say that when someone suggested that the Movies should be cleaned up, as they were always doing, that "the movies cleaned up and didn't write editorials against the lawyers for saying they should." He then added, "Lawyers is everybody's business the same as the movies are." He then went on, after the columnist had said he was once funny but had palled, "I was funny when the joke was on the other fellow," and that the columnist's assertion that "there was a time when a dig at lawyers at the Bijou Theatre was a sure fire laugh, but now even the so-called humorists have sensed the distaste in the mouths of the public for such efforts at humor," was muchly mistaken. He added]:

Well, I wish he could have read a "so-called humorist's" mail. Never did I have so much approving mail on one article, and not a half dozen dissenting ones, and they were from lawyers. Every laymen approved. It batted about 98 percent. I wish I could think of something else as good and as true.

My little movies have been fairly clean, but when the well-chosen roar against pictures come, I didn't get sore, and rise on my hind legs and write any editorials. I knew it was coming to us and took it in good faith for I knew in the long run it would do good, and if this old boy don't think that the audience will still laugh at the lawyers at the Bijou Theatre just let him book me for a lecture on lawyers at the Bijou, and come and sit and listen to 'em roar.

The banker, the lawyer, and the politician are still our best bets for a laugh. Audiences haven't changed at all, and neither has the three above professions.

And, incidentally, comedians haven't improved. Nothing has improved but taxes.

[In August, 1935, after a leisurely trip to Seattle, Washington, Will headed for Alaska with Wiley Post. On August 10, 1935, he wired Betty, from Fairbanks, "Most marvelous trip. No danger with this guy. Wire me all the news. Love."

On August 15, at Point Barrow, their plane crashed on a lonely tundra, killing both of them.

If there be a place where, after death, one can look down and watch what is happening in this old world, and Will is there, one thing is certain. He is certain to be saying to anyone who looks under the chip to expose foibles and chicanery, "Sic 'em, Tige."]